C000197261

Memoirs of a Victorian

Master Mariner

Memoirs of a Victorian Master Mariner

By Captain Hilary Marquand

Edited by

Eric B. Marquand

with an Introduction by

Philip Riden

MERTON PRIORY PRESS

Published by Merton Priory Press Ltd
7 Nant Fawr Road, Cardiff CF2 6JQ

First published 1996

ISBN 1 898937 22 2

Printed by Hillman Printers (Frome) Ltd
Handlemaker Road
Marston Trading Estate
Frome, Somerset BA11 4RW

Contents

List of Plates vii

Acknowledgements viii

Introduction ix

Plates xxxv

Childhood 1

First Voyage (1839–40) 58

Second Voyage (1841) 122

Third Voyage (1842–44) 139

He Falls in Love 158

The Nautical Story is Resumed (1844) 165

Fourth Voyage (1844) 168

Fifth Voyage (1845) 173

Sixth Voyage (1845) 175

Seventh Voyage (1846) 179

Eighth Voyage (1846) 198

Ninth Voyage (1847) 200

Tenth Voyage (1847) 205

Eleventh Voyage (1848) 223

Twelfth Voyage (1849) 237

Thirteenth Voyage (1849–50) 239

Fourteenth Voyage (1850) 253

Appendix: A Letter from Hilary Marquand to his Wife, 1866 261

Index 269

List of Plates

1. Portrait of Hilary Marquand xxxv
2. Portrait of Hilary's father, David Marquand xxxvi
3. Portrait of Hilary's mother, Margaret (Thoume) xxxvi
4. The Marquand family's home, La Brigade xxxvii
5. La Brigade today xxxvii
6. Castel Church, Guernsey xxxviii
7. The Quay, St Peter Port xxxviii
8. Hilary and Louisa's first married home in St Peter Port xxxix
9. Hilary and Louisa's later home in St Peter Port at 30 Hauteville xxxix
10. The SS *Adelaide* xl
11. A contemporary engraving of Havana xli
12. A contemporary engraving of Pernambuco (Recife) xli
13. A photograph taken in 1866 at Nantes, where Hilary Blondel Marquand was at school xlii
14. A photograph of H.B. Marquand as young man xliii
15. A photograph of H.B. Marquand in middle age xliii

16. The SS *Earl of Dumfries* xliv

17. The SS *Earl of Roseberry* xliv

18. 11 East Grove, Tredegarville, Cardiff xlv

19. 73 Cowbridge Road, Cardiff xlv

20. 57 Cathedral Road, Cardiff xlv

21. Well Close, Penylan, Cardiff, in about 1930 xlvi

22. Leonard Marquand xlvi

Acknowledgements

We should like to thank the following for their help in the preparation of this edition: Guernsey Museums & Galleries (Mr Brian Owen), the Priaulx Library (Dr Harry Tonlinson), La Société Guernesiaise (Mrs M.G. Vidamour and Mrs Lawney Sherwill), and Mr Richard Hocart in Guernsey; the Welsh Industrial & Maritime Museum (Dr David Jenkins), the BBC Wales Library, Glamorgan Record Office and South Glamorgan County Library in Cardiff; Newport Central Library; Essex County Library; the Library of Canning House, London; Max Justo Guedes, Director of the Serviço de Documentação da Marinha, Rio de Janeiro; Mike Day, Dr Philip Durkin (Oxford English Dictionary), André Gantée, Dr Alan Jamieson, the Revd Simon Morgan, Mrs Marta Sanchez and Mrs Val Williams.

EBM
PJR

Introduction

Hilary Marquand was born on 29 October 1825, the third son of David Marquand of La Brigade, a substantial farm in the parish of St Andrew, Guernsey. At the age of fourteen Hilary went to sea as a cabin-boy in a ship partly owned by an uncle and progressed from there, via able seaman, second mate and first officer, to assume command of his own ship in 1849, when he was still only 23. Two years later he married and settled in St Peter Port, the capital of Guernsey, where he and his wife, Louisa Blondel, had a total of seven children. In the mid-1860s Hilary gave up his career as a sea captain (and part-owner of several vessels) and moved, with his family, to Cardiff, where he joined an old friend, William Henry Martin, in a ship-broking business. The partnership lasted only a few years, however, since Hilary died of smallpox, aged 46, in October 1872. His widow remained in Cardiff for the rest of her life (she died in 1919) and the family continued to be involved in ship-owning in the city until the 1930s.

Such, in outline, is the story of the Marquand family of Guernsey and Cardiff since the early nineteenth century, part of which is narrated in much greater detail in the volume of memoirs published here. In 1855 Hilary compiled a lengthy manuscript autobiography, rather grandly entitled 'A Retrospect of Twenty Years of my Life written as a Pastime of Idle Hours at Sea for the sole amusement of the Author', in which he describes his education from the age of six until he left school at thirteen, followed by an unhappy year as a clerk in a lawyer's office until he persuaded his father to let him go to sea. The rest of the text is mainly concerned with a series of fourteen voyages undertaken between 1839 and 1851, the last three as master; the only other aspect of his early life which Hilary describes is his protracted courtship of Louisa Blondel and the narrative ends with their marriage in January 1851.

Since Hilary remained the master of an ocean-going ship after he married, he would have had ample time alone at sea to compose quite an ambitious volume of memoirs. Indeed, towards the end of his work, he recommends that a master should keep his mind active during long voyages, suggesting both reading and writing as suitable pastimes.[1] There is no internal evidence to suggest that he proposed to publish the work, which is occasionally addressed to 'Dear Reader' but may have been intended more for his wife, especially as it ends on a happy and triumphant note with their marriage. A number of slightly similar memoirs written by Channel Island sea captains survive in manuscript for this period (although few are on the same scale as Hilary's, which runs to over 120,000 words), but the only published volume which might have inspired him was John Berchervaise's *Thirty-six Years of a Seafaring Life* (1836), written by a Jersey captain born in 1789, who spent his later years in the Royal Navy.[2] It is possible that Hilary might have considered publishing his memoirs had he not died so young but in the event the work remained in manuscript, passing through successive generations of the family to its present owner, a great-grandson of the author. The text formed the basis of a wireless serial in 1954 and was drawn on extensively by Dr Alan Jamieson for his major study of the maritime history of the Channel Islands, but this volume represents its first publication in full.[3]

*

[1] Below, p. 251.

[2] A.G. Jamieson (ed.), *A People of the Sea. The Maritime History of the Channel Islands* (1986), pp. 336–47. I have drawn heavily on this excellent book for the general background to Hilary Marquand's career.

[3] The serial was broadcast on the BBC Welsh Home Service in ten 15-minute instalments at 11.45 a.m. between 19 and 30 July 1954 under the title 'First Voyage', 'selected and edited from the unpublished manuscript by Michael Stephens. Reader, Roger Delgado'; see *Radio Times*, 16 and 23 July 1954, including an introductory article by H.A. Marquand MP, 'A Mariner from Guernsey', on p. 4 of the earlier issue. Jamieson, *People of the Sea*, makes use of the memoirs on pp. 339–43.

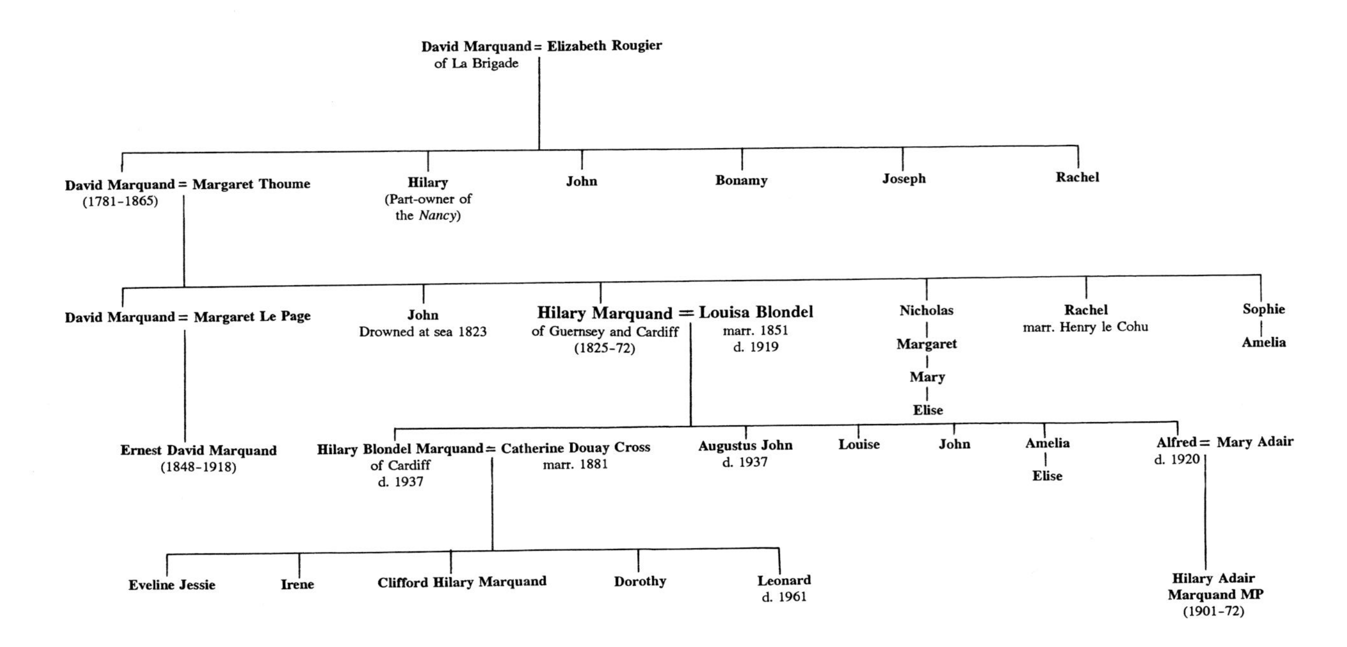

The Marquand Family of Guernsey and Cardiff

Hilary's father, David Marquand (1781–1865), was the sixth generation of his family to live and farm at La Brigade, which had been built by Pierre Marquand, who died in 1668.[1] During the eighteenth century the estate grew in size through a combination of the judicious purchase of additional land and careful arrangements made when each owner died to ensure inheritance of the entire property by the eldest son, rather than subdivision among coheirs. In Hilary's day the farm extended to some 40 acres.[2] At the same time, successive owners added to the house itself, which by the early nineteenth century was a substantial L-shaped, two-storey building in local granite, with a thatched roof. David was in fact the last head of the family to live at La Brigade: with no son willing to take on the farm, he sold the property in February 1865, a month before his death, to a farmer who was already the tenant there.

Hilary was the third son born to David Marquand and his wife Margaret Thoume. The eldest, David, who might otherwise have succeeded to La Brigade, emigrated to the United States in the early 1850s, although his son Ernest (1848–1918) returned to Guernsey and in 1901 published a well-known *Flora* of the island.[3] The second son, John, born in 1823, went to sea but was drowned during a passage from Havana in September 1837, a sequence of events which may help to explain both Hilary's keenness to become a sailor and his parents' adamant opposition to the idea. Hilary had one younger brother, Nicholas, and no fewer than six sisters.

The girls make little showing in his memoirs, but the text opens with Hilary's account of his and his brothers' schooldays, which for him began at the age of six at a local dame school. Hilary does not say how long he stayed there, although he recalled it as a

[1] For a comprehensive history of the family and the estate see R.P. Hocart, 'The Marquands of La Brigade', Report and Transactions of La Société Guernesiaise (1976), 104–26, on which the following is based.

[2] Below, p. 8.

[3] See B.T. Rowswell, 'In Memoriam. Ernest David Marquand, born 8th February, 1848; died 16th February, 1918', *Trans. Soc. Guernesiaise* (1918), 83–90.

happy time. This was less true of his subsequent education at no fewer than four private schools which he attended up to the age of thirteen, when he first asked his father to let him go to sea. By Hilary's own account, most of the masters with whom he came into contact were either drunkards or bullies or simply incompetent, and it may strike the reader as remarkable that Hilary appears to have survived the experience not merely unscathed but with a reasonably wide and thorough education, including presumably a love of literature and creative writing which later encouraged him to compose his memoirs on such ambitious lines. Although some of the stories from his schooldays may have gained in colour with the passage of time, this opening chapter gives a good impression of the education which a prosperous Guernsey farmer of the early nineteenth century thought appropriate for his sons.

Hilary also describes his home life as a child, which was clearly dominated by a very strict father: in particular Sundays were largely occupied by attendance at church and readings from the Bible for the rest of the day. Initially his father refused to allow Hilary to go to sea, no doubt partly because of the loss of his elder brother and despite a tradition of seafaring and ship-owning in the family. Instead he was given a choice: he could either stay at school for another year until he was fourteen or leave and go into a law office as a clerk. Not unreasonably, given his experience of school thus far, Hilary chose the latter and spent an unhappy year at a desk to satisfy his parents' wishes.

Towards the end of this period he tried again. His uncle Hilary, David Marquand's brother, was part-owner of a brig named the *Nancy*,[1] and he implored his father to let him join the ship as cabin-boy. This time his father gave way, although he refused to allow Hilary to take part in the first voyage which the *Nancy* was to make after he had agreed in principle that he should go to sea, a sailing from Guernsey to Antwerp. This may have been a tactical error on David's part, for when Hilary did finally join the *Nancy*

[1] I am indebted to Dr Jamieson for details of the ships on which Hilary served during the period of his memoirs, which he has kindly supplied from the Public Record Office copies (BT 107) of the Guernsey register of shipping.

he was violently sea-sick (as well as homesick) during the first few days of the voyage, as was no doubt commonly the case in such situations. On this occasion, however, the *Nancy* was bound for Havana and remained at sea for over a year; there was thus little for an ill and unhappy cabin-boy to do but get better and learn his trade, whereas the same experience on a short crossing to Antwerp might have been sufficient to put him off the sea for ever.

Hilary did pull himself together after a few weeks at sea and enjoyed the rest of his time on the *Nancy*, which took him to the Leeward Islands and then Havana, before the ship sailed back across the Atlantic to Trieste, finally returning via Gibraltar and London to reach Guernsey in October 1840. In his 'Retrospect' Hilary devotes considerably more space to this first voyage than any of those which follow; indeed, this chapter and that describing his schooldays occupy nearly half the entire text. Besides descriptions of the Caribbean islands they saw on the voyage, Hilary also recounts a bizarre experience on the leg from Trieste to London, when the master of the *Nancy*, Nicholas Le Cheminant, became mentally ill while crossing the Mediterranean and, after endangering his vessel by nearly allowing pirates to attack them off the North African coast, put into Gibraltar, where he reported his crew as mutineers to the Royal Navy. The officers from the warship concerned eventually realised that the master was ill, abandoned their threat to imprison the crew, installed the first officer, Henry Cohu, in his place and allowed the *Nancy* to continue to London, where Le Cheminant was admitted to an asylum.

After this first experience, Hilary was convinced that he wished to make the sea his life and his parents raised no objections. Most of the rest of his 'Retrospect' is therefore concerned with the succession of voyages he made between January 1841, when he rejoined the *Nancy*, this time as an ordinary seaman under a new master, Moses Reeves, and January 1851, when for the third time he brought his own ship, the *Swift*, into her home port. Two days later he was married and his narrative ends. Altogether, a further thirteen voyages are described, some in more detail than others but none so fully as the first. After another trip to Havana and Trieste in the *Nancy*, during which Hilary contracted yellow fever in Cuba and nearly had a leg amputated, he joined a slightly larger brig, the

Adelaide, where he and the rest of the crew suffered for over two years at the hands of a sadistic master named Robert Taylor, with whom Hilary at one stage became involved in a fight. Not surprisingly, when the *Adelaide* put in to Guernsey on Easter Sunday 1844, Hilary decided that he had had enough, declined the offer of an appointment as Taylor's second officer, and looked around for another ship. In May that year he sailed again, this time under Captain John Touzeau in the brig *Duke of Gloucester*.[1]

He stayed with Touzeau for only one voyage but his next move was to be his last for some years. He joined the *Swift*, a brig of 195 tons built at St Peter Port in 1842, as second mate under John David, whom Jamieson describes as one of the outstanding Guernsey master mariners of the nineteenth century.[2] A staunch Methodist (as is clear from Hilary's account of their stay in Jamaica on one occasion), he was a skilled and fair master who was offered the command of some of the biggest and best Guernsey ships at sea between 1849 and the mid-1860s; he also owned shares in most of them. Hilary made three voyages in the *Swift* in 1845–6 as David's second officer and was then promoted to chief officer, still under the same master, for a further four voyages in 1846–7. On his second trip in the *Swift* Hilary fell into the hold while unloading pigs of lead and spent three weeks in the London Hospital; on his next voyage he recounts a more dramatic mishap off the coast of Jamaica, when a thunderstorm nearly sank one of the ship's boats which Hilary and some of the crew had taken to a neighbouring port in search of fresh water.

At the beginning of 1849 John David gave up command of the *Swift* in favour of a larger vessel, the *Dispatch*, 338 tons, in which he also owned a one-eighth share. On 4 January that year the owners of the *Swift* appointed Hilary master, but without any share in the ownership. This was clearly an important turning-point in his career and, before describing his first three voyages as captain of the ship in which he had been an officer for the previous seven

[1] According to Hilary's own account, he was second mate in the *Duke of Gloucester*, but see below, pp. 166, 168.

[2] Jamieson, *People of the Sea*, pp. 342–3.

years, Hilary digresses at some length on the burdens of command, especially of a tramp vessel where the master had frequently to conduct detailed negotiations with rapacious brokers and merchants in distant ports, armed with minimal instructions from the vessel's owners at home. Later in the narrative, he discusses such familiar problems as the loneliness of command at sea, the need to keep body and mind active and the dangers of excessive drinking by merchant captains.[1]

The three voyages he made before his marriage in 1851 were in fact among the least eventful of those described in his 'Retrospect': the only incident of note seems to have been an unscheduled, but not unwelcome, call at Guernsey to repair a leak to the *Swift* and put two sick seamen ashore. His account of the last voyage ends on an unexpected but happy note, with Hilary putting into Guernsey with a cargo of coal from Tyneside, hoping to come ashore for his marriage, only to find that the owners proposed to send him and the coal on to Havana in search of a better market. He objected strongly, the owners gave way and he was married two days later.

This event marks the end of both the sequence of voyages and the only other theme which runs through the 'Retrospect', his courtship of Louisa Blondel, the daughter of a Guernsey sea captain, to whom he was first introduced in 1840 or 1841. The courtship proceeds slowly, as would have been the case anyway in this period for a couple of their social class, but more so given Hilary's profession. As the friendship deepens into love, and what contemporaries would have called 'an understanding', so the accounts of his partings from Louise at the start of each voyage become more mournful and those of his first meeting with her on his return more joyful. Much of the courtship must have been conducted by correspondence and one of the lighter stories in the 'Retrospect' concerns an episode at Newport in 1847 when two of Hilary's friends chase after the *Swift* with a letter from Louisa as the ship is going down the Usk.

[1] Below, pp. 229–36, 248–51.

*

Hilary Marquand's memoirs cover a period in which ship-building and ship-owning in both Jersey and Guernsey were expanding and local owners were taking part in a wider range of trades than had been the case before the Napoleonic War.[1] In the eighteenth century, Channel Island ships had been engaged chiefly in the coasting trade with Britain, plus some Atlantic routes, notably the Newfoundland cod trade. Both these activities remained important after 1815 but to them were added new links with the Caribbean and South America. In particular, the backbone of Guernsey's trade was the shipment of goods, chiefly wines and spirits, from Iberia to South America, and the import of coffee, sugar and other tropical produce to continental Europe, particularly Trieste. In the 1840s, however, the lion's share of the South American trade began to be lost to other countries and Guernsey merchants turned instead to the coal trade, mainly with South Wales and North East England, the carriage of building stone from Guernsey to London, and the fruit trade between the Azores and London. More ships also took up tramping, sailing from port to port in search of a cargo.

The pattern of Hilary's voyages in the 1840s entirely conforms to this general picture. Although a variety of ports and cargoes are mentioned in the text, the story is dominated by the trade between the Caribbean or Brazil and either England or the Continent—as Hilary himself says during his account of his sufferings at the hands of Captain Taylor, 'Back and Forth across the Atlantic'. Typically, the ships in which he sailed went out in ballast to Cuba, Jamaica or one of the Brazilian ports, such as Pernambuco, Bahia or Rio de Janeiro, collected a cargo of sugar, coffee or whatever, and then sailed for Trieste. There a fresh cargo was loaded and it was this, rather than the produce of the West Indies or Brazil, that finally came back to London.

The one variation on this theme in the early years of his career was a voyage to Ichaboe, a small island in Lüderitz Bay off the

[1] Jamieson, *People of the Sea*, Chapters 13 and 14.

coast of what later became South West Africa, to collect a cargo of guano, a natural manure composed of bird droppings. The enormous deposits of this valuable fertiliser were discovered by British ship-owners and merchants in 1843 and by the time the *Duke of Gloucester* set off for Africa in May the following year the business was in full swing, with probably upwards of 400 vessels involved. It was a shortlived boom, and by January 1845 most of the guano had been removed from Ichaboe. Interestingly, the details Hilary gives of his voyage there precisely bear out features of the trade mentioned in other contemporary accounts, notably the extreme congestion of shipping around the island and the difficulty of finding a secure anchorage in the surf. Like many other ships, the *Duke of Gloucester* lost some of her anchors off Ichaboe and had to go to Rio de Janeiro to replace them.[1]

Although Hilary's narrative covers only a decade or so, a shift is perceptible towards the end of the text, when the *Swift* began calling at Newport, then the most important of the three main ports serving the South Wales coalfield, to load cargoes of what he calls 'Black Diamonds', which he ships to the Spanish ports of Cádiz or Málaga. He also calls on one occasion at South Shields in the North East, and makes two trips to Hamburg or Stettin, on one occasion having to unload his cargo at Stralsund to avoid the blockade imposed during the Schleswig-Holstein dispute of 1848. There are thus indications of closer links developing with the South Wales coal trade, a rapidly expanding business in these years which attracted ships from all parts of the British Isles, some of whose masters eventually decided to come ashore, as Hilary did at Cardiff in the 1860s, and set up as merchants and ship-owners. In the 1840s, however, Cardiff was not yet the 'Coal Metropolis' it would later become and on no occasion during the period covered by his memoirs did Hilary put in to the Bute Docks there.

*

[1] See generally R. Craig, 'The African guano trade', *Mariner's Mirror*, 50 (1964), 25–55, which does not make use of Hilary's 'Retrospect'.

Hilary's 'Retrospect', although not written until 1855, ends with his marriage to Louisa Blondel on 29 January 1851 at Castel church,[1] and thus the remainder of his career must be pieced together from external evidence. Hilary and Louisa made their home in St Peter Port for the first fifteen years or so of their married life, during which time they had seven children, four boys (one of whom, John, died young) and three girls.[2] Initially they lived in a small terraced house, 35 Mount Durand, but later moved to a much larger double-fronted detached house at 30 Hauteville, which belonged to his uncle Hilary and stood four doors away from Victor Hugo's home.[3]

Throughout these years Hilary continued to serve at sea and was also a part-owner of various ships. In 1854 he took command of the brig *Secret*, in which he owned a quarter share and of which he remained master until 1862, when he became captain of the schooner *Jessie*, in which he had an eighth share. He left the *Jessie* in 1864 when he was chosen to command one of the finest ships ever built in Guernsey, the 609-ton *Channel Queen*, launched that year and designed to trade to ports in the Indian Ocean and Far East. Hilary was master of the *Channel Queen* for three years and in February 1866 was at Mangalore, on the Malabar Coast of India, when he and four of his crew narrowly escaped death when the ship's boat overturned in the surf, as he told his wife in a lengthy and detailed letter, written in a style not dissimilar to that adopted in the 'Retrospect' when recalling similar episodes.[4]

Although he was only 41 when this particular incident occurred, Hilary (and perhaps also his wife) may have concluded that the

[1] I am indebted to Mrs M.G. Vidamour of the Family History Section of La Société Guernesiaise for locating the original entry; the marriage was by licence.

[2] All of whom were baptised at the Town Church (once again I am grateful to Mrs Vidamour for details of the relevant entries).

[3] Louisa was enumerated at 35 Mount Durand in the 1851 Census (Public Record Office, HO 107/2530, f. 357v), when Hilary was presumably away at sea and his uncle was still living at Hauteville (HO 107/2530, f. 529). Hilary junior is holding a letter addressed to him at Hauteville in the portrait published here as Plate 1.

[4] Jamieson, *People of the Sea*, p. 341; the letter, which survives with the 'Retrospect' among the Marquand family papers, is printed below, pp. 261–8.

time had come to give up his arduous and hazardous life as master of an ocean-going merchant ship and seek a new career ashore. Whatever the reason, after returning to Guernsey in 1867 Hilary decided to move with his family from Guernsey to Cardiff, by this date the largest and most rapidly expanding of the South Wales coal-shipping ports, to become a ship-broker, ironically one of the professions about which he was most disparaging in his 'Retrospect' when he first became a master. Although in his early years at sea Hilary called at Newport, rather than Cardiff, for cargoes of coal, in later years, as the latter gradually overhauled the former, he would presumably have become familiar with the place and realised that it offered better prospects for someone who wished to make the transition from master to broker or owner than either Newport or, even more so, Guernsey itself. This was a view shared by dozens of men in a similar position, from many parts of the British Isles, who began life on board ships trading with Cardiff and eventually decided to settle in the town and make a new career ashore. At least two other Channel Island families followed this route—the Morels and the Hacquoils—who both left Jersey for Cardiff in the 1850s to become successful ship-owners there.[1]

Although none of Hilary's family had preceded him to Cardiff, he had a connection with the port through his old friend William Henry Martin, who first appears in the 'Retrospect' in October 1847 in the episode already mentioned, when the *Nancy* called at Newport to load a cargo of coal destined for Cádiz. Martin was then a Custom House clerk in the office of the consignee and ship-broker for the voyage, Stonehouse & Co. He and Hilary, who were the same age and both engaged to be married, became firm friends and Martin, together with another young clerk named Thomas Williams, were involved in the escapade already mentioned in which they tried to deliver a letter from Louisa to Hilary which

[1] See J.M. Gibbs, *Morels of Cardiff. The history of a family shipping firm* (Cardiff, 1982) for the better known of the two. For Cardiff generally in this period see John Davies, *Cardiff and the Marquesses of Bute* (Cardiff, 1981) and M.J. Daunton, *Coal Metropolis. Cardiff 1870–1914* (Leicester, 1977).

arrived after the *Nancy* had set sail from Newport.[1]

Martin was still living in Newport in May 1850, when, during another voyage, Hilary stayed with him and his wife Ellen, whom he had married the previous January, but later the same year he decided to set up as a ship-broker on his own account and to move from Newport to Cardiff. Martin lived initially at 2 James Street, one of the newly built roads forming Butetown, the district developed by the second Marquess of Bute to serve his docks at Cardiff, and, in common with almost all the first generation of merchants and middlemen there, he ran his business from home.[2] By 1863 the firm had become W.H. Martin & Co. and was still at the same address.[3] A few years later—certainly by 1868—Martin had moved both home and business to the rather grander surroundings of 39 Mount Stuart Square, which lay at the heart of the southern half of Butetown.[4]

It was about this time that he was joined by his old friend Hilary Marquand and the firm became Martin & Marquand. Hilary moved to Cardiff in 1867, although he does not appear on the town's Burgess Roll until 1869, when he was living at 11 East Grove, Tredegarville, a high-status suburb developed in the 1850s and 1860s off Newport Road by Sir Charles Morgan of Tredegar Park near Newport.[5] Tredegarville lay on the eastern edge of the

[1] Below, pp. 207–14.

[2] For Martin see a lengthy obituary in the *Western Mail*, 31 Dec. 1887. His marriage to Ellen, the daughter of John Davies, innkeeper of David Street, Cardiff, took place at St Mary's, Bute Road, on 8 Jan. 1850, when Martin gave his address as Newport. He is listed at James Street in Ewen's Cardiff Directory (1855) (For full details of local directories cited in this section see H. Llewellyn, *A Bibliography of Cardiff Directories, 1795–1978* (Cardiff, 1990).)

[3] Wakeford's Cardiff Directory (1863); Duncan & Ward's Directory (1863).

[4] Martin appears in the Burgess Rolls of 1860–66 (Cardiff Central Library) at James Street; the Library lacks the Roll for the South Ward (which included Butetown) for 1867 and in 1868-69 he is listed at 39 Mount Stuart Square. See generally M. Parker and N. Carter, *Butetown. A Visitor's Guide* (Cardiff, 1989).

[5] Hilary does not appear in the Burgess Rolls for North Ward, which included Tredegarville, in 1867–68, nor in the South Ward Roll for the latter year (the South Ward Roll for 1867 is lost). Presumably he lived in lodgings when he first came to Cardiff and would not therefore have had a vote. For Tredegarville see G. Dart, P. Riden and S.M. Romaya, *The Mansion House and its Environs* (Cardiff, 1990).

older built-up area and over a mile from Butetown and the Docks. Together with similar developments to the north of the town centre along Park Place and to the west on Cathedral Road, it was one of the districts to which docksmen were moving as Butetown, despite its builder's early hopes, rapidly declined into a mixture of slum housing and commercial premises, where merchants and brokers continued to have offices but no longer wished to live. Hilary obviously recognised what was happening and had no desire to live in the area in which Martin had made his home for the previous ten years. As a reminder of his origins, Hilary named his house in East Grove 'Guernsey Villa' and when the census was taken in the spring of 1871 the household included his wife Louisa, their eldest son Hilary Blondel Marquand, who had joined his father's business as a clerk three years before after an education received partly at Nantes in Britanny, and the two younger daughters, Amelia and Elise. The two other surviving boys, Augustus John and Alfred, were presumably away at school and the eldest daughter, Louise, had been married the previous year. The family had one living-in servant.[1]

At about the time Hilary senior joined the firm, Martin evidently also decided to leave Mount Stuart Square. Whereas some men in his position kept on their former home as offices, Martin and his partner made a clean break and moved the business to what were then the only purpose-built office premises in Butetown, Dock Chambers, an imposing range erected in the early 1850s by the Bute Estate on the east side of Bute Street not far from the entrance to the West Dock, consisting of sets of offices arranged on separate staircases. Here the firm was to remain for many years, during which time most of the houses nearby were either demolished to make way for much larger commercial premises or were converted to offices. Martin & Marquand were installed at 2 Dock Chambers by 1873, if not a year or two before,

[1] PRO, RG 10/5357, f. 20; Kelly's Directory (1871). For H.B. Marquand see his entry in *Contemporary Portraits* (Cardiff, 1896), p. xxix, which notes that he was educated partly in France; the photograph of Hilary (aged 12) and his parents reproduced here as Plate 13 was taken at Nantes while he was at school there.

by which time Martin himself had moved from Butetown to 7 Edward Terrace, part of a new development on the south-eastern edge of the town centre.[1]

Before the partnership had been in existence for more than a few years, it was brought to a tragic end by Hilary's death on 25 October 1872 from smallpox, aged only 46.[2] For someone who had, by his own account, survived so many hazards at sea as a young man and had only recently settled ashore with his wife and a growing family, it was an especially sad, as well as very unpleasant, way in which to die. His death took place at 5 Westbourne Crescent, a row of houses on Cowbridge Road just to the west of Cardiff Bridge, on the opposite side of the town from Tredegarville, to which the family had moved only a few months earlier and where Louisa Marquand and some of her children remained for several years afterwards. Her husband, as one might expect from his age and circumstances, left a comparatively modest estate, valued for probate at £2,000, although the family appear to have lived comfortably in the years following his death, partly no doubt because Hilary and Louisa's eldest son, Hilary Blondel Marquand, who was only 18 when his father died, became a partner in Martin & Marquand and the firm continued to prosper.

The most important change following H.B. Marquand's entry into the partnership came in the early 1880s, when the firm, who had previously described themselves in directories simply as ship-brokers, also became ship-owners. Although W.H. Martin is said to have been a tug-owner in his early years in Cardiff, as well as a broker, the move is first clearly signalled in the census of 1881,

[1] The firm is listed at 2 Dock Chambers in Butcher's Directory of 1873, in which Martin appears as a private resident at 7 Edward Terrace. There are no directories for the years immediately before this date and Martin is not listed anywhere in the Burgess Roll of 1871 (the South Ward Roll for 1870 is lost).

[2] This is the age given on his death certificate; his monument in Cathays Cemetery (Plot L.1057) says 47. Since he was born on 29 Oct. 1825, he was in fact a few days short of his 47th birthday at the time of his death, which was not recorded in the *Cardiff & Merthyr Guardian*, the town's only local newspaper of this period.

when H.B. Marquand gave his occupation as ship-owner.[1] The following year the local directory uses the ambiguous phrase 'Ship Brokers &c.' of the company, which in 1883, still at 2 Dock Chambers, is listed for the first time as 'Steam Ship Brokers & Owners'.[2] One of the first ships they owned, if not the very first, was the tramp steamer *Earl of Dumfries*, built for them in 1882; by 1894 they had five other vessels, including two similar tramp steamers (the *Earl of Roseberry* and *Rosehill*) and three steam paddle tugs, *Earl of Bute*, *Earl of Dunraven* and *Earl of Jersey*. The fleet gradually grew in size and by the outbreak of the First World War the company operated three steamers of over 2,000 tons each, the *Dauntless*, *Relentless* and *Silvia*.[3]

Well before this period, the business had passed entirely into the hands of the Marquand family, following the death of W.H. Martin in 1887, at the comparatively early age of 62. He died at 44 The Parade, Tredegarville (to which he had moved from Edward Terrace sometime between 1875 and 1880), leaving an estate valued at £6,900 but no children.[4] Thereafter H.B. Marquand became the head of the firm, which retained the name Martin & Marquand. By the 1890s Marquand was also a director of Hill's Dry Dock & Engineering Co., one of the largest firms of

[1] PRO, RG 11/5278, f. 29. Martin's obituary (p. xxi, n. 2) describes him as a tug-owner when he first came to Cardiff.

[2] See Butcher's Cardiff Directory of 1882, Slater's Directory of 1883 and Wright's of 1883; the two latter are the first to describe Martin & Marquand as owners as well as brokers and both specifically describe them as owners of *steamships*.

[3] J.G. Jenkins and D. Jenkins, *Cardiff Shipowners* (1986), pp. 22–3, where it is stated that the three tugs were owned by Martin rather than the firm. The *Earl of Dumfries* is illustrated on p. 23. Mr Eric Marquand recalls that his grandfather told him that Martin & Marquand also operated a steam ferry service between Cardiff and Weston super Mare called the Red Funnel Line, precursor of the better known White Funnel Line of P. & A. Campbell.

[4] See the *Western Mail*, 5 Jan. 1888, for a lengthy report of his funeral. Mrs Martin bought a double plot in Cathays Cemetery (L.984/960) in which her husband is buried beneath a rough-hewn cross resting on a plinth which stands over a vault in which she, both her parents, a sister, a niece and what appears to be a nephew were also later buried. The monument is only a few feet away from the much more modest headstone marking the last resting place of Hilary and Louisa Marquand.

its type in Cardiff, and a member of the Bristol Channel Tug Owners' Association.[1]

Two of Hilary's other sons also worked in the family business. Augustus became an engineer: when the 1881 census was taken he was chief engineer in the *Earl of Roseberry,* then lying ten miles off Cape St Vincent on the southern coast of Portugal.[2] In about 1889 he came ashore and set up as a consulting engineer at 2 Dock Chambers. His younger brother Alfred was a clerk in the family business.[3]

H.B. Marquand continued to live with his mother and the rest of the family at Westbourne Crescent until his marriage in September 1881 to Catherine Douay Cross, when he and his wife made their home a short distance away at 73 Cowbridge Road.[4] He named the house 'Roseberry Villa', although the connection with the Liberal peer evident in both this name and that of the ship the company acquired a couple of years later remains obscure. In 1890 the Marquands moved to 'Eastwood', 57 Cathedral Road, a slightly larger house in a street much favoured in this period by wealthy docksmen, where among his neighbours was a fellow Channel Island ship-owner, F.P. Hacquoil.[5] Just after the turn of the century, Hilary and Catherine moved again, this time to a much grander detached house in substantial grounds on the other side of Cardiff, 'Wellclose', Penylan. Meanwhile, Hilary's mother Louisa gave up the house in Westbourne Crescent in about 1882 in favour of Castle Road (i.e. the modern City Road), which was then being developed on the eastern edge of the built-up area, just

[1] *Contemporary Portraits*, p. xxix, which also confirms that H.B. Marquand became a partner in Martin & Marquand in 1872, on his father's death.

[2] PRO, RG 11/5291, f. 33.

[3] PRO, RG 11/5278, f. 29.

[4] He was still living with his mother when the census was taken in April 1881 (PRO, RG 11/5278, f. 29), but both Slater's and Wright's directories of 1883 list him at 'Roseberry Villa'.

[5] See the Cardiff Directory of 1890, the first to list Marquand at Cathedral Road.

beyond Tredegarville.[1] She continued to live on Castle Road for several years but by 1894 had moved a short distance from what was now becoming a busy commercial street surrounded by working-class housing to the much quieter surroundings of 13 Richmond Crescent, close to her first home in Cardiff in Tredegarville.[2] Mrs Marquand lived on until 1919, when she died, aged 95, at 27 Tydfil Place, Cathays.[3]

The firm of Martin & Marquand was wound up after the First World War, although H.B. Marquand did not die until 1937.[4] The family's connection with ship-owning, however, was maintained into the next generation: in 1922 Hilary's younger son Leonard Blondel Marquand joined forces with Edward Richard Care, the son of another long-established Cardiff docksman, Richard Care, to establish the Care & Marquand Shipping Co. Ltd with three tramp steamers employed principally in the South American trade. The company was liquidated in about 1935, a victim of the slump in shipping during the Depression, although the Care family remained ship-owners in Cardiff until the 1960s.[5] The Marquands' connection with Cardiff was sustained into the next generation by Alfred's only son, Hilary Adair Marquand (1901–72). After a brilliant academic career that began at Cardiff High School and ended with his appointment as Professor of Industrial Relations at University College, Cardiff, at the age of 29, H.A. Marquand

[1] The last directory entry for Mrs Marquand at Westbourne Crescent is in Butcher (1880); the same directory for 1882 gives her address as Castle Road.

[2] Mrs Marquand appears at 179 Castle Road in the 1892 Directory and at 13 Richmond Crescent in 1894.

[3] She is buried with her husband in plot L.1057 at Cathays Cemetery. In her will, proved 13 May 1919, she left effects valued at £4,320; her executors were her sons H.B. and A.J. Marquand.

[4] Jenkins and Jenkins, *Cardiff Shipowners*, p. 22. H.B. Marquand died at 'Wellclose' on 24 Nov. 1937. His younger brother Augustus, the consulting engineer, died on 3 July 1937, and his other brother Alfred, a clerk in the family business, died in July 1920. All three lived within a mile of each other: Augustus on Marlborough Road and Alfred on Albany Road.

[5] Jenkins and Jenkins, *Cardiff Shipowners*, pp. 22–3, drawing on information supplied by Mr Paul Marquand (Leonard's younger son) of Cheltenham and by members of the Care family.

undertook important investigative work for the government in South Wales during the 1930s and was a senior civil servant during the war. He entered Parliament in 1945 as the Labour Member for Cardiff East and was immediately appointed a minister. The Cardiff seat disappeared in a rearrangement of boundaries in 1950 but Marquand continued to sit in the Commons for Middlesbrough East until he retired in 1961 to take up an ILO appointment in Geneva.[1]

*

Although Hilary disclaimed any wish that anyone should read his 'Retrospect', it is clearly an ambitious and polished, as well as lengthy, piece of work which reflects considerable credit on its author, bearing in mind his distinctly limited, not to say unsettled, school career. Indeed, the very obviously 'literary' feel of the piece suggests that he must have spent a good deal of time at sea following his own advice and reading widely so as to improve his creative writing skills. The work is not only of some length, it is also much more than a series of jottings worked up from a diary or log. On the other hand, the text is unbalanced, with nearly half devoted to his school days and first voyage. Although one might expect the second (but perhaps not the first) of these topics to be treated more fully than the later voyages, in which there would be less that was new to report, the arrangement of the material suggests that Hilary planned a much fuller work, with longer chapters on the other voyages, which he failed to execute.

Only in one instance does Hilary identify a published source from which he has taken passages to insert into his own narrative. Parts of his descriptions of the main Brazilian ports at which he called are taken from a French navigation guide to Brazil, which he presumably kept in his sea-chest as a ready reference book.[2] There are a few other literary, or at least bibliographical, references in the text, one to the standard navigation guide to the Indian

[1] See *The Times* obituary, 8 Nov. 1972; *Who's Who* etc.

[2] Below, pp. 219, 228, 241.

Ocean by James Horsburgh, and another to a second work on Brazil, this time by the botanist John Forbes, while at one point Hilary inserts a poem published in the *London Journal*.[1]

A notable feature of the entire work, including the later chapters as well as the first two, is the amount of detail Hilary is able to recall, such as the exact dates of sailings or the precise cargo his ship was carrying. His account of his schooldays is also very full, considering that they ended more than fifteen years before he was writing. Equally, it seems remarkable that he could rely on memory alone to distinguish the events of no fewer than fourteen separate voyages, some of which followed very similar routes, undertaken between 1839 and 1851. Nowhere in the text does he mention any sources of information on which he might draw: no diary or log, covering either his early years at sea or the period after he became master, nor any letters to Louisa to which he might refer to refresh his knowledge of dates and places, although he presumably wrote to her before they were married, possibly in as much detail as the example of 1866 illustrates his style in later years. But on the face of it, the entire 'Retrospect' was composed simply from memory, even though it dealt with events covering a period which ended four years before he actually sat down to write.

It is impossible to be certain how accurately Hilary recalls the events of his youth, if only because most of them cannot be traced in other source. What one can say is that the 'Retrospect' appears to form a complete account of his career at sea between the ages of 14 and 36, since the dates he assigns to voyages form a continuous record, with no gaps in which others might have taken place. The destinations and cargoes he mentions are those one would expect to find Guernsey ships of this period carrying, and all the details he gives of the ships in which he served and their masters tally with the island's statutory shipping registers.[2]

[1] See pp. 256, 244–5, 212–13.

[2] Once again, I am indebted to Dr Jamieson for kindly supplying details of the ships in question from the PRO copies (BT 107) of the Guernsey shipping registers of the period.

Furthermore, although information is lacking for the first three voyages, for the other eleven, beginning with his trip to south west Africa and Brazil in the *Duke of Gloucester* in 1844–45, crew lists and agreements survive to confirm the accuracy of Hilary's own account of dates of departure and arrival, ports of call and (apart from some uncertainty over the voyage to Ichaboe) his own position on board each ship, whether as ordinary seaman, mate or master.[1] Indeed, the details match so precisely that it seems almost certain that Hilary did keep a diary, even though he makes no mention of such a source in his text.

As it happens, a diary kept by one of Hilary's colleagues on two of the voyages included in the 'Retrospect' *does* survive and further confirms the reliability of his narrative. William Day was first mate in the *Swift* for several years, including the second and third occasions on which Hilary served as second mate (i.e. the sixth and seventh voyages in the 'Retrospect'); on his first voyage the mate was William Day's younger brother Clement, of whom Hilary did not have a high opinion.[2] Not only do the dates given in the diary correspond exactly with those given by Hilary (and with the crew lists and agreements) but Day also mentions the same delays caused by adverse winds as Hilary does, the high value of the cargo of fruit which the *Swift* brought back from Málaga in 1845, and (perhaps most interestingly) a mishap when the *Swift* moored at Dry Harbour, Jamaica, when Hilary nearly drowned.[3] Day's diary is thus invaluable independent evidence of the detailed accuracy of Hilary's own memoirs and the two make

[1] The crew lists and agreements for this period are in PRO, BT 98: full details of those for each voyage described in the 'Retrospect' are given in footnotes at appropriate points in the text. See in general N. Cox, 'Sources for maritime history (II): the records of the Registrar General of Shipping and Seamen', *Maritime History*, 2 (1978), 168–88. No other references to Marquand were noted in the bundles of crew lists examined during the search for those relating to the voyages described in the 'Retrospect', which tends to confirm that his own account of his career is complete, as well as accurate.

[2] Below, p. 173 for Clement Day. William Day's diary is in the possession of his descendant, Mr Mike Day of Edinburgh, who has kindly made available his typed transcript of the work and allowed me to quote passages therefrom.

[3] Below, pp. 176, 181, where full cross-references are given.

a striking contrast, most notably in the case of Day's laconic record of the loss of tackle from the overturned jolly boat at Dry Harbour and Hilary's lengthy and emotional account of an accident in which he came close to losing his life.

On the other hand, where readers may feel some unease is with Hilary's capacity to recall lengthy passages of direct speech from both his school days and later, and indeed the content and tone of many of these exchanges. No doubt some conversations of the sort included in the narrative with his school friends, teachers, parents and fellow sailors did take place, but it is sometimes difficult to believe in the actual words used in the text, which often sound as if they have strayed from the pages of contemporary light fiction. This is perhaps especially true of Hilary's account of his courtship, culminating in his proposal to Louisa, whose reply is a conventional response that could no doubt be found in dozens of novels of the period and surely cannot be what she actually said. On a different note, it seems unlikely that a young man of 25, who had only been master of his own vessel for two years, would speak to his owners in quite the way Hilary claims he did when told to go to Havana in January 1851, when he really wanted to stay in Guernsey and get married. Equally, some of the exchanges with his father, or the passages in French in which one of his school friends tries to get the better of their master, sound contrived.

Doubts on this score may in turn raise questions concerning the accuracy of some of Hilary's actual narrative. Presumably most if not all the events on board ship which he describes so fully did occur, but one suspects that the details may sometimes have been modified to make a better tale. Thus the story of Captain Le Cheminant's madness and his meetings with the naval officers at Gibraltar, which is perhaps the highlight of Hilary's first voyage in the *Nancy*, is so detailed that it must be basically sound, although there may be some doubts over the way in which he is able to recall so much direct speech.[1]

In this case there is also a problem with Hilary's identification of the naval vessel from which officers boarded the *Nancy*, which

[1] Below, pp. 102–16.

he names as HMS *Vanguard*. Precisely when the incident took place is not stated but it appears to have been about a month before the ship returned to London in October 1840. The *Vanguard*, having spent the earlier part of the year at Portsmouth and Spithead, sailed from Plymouth for Cork on 6 September 1840. She left Cork on the 13th and passed through the Straits of Gibraltar on 20th on her way to Malta, where she arrived on 4 October. Her log makes no mention of an encounter with a merchantman while she was near Gibraltar and she certainly did not call there. She hove-to briefly near the Rock on the afternoon of 20 September in a vain attempt to recover a man lost overboard, but otherwise continued on her passage to Malta and remained in the eastern Mediterranean until the end of the year.[1] Hilary's account of the *Nancy* putting into Gibraltar and summoning help from a warship moored in harbour, although it sounds authentic, cannot therefore be reconciled with the captain's log of the ship in question, even though the vessel was in the right area at the right time. Given the high degree of accuracy of the rest of his narrative, where other events can be checked against independent evidence, the most likely explanation is that Hilary simply got the ship's name wrong, possibly because he had in fact seen HMS *Vanguard* on another occasion during the voyage.

A further aspect of the 'Retrospect', which modern readers may simply find unattractive, rather than unconvincing, is the way in which Hilary emerges as the hero of every story, beginning with the episode at Gibraltar, where he conceals himself beneath a hatch to listen to what Captain Le Cheminant is saying to the naval officers. Later, as he gains in experience, Hilary is rarely slow to stress his own talents and usefulness to those in command. A good knowledge of French would be expected of a Channel Islander, but Hilary also picks up Spanish with remarkable facility and is soon put in charge of ordering supplies when his ship puts into a Spanish-speaking port; similarly he is able to speak Italian after a

[1] HMS *Vanguard*'s day-by-day movements can be reconstructed from the captain's log (PRO, ADM 51/3521 and ADM 51/3643).

couple of visits to Trieste.[1] He is one of only two members of Captain Taylor's unhappy crew who stays the course and is also prepared to take on the tyrant with his fists.[2] When he becomes a second officer he deals firmly with an older and more experienced able seaman who attempts to undermine his authority.[3]

After such a successful early career, it seems to come as no surprise to Hilary that he is given his own command at a relatively young age, or that Louisa is suitably impressed.[4] To some extent, he appears to have taken the events of his life, colourful as they undoubtedly were, and woven them into a story which could have been passed off as fiction, although Hilary clearly intended his work to be read as an autobiography, not a novel.

This impression is reinforced by the way in which every story ends happily, with right triumphing over evil. Similarly, the conventions of contemporary light fiction are maintained in that Hilary has something good to say about even the villains of his piece, or at least tactfully follows the dictum he quotes twice in his narrative, *De mortuis nil nisi bonum*. Both the mad Captain Le Cheminant and the bad Captain Taylor are treated gently at the end of their respective appearances in the drama.[5] And, as one would expect, the good are always very good, at any rate if they are English. The ships' companies in which Hilary served are always the finest fellows who sailed beneath the Red Ensign, the vessels the smartest in the merchant service. Foreigners fare less well: a battalion of British red-coats would easily out-do a whole regiment of Brazilian soldiers if it came to a fight; the Brazilian ports are shabby and dirty (as they may well have been); the women of Spain, though beautiful, cannot compare with those of England (as Hilary invariably describes his home), if only because they are

[1] Below, pp. 76, 122–4.

[2] Below, pp. 146–55.

[3] See below, pp. 168–9; there appears to be some doubt as to Hilary's appointment as second mate on this voyage, which may account for the problem he faced.

[4] Below, pp. 229–31, 236.

[5] Below, pp. 118, 137–8, 155–7.

given to smoking.[1] Comments such as these, which pepper the narrative, may tell us something about Hilary's own outlook on life, or else they merely reflect the conventional views of his age.

None of these criticisms detracts from the value of Hilary's 'Retrospect' as a source for the day-to-day life of a young Guernseyman who, like generations of his fellow islanders before him (and, to a lesser extent, since), felt called to a career at sea, and who may also have considered, as the younger son of a farmer, his limited prospects if he stayed ashore. The text published here for the first time is a fascinating, if at times somewhat highly coloured, memoir which relates, accurately and in detail, its author's progress from cabin-boy to captain during a decade falling towards the end of Guernsey's heyday as a ship-owning centre. The book provides useful evidence as to how a young man might progress in the merchant navy, what cargoes Channel Island ships were carrying in the 1840s and between which ports, and what life was like on board ocean-going sailing ships in this period. The introductory chapter throws valuable light on the upbringing and education of a boy from a comfortably off Guernsey farming family, while Hilary's later career, after his narrative ends, is an interesting example of the way in which sea captains from all parts of the British Isles viewed Cardiff, the most rapidly expanding port in the region of which the Channel Islands were part, as an ideal place in which to settle and make a new life ashore, hopefully (as in Hilary's case) establishing a business which would long outlive its founder. Even the literary gloss which has clearly been added to the basic narrative has its value, since it probably illustrates what sort of books Hilary read in his leisure hours and how they influenced him when he came to write one of his own. His 'Retrospect', however, is certainly not to be dismissed as fiction but is a solid, reliable historical source which well merits publication in full, nearly a century and a half after it was composed, ostensibly for the entertainment of none but its author.

*

[1] Below, pp. 226, 217–19, 240–4.

Hilary Marquand's 'Retrospect' is written in a neat copperplate hand, with a few contemporary revisions to words and phrases, in two bound foolscap volumes, one of which has a label on which is written 'HMQ 1850' on the cover, indicating that he had had the book by him for a few years before starting to write. Comparison of the text with surviving letters from Hilary to his wife indicates that the work is autograph. The books have descended in the Marquand family since Hilary's death in 1872 and now belong to Eric Blondel Marquand, the author's great-grandson, who a few years ago supervised their transcription into a typescript which forms the basis of this edition. Mr Marquand is also responsible for dividing the text into chapters and inserting the chapter headings and subheadings used for this edition. In preparing the work for publication, nothing has been added to or omitted from Hilary's own words, apart from some tidying of the punctuation to make the text easier to read and a few minor rephrasings which have been explained in the footnotes. Occasional archaic and dialect spellings have been retained, as has the orthography of the passages in French and Spanish.

Hilary included a thin sprinkling of footnotes in his text, glossing some nautical terms which might be unfamiliar to the general reader, translating Latin proverbs or adding sentences to amplify the main text. These have been retained in this edition and are identified by the initials [HM] at the end of the note. Other footnotes not so flagged are my own work, although these have been kept to a minimum to avoid overburdening a book intended for a general rather than specialist readership. I have assumed that the reader will be able to cope with the short passages of direct speech in French but have translated the occasional phrases in Spanish. I have resisted the temptation to discuss every place mentioned in the text, unless its name has changed since 1855 or I have felt that some comment by Hilary required further explanation. I have, however, glossed obscure words or ones whose usage by Hilary seems to be of particular interest.

University of Wales
Cardiff

Philip Riden

1. Portrait of Hilary Marquand by A. Royer, 1853.

2. Portrait of Hilary's father, David Marquand. Undated and unsigned, but presumably also by Royer, *c*. 1853–4.

3. Portrait of Hilary's mother, Margaret (Thoume), by A. Royer, 1854.

4. The Marquand family's Guernsey home, La Brigade, painted by the Cardiff artist, Sydney Broad, *c.* 1910.

5. La Brigade today.

6. Castel Church, from a drawing by W. Berry, where Hilary and Louisa were married on 29 January 1851. (*States of Guernsey Heritage Committee*)

7. The Quay at St Peter Port in Hilary's day, from a lithograph by P.J. Naftel. (*States of Guernsey Heritage Committee*)

8. Hilary and Louisa's first married home in St Peter Port at 35 Mount Durand.

9. Hilary and Louisa's later home in St Peter Port at 30 Hauteville, owned by his uncle Hilary.

10. The SS *Adelaide*, on which Hilary served as an ordinary seaman in 1842–44, under the tyrannical command of Capt. Robert Taylor. (*States of*

11. A contemporary engraving of the Cuban port of Havana, which Hilary visited on his first voyage (from S. Hazard, *Cuba with pen and pencil* (1873)).

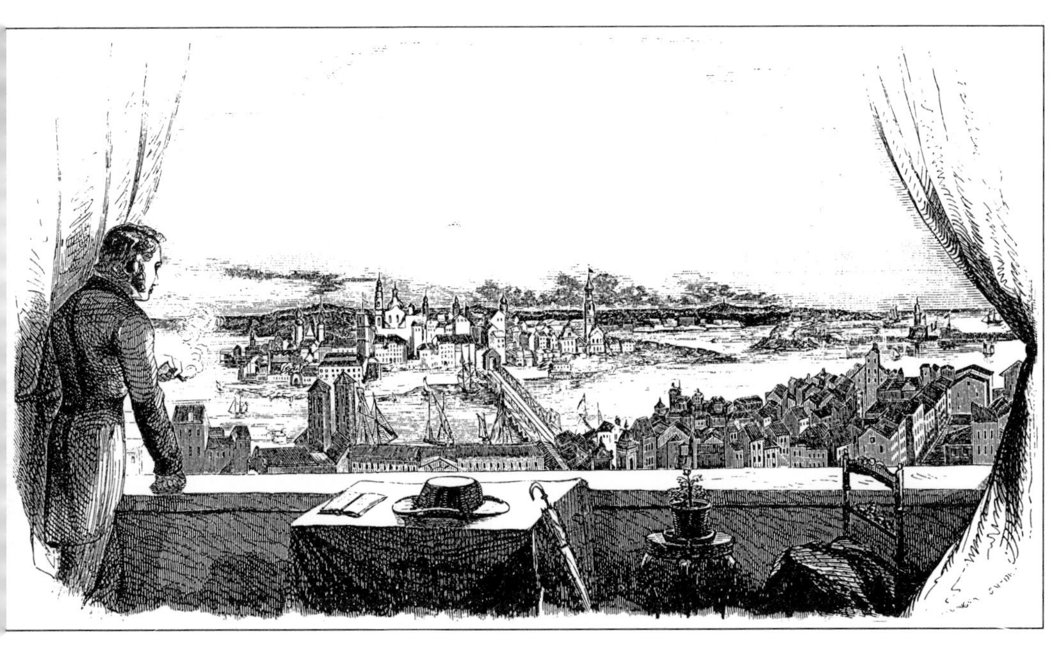

12. A contemporary engraving of the Brazilian port of Pernambuco (the modern Recife), which Hilary mentions on several occasions in his autobiography (from D.P. Kidder and J.C. Fletcher, *Brazil and the Brazilians, portrayed in historical and descriptive sketches* (Philadelphia and New York, 1857).

13. A photograph of Hilary and Louisa Marquand and their son Hilary Blondel (aged 12), taken in 1866 at Nantes, when the boy was at school there.

14. A photograph of H.B. Marquand as a young man, published (probably some years after it was taken) in 1896. (*Welsh Industrial & Maritime Museum*)

15. A photograph of H.B. Marquand in middle age, probably taken about 1900.

16. The SS *Earl of Dumfries*, built at Sunderland in 1882 for Martin & Marquand of Cardiff. (*Welsh Industrial & Maritime Museum*)

17. The SS *Earl of Roseberry*, another of Martin & Marquand's ships, in the entrance basin of Bute East Dock, Cardiff. (*Welsh Industrial & Maritime Museum*)

18. 'Guernsey Villa', 11 East Grove, Tredegarville, Hilary and Louisa's first home in Cardiff.

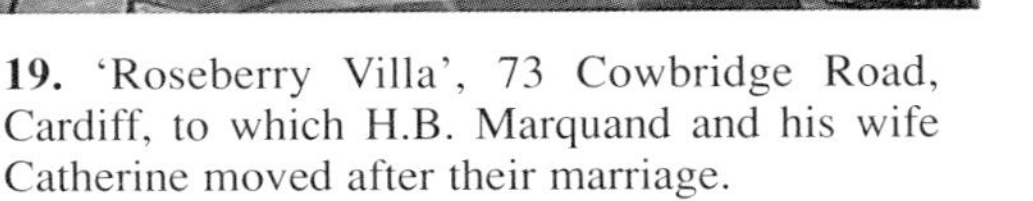

19. 'Roseberry Villa', 73 Cowbridge Road, Cardiff, to which H.B. Marquand and his wife Catherine moved after their marriage.

20. 'Eastwood', 57 Cathedral Road, Hilary and Catherine Marquand's second married home.

21. Hilary and Catherine Marquand in the grounds of 'Wellclose', Penylan, in about 1930.

22. Hilary and Catherine's son Leonard Marquand, who also became a ship-owner in Cardiff. (*Welsh Industrial & Maritime Museum*)

– 1825 –

Childhood

I was born in the year of our Lord one thousand eight hundred and twenty five and since that time have seen a little of the rough and smooth, ups and downs of this world, though perhaps not so much of the first and last as many of my fellow creatures in the same course as I have pursued. Yet it is, I believe, a natural feeling with us all, when arrived at a certain period of our existence and casting a retrospective view on the past, to think that we have seen and encountered a great deal.

Since the period I have above mentioned until the age of six years I cannot give any account of myself that would tend to be of any satisfaction, or amusement, to any of my gentle readers who may chance to lay hold of this fragment, though it is not my intention that many should indulge in the amusement of its perusal, if indeed amusement can be found within its space. I have not undertaken to trace out these lines for any other purpose than to gratify 'my own' inclination. I have never had the intention of giving them publicity; but should they chance against my will in after years to meet the eyes of the world, I trust that at least they will not be found to merit ridicule.

At the period which I have just mentioned I recollect that I was 'a naughty boy' running about the house, gambolling about the yards and fields with the remainder of my brothers, three in number, two of which were my seniors, and which two had been placed at school already some time. It was at this time that I also was placed in company with them, and indeed it might be said that we were never out of school, for though we were only confined there for seven hours during the day, yet we were so strictly attended to by our honoured parents at home that we looked upon it as continual confinement.

My father, a rigid disciplinarian, always maintained a particular strictness with us, and endeavoured always to check the first symptoms of a wild habit in us. He was, moreover, a zealous member of the Church and determined to follow its precepts to bring up his children in the 'nurture and admonition of the Lord', which indeed I have cause to bless him for now, and his memory hereafter if spared since him.[1] My mother also did not lack in duty towards her offspring: ever affectionately attached to us, she would always do her utmost to inculcate in us the principles of virtue, and indeed her remonstrances, whensoever we gave cause for them, were oftener attended to with more caution from us and more satisfaction to herself than were those of my father, though perhaps given out with a much greater degree of austerity, but such were our feelings towards our parents, we were ruled by fear from the one, and by love from the other.[2]

The lolly-pop school and life at home

The school that we were placed at lay at some distance from our home so that it was necessary to be got in readiness at an early hour. The schoolmaster was an old lady who was, or seemed to be, fond of punctuality, and strictly enforced it upon her pupils, and whenever that rule of her school was broken, the culprit was sure of his punishment, which generally was a rap on the head with her sewing thimble, or even sometimes a more disgracing punishment was inflicted with the sprig of an elm tree, which was by laying us across her knees and rising up the hinder part of our little plaid surtouts[3] would apply the said sprig to a fleshy part that I shall not name with such power that made us resolve never to loiter on the way to school again. Indeed we found such a pricking sensation after the punishment that we invariably sought relief with

[1] A slightly obscure construction, apparently intended to mean 'if I survive him'.

[2] Mr Eric Marquand recalls that his grandfather, Hilary's son H.B. Marquand, maintained a like regime and was a very severe father much addicted to the rod.

[3] The standard dictionary definition (overcoat or greatcoat) may be intended here, unless Hilary is using the word in its literal sense to mean an 'overall', perhaps a smock or similar garment worn by young children.

both our hands behind us grasping the aching part with as much seeming earnestness as if we had feared its abduction. We therefore after having smarted once for our non-attendance to punctuality, made a virtue of necessity as it were, and hurried on every morning, often for a few successive days arriving much before the time of entering, which time was spent in innocent amusement upon a grass plot that lay close to the house until at last the harsh voice of our worthy preceptress disturbed us in our unbounded pleasures, and hurried us to our respective seats. Which each having occupied, a stillness reigned throughout the room such as would have made the fall of a feather on the floor audible, but however it was seldom this silence peculiar to the entering of the schoolroom after the fatigue of some half-hour's play lasted long. It was sure to be broken by the roaring out of some of the young urchins, who when interrogated as to the cause of his cries would answer with distorted features, 'John is pinching me' or 'Thom is pricking me with a pin', or if some of the female sex (for there were as many girls as boys), 'That boy is stealing my thread' or 'This boy has torn my apron' etc, etc. Such were the usual disturbances in the school until the 'Mistress' had again made use of her switch and thereby restored a temporary peace.

But not withstanding her severity when necessary, in justice to her I must say that if we behaved well, we were also treated well. If, for instance, we learnt and repeated our lesson correctly, which consisted of six words of one syllable such as CAT, DOG, and suchlike, we were rewarded the very next time she washed her parrot with a wing feather; that is if he happened to lose one, and if not we anxiously awaited for the next washing day for Polly, when we did not forget to remind her of the promise she had made us and indeed, to her credit, be it said she seldom failed to accomplish it, though sometimes there were more promises than feathers but the deficiency on such occasions was soon made up by the division of a lolly-pop amongst three or four.

The good old dame sold lolly-pops as well as kept school and many an honest penny she made by them, as it was seldom that many of us were without our double (half a farthing)[1] every morning on coming to school, which we managed to draw by our entreaties from our good-natured mothers, indeed I have often thought upon her plan of selling such tempting bait and have always approved of it. It was a source of gain to her in more than one way for albeit we paid her many pennies amongst us all in the course of half a year, yet that was not her only way of gain. All the children in the neighbourhood knew of this lolly-pop school and therefore entreated their parents to send them to school even before they were able to walk there themselves. Our parents also found the beneficial results of this, to us, allurement, for when not exactly in school humour and perhaps objecting to be washed, or dressed for school, the promise of a double would dispel all our sourness in an instant, and the process of washing, dressing, and combing down the hair was done as quick as ever it lay in the power of the mother to do it, and that without the least signs of murmuring or discontentment on our parts. Indeed it often happened that this process which we had to undergo every morning was not gone through with sufficient dexterity to please us. Often after the promise of my double to go to school with, have I reminded my mother that it was getting late, and under pretence of my earnest desire of keeping up the rules of punctuality have pressed upon her to attend to my fitness for school when other and more pressing duty called her away.

One instance of the force of these sugar plums upon our fondness for school I recollect, and will mention. It happened one day between the hours of twelve and one, our dinner hour, that having finished our repast which, by the way, did not occupy much time, especially if we had some preconcerted game to go through, we had all repaired to the aforementioned grass plot, our play ground, and were exhibiting our skill in architecture by building houses with small stones and sticks picked up on the adjacent premises, when a carriage passed by in which were comfortably seated a lady and gentleman. Struck, I suppose, by our appearance

[1] Hilary's gloss (presumably for the benefit of readers outside Guernsey) is correct (cf. *OED*).

'en masse', so many young urchins grouped up together in innocent play, all young, but many younger, many not being able to pronounce their names distinctly. Struck, I say by the appearance of our youth and innocence or by the youthful beauty which some of us possessed, perhaps by both, the lady called out to us and asked us if we all were good children, when most of us hung down our heads and could not venture a reply to such a serious question fearing to offend our Maker by telling a falsehood and ashamed of telling the truth. However, on the second repetition of the question one little fellow yet habited in petticoats ventured to mutter out a response as plain and as loud as he could, 'O yes, Mam, we is all very good, for the Missus told us so dis-morning'. Satisfied that a spokesman had arisen among us, we all ventured to raise our eyes from the ground to the carriage when to our inexpressible joy we heard the chink of money, and soon after were told to 'look out for scrambles', and the next moment a volley of doubles fell among us; when of a certainty there was a scramble, one rolling over the other, each trying to outdo his companion, one moment picking up the coins, the next losing them again trying to pick up more; till at last worn out and fatigued each began to content himself with what he had and to withdraw, but the strongest party came off the richest; I being of that number had as many as five for my booty whilst of the youngest many had none. However, when the affray was over, everything was arranged very satisfactory, as the good lady gave to them that had none, and made those that had many divide about equal with the others, so that when this degree of equalization was accomplished among us, everybody seemed satisfied and thought of nothing next but the lolly-pops. Nor do I recollect that any even thought of expressing their gratitude to the donor, so much were we all engrossed with the thoughts of the coming sweetmeats. However, I do not think they expected any expression of gratitude from us. I now feel confident they must have been highly amused at our scramble and thought themselves sufficiently thanked at the evident manifestation of joy which was visible in each countenance. No sooner had the carriage drove away than we hurried to the school and made our wealth known to our worthy governess, which promised inevitable destruction to her store of lolly-pops. But however she was not ignorant of our possession of some booty, but more or less she could not tell, she had been an unseen gazer at the transaction on the grass plot, and smiled good naturedly at our good disposition in making a right use of it. She therefore bid us all take her advice and deposit the money into her hands, and that after giving us each a lolly-pop said she would make some fresh ones and that every morning on our punctual arrival at school we should receive another so long as the money lasted; and moreover since we had evinced such readiness to let her take care of our money, that she would, being about to make fresh ones, give us two for the price of one, a promise which made all our hands as by magic stretched out towards her with their entire contents, nor did we evince the slightest scruple at making her the possessor of our small fortunes under the circumstances of such sweet reward.

Having therefore signed and sealed this mutual agreement so satisfactory to all parties, the money was carefully deposited in the savings bank of the good dame, a large pocket that hung on her right hip fastened around her by no means slender waist by the aid of at least a fathom of broad tape, the whole being carefully concealed by the skirts of her upper garment which descended just low enough to conceal from the view of more inquisitive eyes than ours, the numberless gatherings of I do not pretend to know what formed there.

One thing, however, I can still recollect which happened one day and gave some of us reason to form an idea of the immense rotundity of her seating side, this happened I believe after a tremendous excursion about the schoolroom after her deserting inclined parrot, who was nevertheless ultimately captured and rechained to its wonted post, some of us perceived the floor all strewed over with bran leaving a well marked out trace of the old woman's course, and indeed on closer investigation beheld to our utter consternation the track following in close connection with her heels, wither she directed her steps. One of the youngest pupils of her sex, on perceiving this strange phenomenon immediately cried out, 'O Missus, look here!' but was soon hushed by the good lady who, on perceiving the cause of the child's wonderment, immediately ordered one of the seniors to take a sweeping brush and make the floor clean again, placing the bran in a basket given to her for the purpose, then immediately retired from our presence for half an hour. Now I did not pretend to know where the bran proceeded from, but many were the conjectures formed during her absence. Perhaps if this should meet the eyes of some of the knowing fair,[1] they may easily find a solution to this so strange an occurrence.

Now to resume my former reminiscence, after the security of our money by the good old lady we were presented each with a lolly-pop and sent to our seats where soon our wonted avocations were resumed. The afternoon delightfully passed away, and we were again on the way to our homes. The next morning, contrary to our usual habits, we were up at an early hour, and with our little spelling book in hand would fain have made our way to school an hour before the time, and in our *déshabillé*, but however notwithstanding our impatience which indeed pleased my mother very much, while it made her wonder at the great change that had taken place in us. She was too careful a mother to permit us to take our leave of her without having first gone through our morning toilet. That gone through to her satisfaction we were then called 'good boys' and made to take each other's hand, and with several injunctions as to our safety from the carts, carriages etc on the road, and finally with her blessing we took our departure. Our eagerness to arrive before any of our schoolfellows so as to have the first choice of the sweets made us hurry on our way, leaving on such mornings all the butterflies and blue-bottles and even the robin's nest which we knew in the moss grown hedge of Farmer B...'s orchard, quite unmolested and unnoticed.

Such was our schoolgoing eagerness and our comportment for one whole week without deviation, which did not fail to attract the notice of our parents at home. Our mother was highly pleased at our good behaviour and indeed prided herself of having dutiful sons, on that account we were always well received on our return at evening, and not unfrequently did we find a nice little pudding or a cake in readiness for us, or in the absence of such, we were sure to obtain whatever we asked for, besides permission to go out

[1] i.e. 'fair sex'.

and play till bedtime, which generally was at dusk. These and numberless other advantages did we reap by being dutiful and school desirous. But oh! little did our poor mother know that the loadstone of our governess's lolly-pops was alone the cause of this great change in us, of this strong attraction to school. At last the doubles had come to an end, and the sweets had all been sucked, consequently the Missus gave us all warning to that effect, but oh what a change took place, the disappointed looks of each gave evidence of our peevishness. One could not learn his lesson, another could not be quiet, the girls could not sew, they pricked their fingers with the needle, in fact, nothing went on well that day, and not unfrequently was the squalling of some young urchin heard smarting under the pain of the sewing thimble.

At home with us things took just such a turn, we would not wait patiently to be washed, the teeth of the comb would hurt our heads, and in a moment of anger we would undo all the nice curls and divisions that had taken my mother so much time and trouble to fashion, in fact, we had, it was plain, taken a directly opposite turn, and nothing could remedy it for some time.

I have often, calling up the days of my childhood, thought upon this, and even now cannot but smile at the powerful influence of sugar plums over children, and indeed have also often admired the subtlety of the worthy old dame in selling them, so much do I admire her plan, that were I to turn my thoughts at keeping an infants' school I should decidedly have an NB at the end of my solicitations for pupils, 'Lolly-pops also sold'.

Having now given the outlines of my first scholarship I will again turn my thoughts towards home where I shall dwell for a few minutes before I give a description of the next school I was placed at, shortly after leaving that of worthy Dame Roberts. My father, whom I have already described as a rigid disciplinarian, was a farmer possessing what was deemed, in that part of the world where I received my birth, an extensive farm consisting of perhaps about 40 acres of fruitful land, and as a man that had himself been brought up on a farm in an active way and had perhaps never known the unpleasantness of an idle day, could not suffer to see in his children the least symptoms of inactiveness, consequently was ever on the watch against such, and though it was far greater pleasure for him to see us with a book in hand employing our youthful minds to some good, yet whenever our propensities led us to the contrary he would always find for us some employment wherewith to keep, if not our minds in employment, at least our bodies in exercise, and whensoever he had set us a task to perform, it was seldom we left it unexecuted, so great was his influence over us through the strict discipline with which he ruled us.

Whenever we were absent from school and remained at home, it was seldom we had the chance of giving free course to our own inclinations. On those occasions and when duty called him away to some further part of the estate, he would generally call away one of two of us with him, and then oblige us to lend a helping hand at whatsoever was going on, whilst the others had some set task to execute on some other part of the farm, such as pulling up weeds, picking stones from the meadows and thereby clearing the ground etc, which stones and weeds we had to produce for his inspection on his return, that our idleness or activeness might be proved, and not unfrequently when we proved the former were we made to confess the cause and receive the merits of our non-attendance to his orders, whilst on the contrary if we proved the latter, we were rewarded with hope of a present at Christmas or New Year and sometimes with a few pence.

On the Saturday, there being no school for us, and duty calling his presence in town, he would invariably shut us up with our books in an outhouse on the premises, when he would give each his lesson to learn, generally a short prayer, or a hymn, and on a promise that we should not ask for our liberty before his return except indeed at mealtime and that we should learn our lessons so as to repeat them correctly, he would present us each with a silver piece, either five or six pence, and so much were we intent upon earning our reward that we seldom found it tiresome to obey his injunctions. At evening when he returned he would summon us to him and having questioned us as to our good behaviour which of course we strongly avouched and referred him to our mother for stronger evidence, and repeating our lessons correctly, we received our promised reward, which generally was the brightest piece that had passed through his hands that day. Then it was that our joy was full, dancing about with our piece in hand, showing it as a trophy to our merits to all the household, then comparing them with each other and ultimately quarrelling together as to whose was the brightest. This money, after we had possessed it for a few days and become used to its brightness and less dazzled with it, we, at the request of our mother, would give it her in charge, when it was afterwards distributed at intervals in small sums generally for the gratification of our sweet teeth.

On Sundays it was a general rule for all the family to attend church regularly twice, and not unfrequently three times a day. And I am sure it must have been great satisfaction for our parents to witness our number, generally walking before them with such a degree of decorum as would have given credit to better children than we were. But I must allow that had we been left to ourselves unguided by our parents, we should likely not have behaved with such a degree of propriety.

At church though, we generally found the time to slip by but very slowly, and though we often had to punish our eyes by keeping them awake against their desire, yet we feared to show the least uneasiness or evince the least degree of carelessness. On our egress from the church we generally sought a friend from whom we begged to know the chapter and verse from whence the text had been taken, which request granted we carefully imprinted it in our memories, and in fact being now wide awake we had no trouble to retain it, nor would we have from the minister's own mouth if he had given it out to us on the road home instead of from his pulpit, but so it was with us, notwithstanding the necessity of knowing the text by heart on our return from church, yet when there we could not exercise any command over our memories, influenced I suppose by the enchantments of Morpheus.[1]

Arrived at home, and dinner being served up, each took his respective seat, nor did we once fall out on that score, as each had his pointed out by a glance of the eye and a motion of my father's finger, whilst he occupied the most honourable place at the head of the table; an unbroken silence reigned whilst the process of

[1] In classical mythology, the god of dreams, son of Hypnus, the god of sleep.

carving was being gone through, which perhaps was only found tedious by our more hungry stomachs on that day than on a week days, not having had access to the orchards which consequently brought them emptier by some pounds of indigestible fruit, at table. At last our unmarked impatience was satisfied by the presence of a good plateful of wholesome food before us, which we only waited for the completion of grace before meat to put out of sight, this done and washed down by a good glass of cider which by the bye occasions my mouth to water now, and perhaps repeated one or twice more, at least if not with the same nutriment, perhaps with a still much more palatable one 'a good fruit pudding'. We were then just fit for a good game at 'hide and go seek' or 'blind man's buff' but not so; we had to undergo an examination which had only been postponed so as not to disturb the masticating qualities of each individual, as well as to give every opportunity of doing ample justice to their stomachs.

But now the table being cleared, the cloth removed, and the wine being set before my father (for we were not allowed to indulge in this luxury), who after emptying the first glass and replenishing it, would send one of us out to the hay rick to procure for him a chosen stem wherewith to pick his teeth,[1] then while in this act he would commence with our dread interrogation.

'Well boys, have you heard a good sermon this morning?'

'Yes Father', was our unanimous reply.

'Do you recollect the text and where it was taken from?'

'Yes Father.'

'Well I am glad to hear that, as it is a proof that you have been attentive.' (A look at each other and a laugh in our sleeve.)

'David, perhaps you will name the chapter and the verse to me.'

'Yes Father', then the chapter and the verse were named.

'John, is that correct?'

'Yes, Father.'

'Is it so Hilary?'

'Yes, Father.'

'Is it so Nicholas?'

[1] This has always been his favourite toothpick. [HM]

'Yes, Father.'

'Well I also agree that is correct, so far you are good boys.'

Now for the words of the said verse, this task was seldom performed without impediment, but if we seemed to know the main part of the whole, he appeared to be satisfied and was lenient enough as seldom to exact from us a correct repetition.

'Now then David, take the Bible from yonder shelf and find the said chapter and read it out, loud and distinctly.'

This was done whilst we others sat round the reader, and appeared as serious as we had done in church, and very often as sleepy. After that chapter was read, another took the reader's seat and read a chapter from some other book directed by our worthy parent, to witness our ability, or inability, in finding it out.

This mode of exercise was gone through every Sunday when we did not attend afternoon service, but when we did, it was dispensed with till the evening, and each in his own turn had to read a chapter until we all had read one apiece, then would our worthy tutor comment on some of the most striking parts of one or more of the chapters for our enlightenment and benefit, though it sometimes happened that before we had concluded our reading he had fallen asleep. On such occasions we would carefully move from our seats and, fearful of disturbing him, walk on tip toe to the door, open it gently and close it in the same manner after us, then finding ourselves once more at liberty, we would indulge in innocent recreation until tea time, checking however any impetuous desire that might arise in our breast for though childlike we were fond of play, yet so much had we been taught to reverence the Sabbath that we were seldom guilty of profaning it; even then at that early age can I say with veneration towards my parents that the principles of piety were already kindled. Seldom did we retire to rest without offering up our supplications unto the throne of grace, and invariably did we, if we felt guilty of any act of disobedience or of having committed any crime in telling a falsehood or in any other way, make an open confession to our mother on retiring to rest and sue for forgiveness, which was always in all cases of true penitence granted us but with strict injunctions to sue also for forgiveness from Him that watcheth over all our actions.

My father had all vicious habits in abhorrence, but if there was any he regarded in a worse light than another it was that of lying. A liar he had in utter detestation, and none of his children could be guilty of that vice with impunity, therefore if ever we made use of a lie to hide a lesser or greater fault and discovered afterwards, we unquestionably incurred his displeasure and were sure of severe chastisement.

I recollect one instance of his severity on such an occasion which I will relate. One day being at play with my brothers in the yard, I accidentally threw a stone in the window of one of our outhouses and consequently broke a pane of glass, but on being questioned by him I protested my innocence, fearing the punishment that his threatening countenance promised the guilty one. My brothers likewise protested theirs, and so matters ended for the present, and I was very joyful at having escaped at so cheap a rate. We retired to rest and I soon forgot in sweet sleep the mischief I had performed, though not so easily the offence I had committed by telling a falsehood. However in the hope of repairing the offence on the morrow with my mother I forgot it all, but behold! on the morrow before I had yet satisfied nature, I was awakened by the removal of the bed clothes over me, and on casting up my eyes beheld my father with a birch in his hand who told me he had come to punish me for two faults, the first for breaking a pane of glass, the second for telling a falsehood; now where or how he had found me out I knew not, but however it mattered little, I could not deny it again, but sought then through tears, entreaties and an open confession for pardon, and with a promise of never telling another falsehood, but all these were of no avail, he could not allow his children to lie with impunity and therefore out of bed I had to jump and receive my justly merited punishment, and by the bye, the birch was so well applied that I kept a strict maintenance to truth for a long time afterwards nor could I forget the shattered pane of glass, and for perhaps the self-same reason do I recollect it now and am able to recall the incident to my memory as fresh as if it had only taken place yesterday.

This short sketch will serve to give the reader an idea of my parents' mode of training up their children, though indeed it is but a very imperfect one, nor can it be denied that the proverb was strictly adhered to 'Train up a child in the way he should walk, and when he becomes old he will not depart from it'. But though no care or pains were spared by my parents to follow up the first part of this essential paraphrase, yet whether the happy results protested in the latter part have been the fruits of their toil remains yet to be told, the sequel of this fragment however will show. But in justice to them I will yet add that whether it has, or has not been the case, they can in their good old age look back with much satisfaction to themselves upon the past, and feel they have done their duty; their children's future moral and spiritual welfare they have cherished and cultivated in their earlier days, and alas! if the carnal mind which is ever at enmity against God, if the sinful lusts of the flesh and the devil have blighted all, or some of their hopes, if indeed the seed sown has been choked by the tares of a depraved world, yet at least can they find assuagement in their grief through a self-conviction of having acted the part of dutiful parents. But though my veneration for them leads me thus far as to point out the crystal fountain, where in the sultry days of disappointment they can draw forth from the refreshing streams of an unblemished conscience; yet I by no means pretend to assert they have ever had the necessity of having recourse to such a valuable provision. However, here I must leave them for the present with all the good wishes of a dutiful son, ever grateful for the numberless cares bestowed upon me in my youth, and now having attained the age of manhood and the summit of my desires, can look back with a tenfold degree of gratitude upon them for the many virtues implanted, and which have ever been the precursors of my present attainments.

The lash-threatening school

I will then endeavour to resume my narrative by following it from that memorable epoch in my life when I was obliged to bid Adieu to all its sweets — The Lolly-Pop Seminary. The next school I was placed at, my two elder brothers in company, was one calculated by my parents to be of a little more note, and more adapted for our growing years; but in truth it was one little adapted to improve our growing morals, a fact which soon disclosed itself in us to the indescribable astonishment of our parents, who had been led to entertain the highest respect for the governor's character, as well as profound esteem of his abilities, through I presume the insinuating method in which he always made his own solicitations personally.

He was an excellent physiognomist and could read deep into a second person's character after a short introduction, consequently was always ready to suit his outward man to the very shadow of his conversationist; upon his introduction with my father he soon found out the necessity of clothing himself with the garb of a strict moralist and even wearing the mark of piety — which indeed answered his purpose very well for after having ingratiated himself thus far and promised to attend to the morals of his pupils as well as to their education otherwise, he found no trouble in adding our names to his already long list. But it will be as well here to remark that the list of names which he carried in his pocket for display when occasion required it, and the list of boys at school greatly differed, there being some five and twenty in the former whilst there was but eleven in the latter after we were added.

The first few days of our initiation to the rules of this academy certainly met with our disapproval, the change being so great in all instances to our former; and we began to evince that it would be difficult to habituate ourselves to it. For instance it was a lash-threatening schoolmaster that overruled us in the present case, whilst in the latter it was a parrot-feather-promising-school-missus. The former had nothing sweet about him, the latter sold 'Lolly-pops'! Here were all wicked boys and we the juniors; there was amiable young girls and we the seniors!.

In fact everything evinced a total change to our established opinion of a schoolhouse; the boys quarrelled, swore, told lies, and fought; the master got occasionally inebriated and either kept himself awake by maltreating us, or fell asleep and left us to maltreat each other. But *malgré* all this, time works its miracles. After a few weeks tuition in these sciences and the promised care of our morals utterly disregarded, we soon made our appearance on the stage as competent actors in the daily tragedies, and found our former dislike to the school was fast retreating into the gloomier shades of oblivion, and more especially after having come off conqueror in two or three of the affairs of honour which daily took place among us, we were duly elected by a majority as 'Cocks of the Walk'.

Proud of our then elevated station it was natural we should feel less dread at going to school and more self-glory at maintaining our pre-eminence when there. There remained now but one more glorious enterprise to achieve, the which if we could effect either by storm or otherwise, our glory would be complete; the nature of it truly was in itself dangerous enough but notwithstanding the envy of the laurels that would follow its achievement it made the parties desirous of wearing them look upon danger only as a mere want of courage and, consequently, a meeting of all the elder schoolboys was summoned and held in which my senior brother occupied the chair.

The downfall of our worthy pedagogue was then moved and pointed out in terms so very applicable that each word seemed to have an instantaneous effect in the breast of the hearers — his downfall was motioned as a necessity, for redress of wrongs — the which eloquent speech was heartily cheered by the worthy vice-president in the rear (your humble servant) and unanimously seconded by the assembly at large; such hearty responses to the feelings of the worthy president could not fail to excite the joy with which he was already prepossessed, to such a degree that he deigned to look over his suit with self-satisfaction and call them 'brave fellows', an appellation which made them rear up the head, each trying to outdo the other in stature while fresh vows were taken to prove themselves worthy of the honour that had just been done them. After the first outbursts of joy had subsided a little, the worthy president again called to order, and immediately a silence reigned equal to the stillness of night. He then moved that it was an incumbent duty he felt on himself to remind them that it was necessary to fix a time and place for carrying their project into execution (hear, hear). He did not doubt for a moment that their own good sense and judgement was quite equal to the task, but at the same time if they would permit him he would give them his own opinion on the subject (hear, hear) (thousands of applause).

He had seriously considered the matter over and over, and weighing one opinion with the other besides consulting with his very worthy and able colleagues, he had concluded by judging there could not be a fitter opportunity than when their enemy had heartily worshipped his idol God Bacchus, and therefore he moved further (a shout of applause) that if their own better judgement had not fixed upon a better plan, but coincided with him, that he should name a committee for the purpose of watching his fervency and zeal to his said god. Among deafening cheers the worthy vice-president made it known to his more powerful friend that the feeling amongst his people was unanimous, therefore a committee was named of four sharp-sighted individuals whose duty it was daily to report to the president how the mercury of our worthy pedagogue's headometer rose or fell. This duty was faithfully performed for two days or upwards but still it was never judged to have risen sufficiently until at last the happy time came, the committee reporting the headometer to be some one hundred and twenty above fahrenheit.

Now was the time, 'strike the iron while it is hot' was the cry, and to the scene of action one and all repaired, and sure enough the report had not been much exaggerated, if at all, for here lay with his back and head reclined against the wall and the remainder of his body resting on the floor, and in a happy state of unconsciousness, the victim of our ire. All around him gazing upon his insensibility and in the act of putting our threat in execution and only waiting then the implement for use to be sufficiently heated, the worthy president said that it being always well to enter into every execution with due precaution he would vote that it should be tested if he actually was in the deep worship of his god, or if he only slept. That being a very necessary precaution the test was put, which was done by tumbling the stool he lay under upon him, which only had the effect of producing two or three unintelligible mutterings which satisfied all parties that he was, as one of our learned associates expressed it, 'not able to see daylight through a nine-barred gate'. Accordingly all parties being satisfied on that score we laid hold of our victim by the lower extremities and dragged him in the centre of the schoolroom where in a short time our long promised punishment was executed without the least resistance on his part and so successfully did we achieve our task that he put us in mind of it at every minute of the day for some weeks afterwards, indeed his continual restlessness and seeming uneasy disposition joined with the momentary application of his right hand to the seat of uneasiness might have induced an ignorant observer to believe that he harboured about him a host of troublesome companions, but it was not so with us. We all knew what ailed him and therefore enjoyed the more with hard suppressed laughter every uneasy motion of his features, which always became more and more perceptible with the increasing height of his headometer, each potion generally having the influence of raising it four degrees and was seldom at a stand till it had reached eighty or ninety. Notwithstanding his uneasiness, as I have already mentioned, in justice to him I must say he bore it valiantly, never once complaining to any of us, nor indeed did he seem to have the least suspicion of the guilt which secretly accused us, but whether it was feigned ignorance or whether he feared to make a discovery knowing the shame that would be his on such an occasion, I know not, but such it was he left us in the full enjoyment of our malice unmolested, nor did we fail to enjoy it, each in his absence mimicking all his motions with such a degree of self-satisfaction and pleasure as would have revived the heart of a dying miser.

The reader may pause ere he has reached this line and ask what was the nature of the punishment inflicted which caused the punished so much uneasiness, and the punishers so much pleasure. But I will here answer that he is too inquisitive, or at least if he is not, I am too reserved to tell him. Let what I have already too lengthedly expressed suffice; taking care always to misapply none of its meanings, nor to infer from what is actually not immodest, any wrong conjectures.

Shortly after this event our moral character was by our parents perceived to be contaminated in a more or less degree, and being both surprised and grieved at this change, not knowing perhaps from whence proceeded the direful cause, an investigation ensued which soon opened their eyes to the truth, consequently an irrevocable warning was given to the master and at the end of the quarter we left his care to be consigned to that of his superior in every quality. Whilst I have dwelt perhaps freely upon his failures,

I have also perhaps done him an injustice in not remarking the progress I had made under his tuition, but I feel it a duty owed him to state that in writing and arithmetic I had decidedly improved, for when I entered his school I was but very indifferently instructed in the rudiments of the spelling book, and as for being an arithmetician I was no more than in being able to calculate that four lolly-pops were worth a half-penny. But when I left him I was already a good writer and had filled many a copybook to his, mine and my parents' satisfaction. In arithmetic I had got on as far as division tolerably to my credit, I knew also in geography that Europe, Asia, Africa and America constituted the four quarters of the globe, whilst in grammar I knew it was the art of speaking and writing the English language with propriety, so that in the short space of some six months it was a tolerable share of learning I had gained.

A gem among schoolmasters

The next personage to whom my youth was consigned was a man as much superior to the latter as I was inferior to a good boy. Indeed he was a gem amongst schoolmasters, and though he made no outward show above his contemporaries, yet he decidedly excelled most of them. I had not been many weeks under his care before all those vices with which I had left the latter school vanished and in their places were deeply inculcated the seed of hopeful virtues.

We were, if my memory does not fail me, seventeen in number, all children of respectable parents and of sensible ages; the youngest must have been about eight years old, but most of them exceeded twelve, and the order and discipline that reigned amongst that number will ever be a credit to him that maintained it. Scarcely ever was a whisper heard during the hours of exercise but every one to his respective task seemed riveted, and I believe the general desire with every one was to give the master satisfaction, at least I am sure such were my feelings towards him, and I am even now proud to say that I seldom failed in that desire.

I had not been long with him before he declared that I was the smartest boy in the school and the one that reflected the most credit upon him. At writing, in which his was a beautiful hand, he declared that if I wished, in a very short time I would excel him and certainly though I tried my utmost, yet I never could but I was nevertheless sure of carrying away the prize always. At German text also I was an adept and in no wonder perhaps, for I was partially fond of it, on account of its many beautiful flourishes I suppose, and was always at it every idle moment I had, whether it was with pen, pencil, or a piece of chalk no matter, but with the first thing that came to hand I was sure to chalk everything in my reach.

In grammar and arithmetic I also made great progress, in fact I was not one of the dullest of boys and when my propensities met with attendance and cultivation they very soon displayed themselves in perceptible measures. I could also relate any particular passage of scripture in the New Testament, and many were the chapters I knew by heart. This was owing to an admirable plan of our governor's, whensoever we were backward in any of our several exercises or had been guilty of misdemeanours, in short deserving of any punishment, instead of applying the rod as is generally the case with most schoolmasters to no good effect, he would in the first place seriously admonish us against the repetition of the like fault, but not even with a fair promise of attending to his injunctions could he let us off with impunity. No, ten or a dozen verses of some chapter in the New Testament were marked out to us and we had to repeat them without a fault or even impediment in our speech, before we left the school. By this mode he spared our backs, kept our intellect unimpaired through ill-treatment, whilst he keened our memories and propagated our general advancement in literature, and besides this gained for himself an affection bordering upon love from us, which contributed in no small degree to his comfort and our good.

Such was Mr Wakeham's mode of training up his pupils, and of him I shall always be able to speak in terms of greatest eulogy, and for him I will always entertain the highest respect coupled with no lesser degree of affection. I shall ever esteem him as an honourable gentleman, a friend to every child, and to every child's parent. Indeed at this moment I know not where he is, or what has become of him; it is many years since I am denied that pleasure, but I sincerely trust he is still carrying on his excellent tutorage to the advancement of a rising generation; but if not, and he has been called away ere this by death I trust he is yet happier in the enjoyment of the reward of an upright life made uprighter still through the virtues of piety. Living or dying his memory will ever be dear to me and thus I wish him a temporary adieu for the present to continue with my narrative.

Nine months had passed away at this very excellent school and it was suggested to my father by an uncle of mine that Mr Wakeham's school was no longer a fit place for the cultivation of my promising abilities and that it was necessary to remove me to another that had lately been established in the vicinity, where every branch of literature necessary to qualify a young man for any station in life was being attended to.

The Butcher

The terms per annum of this university were decidedly exorbitant, but my father, who regarded not the expense in a light to be compared to the completion of a liberal education in his children, agreed in my uncle's views and accordingly I and my senior brothers were placed at this university. And an unhappy moment it was for us when we entered it. Such a great contrast to that we had lately left failed not to produce in us an intimidation which only served to check our capacities and not to enlarge them. However, it is said that 'Eels get used to flaying', and a few weeks served to bring us in a measure to a like resignation, though never properly reconciled to it as long as we were there.

That sufficient was taught at this mart of science cannot be denied, but that much less was learnt was also a truth. I never knew of one of our collegians who was possessed of a capacity sufficiently spacious to store in the multitude of learning that was literally speaking crammed and heaped one over another into our 'knowledge box'. It was a general thing with us to learn our lessons *en masse* at home, and having time to look over them at school the next morning, we thereby freshened our memories. But I can say that it was also a general thing to have entirely forgotten the first before the last was repeated.

We had several teachers or assistants, each having his respective department. In the first place there was the head man, Mr Wadeson whom we designated by the very proper appellation of 'Butcher'. His duty was reading the morning prayers on opening the school, and God knows how unworthy he was of that office; the remainder of the day he did nothing but punish; as no teacher was allowed to exercise that authority, every culprit was sent to him at the head of the school where on interrogation he was obliged to confess what he had been sent up for, and from whom, after which he was pretty nearly served like the eels above mentioned, which was found the more unbearable not having, like them, got used to it yet.

I have witnessed instances of his cruelty over several individuals that would have stained the character of a hangman, nay more, I have myself been sufferer in a like instance, and may find an opportunity to give an account of it in a more distant page. If such shameful treatment is consistent with the duty of a schoolmaster, it were better for their parents to keep their children in ignorance. But no, I am happy to say it is not the case, and it is only the man that is void of all delicate feelings that will prove himself the barbarian over his pupils. Thus it was with Mr Wadeson. That he was a talented man it cannot be denied, his aquirements were almost boundless and could act the perfect gentleman without his rod; he paid a great deal of respect to his assistants and was treated by them equally although with more or less degree of awe.

But alas, albeit these, he had overbalancing faults. One, and certainly not the least, I have already named, the next that worked in conjunction with it and which generally excited the other was that of being like my first tutor, overzealous in the cause of Bacchus, though not like him laying down to worship for, I dare say their zeal was upon a par, yet Mr Wadeson adhered as much as lay in his power to the precept of worshipping in secret, and though he scarcely ever was without his prayer book yet it was only on occasions that he was seen at his devotions.

I remember having seen him once or twice in one week at them and the admirable way in which he indulged in his potions was amusing enough. He had come to school in a state of indisposition, so much so that he could not perform his task at morning prayer but was substituted by one of the assistants, and to say the truth he had a very haggard look that morning, a look that made many tremble in their skins, and in fact one or two soon after prayers trembled 'skins and all' at being sent to him for a misdemeanour during prayers. T'was that morning I took notice of his disposition particularly. A doctor's bottle of large size stood upon his desk with a large label fastened to its neck and a prescription written on it which could not be read by a distant observer. A tumbler lay also close to the bottle and the use of both were had recourse to several times during the forenoon, but each dose was followed by such distortions of the features that everybody must have felt for the great inconvenience he was placed in at having to swallow such bitter drugs.

In the course of the forenoon he had occasion to leave his seat and to go down to the extreme end of the schoolroom, which by the bye was a good length, so that he offered a few of us a good chance to satisfy our curiosity. A discussion arose who should go to his desk and read the label, but at last to save time I stepped up unperceived by him or any of the other tutors, and when I had satisfied myself, I was able to satisfy the others, by telling them the prescription was 'To be taken occasionally', and injunction which, by the bye, he appeared very earnest in complying with, but this did not yet sufficiently satisfy our inquisitiveness or establish our surmises.

Consequently an opportunity was watched for which did not offer itself before noon when he had retired from school and gone home to dinner. At this time a general desire amongst us who dined at school prevailed to ascertain the quality and to have a taste of the drug. But to our utter disappointment, arriving at his desk we found both the bottle and the glass removed, so that we conjectured he had either taken them with him or placed them in confinement within the escritoir. Now to try its security was only the work of a moment, but as surmised, it was carefully locked and the key no doubt in his pocket at the time. What was to be done? A suggestion arose to force it open but then it was as quickly repelled by another, which reminded us of the consequences.

At last it was voted that all the keys of our several desks be tried to fit it, and who can conceive our joy when one was found. The desk was opened and immediately before our eyes lay a similar bottle, with its label attached, to the one we had seen in the forenoon, but evidently not the same, for this one was prime full, whilst the other was partially if not altogether empty. The bottle was examined carefully, the label was found to be attached in too careless a manner to be the work of a doctor, whilst in the superscription we detected the hand writing of our skilful 'Butcher'. Everything tended to corroborate with our suspicions, but one more test yet remained unexecuted and this final one was to be the decision either pro or con — the cork in another instant flew from the bottle, and in as short a time its neck was pointed to at least a dozen noses, each of which was as quickly drawn back with a choking sensation caused by the strong draw we had taken of its yet stronger contents.

All instantaneously agreed that the drug was nothing more or less than French cognac but as a test of his abler judgement one said he would taste, he could not be deceived he said, in the taste, on the contrary he would analyse a mouthful and tell us how much adulteration and of what kind it contained. No sooner said than done, with the bottle in the right and the tumbler in the left hand, he stood pouring out the liquor with a seriousness that would have graced the features of a judge, that done he applied it to his nostrils first, then held it out at arm's length between the light and himself, strictly scrutinising the clearness of its contents, then applying it to his lips took one small sip which he carefully kept in his mouth and dexterously washed it with it, then turned around and spat it on the floor, after which a second sip was taken which was allowed to reach the concaves of his stomach, a smack of the lips followed, whilst the head was thrown upwards with an inclination to the left, the eyes pointing meaningfully to the opposite, and finally the bottle was replaced on the desk. All this had been done with such a degree of majesty that every beholder was riveted to the spot, and feeling assured that such a dexterous hand at tasting a liquor must be an able judge, we awaited his decision with impatience, and I am sure had he pronounced it 'tincture of rhubarb' we would have felt satisfied it was, *malgré* our own test in smelling. But however this was not the case, for after placing himself in an attitude of eloquence and brushing up his hair over the forehead with the palm of his hand he began thus.

'My Friends, after the honour you have done me in giving me the preference of being judge over the liquor contained in that bottle, I should brand myself with base ingratitude if I did not give you my candid opinion towards it. Therefore I wish to assure you that I am about to do as such, and hope you will receive the same without a doubt as to its worthiness. After smelling, viewing, tasting and analysing the said liquor with judgement, I declare it to be real first-rate "Jamaica Rum!" of at least ten years standing, and if there is any adulteration in the said rum (of which I do not think there is), it may peradventure be an extra quantity of aquafortis, and the reason I assign for this, is that I feel it rather overheating in my stomach now, but however this may only be a delusion on my part owing to the quantity taken. I would therefore repeat my assertion and have you to regard it as correct that it is first-rate "Jamaica Rum".'

A shout of applause followed this eloquent discourse, and all hands feeling satisfied as to the quality of the fluid, the bottle was refilled with water to its original mark and placed in the same position it had been taken from, and the desk carefully locked again. This done each gave free course to the exultation that overwhelmed him at the discovery he had made, nor did we keep it a secret. No, before that day's eve every school fellow had shared with us, and it was a subject of mimicry amongst us for a long time afterwards, often in our play hours some of us feigning sick and the able judge of the rum, having been elected as the doctor, would come and tend upon us with all the seriousness he was noted for, and after feeling our pulse, examining our tongues, and otherwise more minutely watching the symptoms of our malady through a host of interrogations, such as, 'How is your appetite?', 'Have you lately been to stool?' etc, etc, he would declare our indisposition only slight which he undertook to remove with a bottle of medicine (presenting us with it), 'To be taken occasionally'. The patient would then take a draught which was followed by all the horrid grimaces that he possibly could form his features into, and finally a speedy cure ensued. But this is only a tithe of the many games this subject brought forward, but it may be however sufficient to give an idea of the whole.

Every morning on the 'Butcher's' entrance in school his physiognomy was strictly scrutinized, when if any menacing traits were discovered, he was unanimously declared to have been at 'Jamaica', if any of us had dealing with him during the forenoon, he was sure to be interrogated by the others on his return, how high the temperature of Jamaica had attained. If any poor fellow was about being measured by the length of the detested cane, he was said to be 'receiving Jamaica', in fact nothing now transpired in school through the interference of Mr Wadeson but was sure to be declared 'influenced by Jamaica'. And ultimately when his dissolution took place and by it our happy emancipation, he was deeply lamented by the school at large with 'Poor fellow! he has then at last succumbed under the overpowering influence of the West Indian climate'. Others exemplified their sorrow for the deceased by remarking that his strong attachment to a West India produce was perhaps a fault, but more to be pitied than blamed, as one observed it, *'Gratis sua quemque voluptas'*;[1] another with uplifted eyes and a long drawn sigh declared that *'In caelo quies'*[2] but myself less hypocritical than any neighbours exclaimed, 'C'est tout fait de lui, et le voilà bien!' and argue it out that it was my opinion the end he had met was *'Recte et suaviter'*.[3]

But more of this anon, now we will let him rest in peace until his turn comes again, and turn our thoughts upon the next subject worthy our commentation upon. This was the next in consequence and the representative of the former. Mr Burman was the gentleman who filled the office (by no means a sinecure) of teacher in writing, arithmetic and dictation, and also as Latin master for the

[1] 'Everyone is led by his own pleasure'. [HM]

[2] 'There is rest in heaven'. [HM]

[3] 'Justly and mildly'. [HM]

2nd and 3rd classes. He was a person in no degree to be compared with Mr Wadeson. No, he was to all intents and purposes, and in every sense of the word 'a gentleman'. He had an admirable store of patience, which indeed must be owned is a very necessary provision for one filling the office that he did. This patience was blended with a no small degree of good humour, which made him the idol of everyone in the school, and many a 'flaying' of the boys' back and hands were avoided through his good nature.

Much may be said of this eminent personage but I will however limit myself to this short sketch for the present, as I will again have an opportunity of describing his merits in another page, having subsequently been placed entirely under his care.

The third person that fills up a very adequate place in my memory was our French teacher for whom I shall always entertain a great degree of respect, for albeit at the time I am speaking of I held him in utter derision, yet through his assiduity and care I became a proficient scholar in that branch of literature and have ever valued it more and more since, having always found it of the utmost usefulness in the several capacities I have filled, and in the different parts of the world I have visited. And now if called upon to give an opinion relating to the use of French or Latin I would unhesitatingly give it in favour of the former. I have found the French language to serve me as a key to the Spanish, Italian and Portugese, and with it I have aquired a sufficient knowledge of these languages to serve my purposes in any case. Whilst with the Latin which I certainly never had a great insight of, I have never been able to do more than now and then embellish a phrase by quoting a word occasionally.

Mon. Bourdic, for so our French teacher was called, had a very particular way of impressing into the minds of his pupils their several tasks by calling on Mr Wadeson, alias 'The Butcher', to open their understanding, which he was always prompt in doing; by this means if any of us ever went up to him with faulty exercises, it certainly was that we could not help it. He also had a way of his own to 'knock it into our heads' which was, when his patience was exhausted, which by the bye always was five minutes after he was in school, by taking us by the hair of the head without any regard to our pride in the neatness of its arrangement and thumping our chins on the edge of the desk he was seated at with such a degree of force that it made it very dangerous to the ivory of our mouths as well as to our tongues if unhappily we allowed them to come in contact. While inflicting this mode of punishment he would squeeze through his teeth, 'Vous êtes aussi bête que le bon Dieu est bon. Vous êtes aussi bête qu'el y'a d'étoilles dans le ciel' etc, etc.

It strikes my memory now of an incident that took place one fine day which of its nature was laughable enough. The party who was the principal actor in the scene was no other than our worthy orator, the judge of liquor. He was altogether a queer character and full of fun as well as wickedness and would run any risk or danger for the sake of gratifying his own inclinations as well as the amusement of others. Besides this his was an undaunted spirit and if once excited would have faced a lion. This same lad was also a pupil in Mons. Bourdic's department, but altogether a troublesome one, as he paid no attention whatever to his lessons nor seemed to care about ever learning anything of 'Johnny petite's' language as he called it. One day, however, he felt himself more ignorant of his duty than ever he had, and as to his exercise it was so carelessly translated that every word was a perceptible mistake. Just before being called up he had brought his exercise to me for examination, but I could not help laughing at the seeming purposely made mistakes. However, I corrected a few but had not time to correct all before I was summoned.

Conscious of his desserts he ruminated in his mind how he could manage to avoid them. I told him there could be no remedy; he was sure of being sent to 'Jamaica'! but notwithstanding he yet hoped for the best. At length his name was called. Everybody's eyes were instantaneously turned towards his seat where he was seen to the indescribable amusement of all of us with his pocket handkerchief tied around his head and face, from the lower jaw upwards, and a great piece of blotting paper stuffed in his left cheek causing such a visible protruberance as would have forced anyone into the belief that at least half a dozen of his teeth were in a disordered state. Besides this well carried out deceit, he put on a countenance to suit the occasion, which would have forced a fit of laughter from a monument of stone. With his books in his right hand and his left to his cheek he approached Mon. Bourdic, who upon casting his eyes upon him shrunk back in amazement, and asked him

'Qui est ce que vous avez donc? Est ce que vous êtes malade?'

'Ah! oui monsieur, moi beaucoup malade. Moi mal ici', pointing to the swelled cheek.

'Comment! O, Mon Dieu! Vous avez une joue de détrisse pourquoi venir a l'école dans un état pareil?'

'Moi bien malade, Monsieur.'

'Retirez vous je m'en vas demander à Mr Wadeson de vous permitter de vous en allez chez vous et ne revenez plus que quand vous serez parfaitement guéri.'

'A non, Monsieur, ne demandez pas a lui je prie a vous moi aime mieux rester ici.'

'Comment donc vous êtes bête, vous ne connaisez pas le danger que vous courez a rester ici, mais enfin ce sera comme vous le souhaitez.'

'Merci, merci, Monsieur' and he presented his books. But *O bonas mores*! how was his sympathy changed when he viewed the faulty scrap. One thrust of his hand was made to seize him by the hair, when lo! the handkerchief and the swelled cheek presented themselves to his gaze, and instantly his hand dropped, but his rage being so great and not being able to satisfy it, he threw his pen in half a dozen different ways over the exercise and utterly disfigured it, then turning to the pretended sufferer addressed him.

'Bête que vous êtes si ce n'etait pas que vous êtes malade je vous fenez allez à Mr Wadeson et je lui demanderez de vous punir severement, car en verité vous le meritez.'

'Merci, Monsieur, moi malade', was the reply.

'Oui, c'est bien pour vous que vous l'êtes; mais tenez, voilà vos livres et si vous me les rapportez dans un état pareil. Je vous en ferai avoir comme il faut, allez vous en.'

Our pretender did not wait for a second command but was instantly at his seat which fortunately for him was in that position of the school that screened him from the gaze of his dupe. The handkerchief was soon removed and with his face concealed by the lid of his desk he indulged in an immoderate fit of laughter. Monsieur Bourdic, having completed his duty, walked up to the head of the school, whilst our friend trembled in his shoes for fear that his humanity should have taken the ascendancy and prompted him to intercede in the sufferer's behalf, but however he was soon happily released from this state of uneasiness when he saw he had only walked up as customary to make his bow to his superior and retire. Thus having dexterously avoided 'flaying' and twelve o'clock having arrived our friend gave unlimited course to his boundless joy on the play ground of the school admidst the congratulations of a host of others equally as wicked as himself but far less daring, invariably bursting out in exclamations such as 'Bête que vous êtes, moi beaucoup malade, Mons.'

'Ah, didn't I tell you I'd get off scot free?'

'Leave Harry alone for a clean trick', etc, etc, but however it was suggested to him that he would be paid with interest on the morrow if he brought his exercises incorrect again but all the coincidence that his had with our views was 'That he did not think so.'

'If Johnny petite', says he, 'gets to windward of me I'll give him leave to run me down and sink me if he likes'.

The morrow came however and with his exercises untouched, in fact they had not moved from the position he had placed them in when handed back to him the day before, but of this he evinced not the least uneasiness, nor could we conceive what plan he was about to practise that day, that he would dare to return his former one we could not believe as he would not only have been in danger of being found out by Monsieur Bourdic, but he would evidently have been represented to Mr Wadeson by the former who had strictly prohibited him from attending the school in that state. Therefore another device was necessary, the practise of which made us all impatient to witness. However as 'Time and tide wait for no man' the hour came in which Mons. Bourdic made his ingress and with it the shuffling of books, the repetition of lessons in whispers, the conjugation of verbs, *j'aime, tu aime, il aime. Je finis, tu finis, il finit*, etc, etc, but amidst all this disquietude and continued reverberation of different sounds, our worthy friend was at his desk in an attitude of composure satisfactorily amusing himself in drawing upon a sheet of foolscap a huge Frenchman running away at his maximum speed from a little

English boy from whose mouth protruded in small but legible characters, 'I'll get ye, if I can only catch ye, ye frog-eating French gander.' This completed to his satisfaction he put it away to prepare for answering to his name when called. At length it was called, and as quickly answered with 'Oui Monsieur' by our worthy friend who was seen shuffling his way onwards to the summoner without as much as a book in his hand, but not before he had thrust a large chestnut with which he had provided himself for the purpose in his left jaw.

Now what could he be up to this time? Without his books too! was a question that reverberated through the schoolroom. Having reached the desk he made a more polite bow than ever whilst he drew forth from his waistcoat pocket and handed to Monsieur Bourdic a neat folded note of satin paper with gilt edge. All this was done without the exchange of a word, but not without that of a glance which proceeded from the sharp bright eyes of the teacher to the yet disfigured cheek of the pupil. Unfolding the note with his hands whilst his eyes were still in this occupation he held it up before him unread, still contemplating the unfortunate sufferer, who met his gaze with such an unaltered countenance as would have graced a Nelson. Having at length altered the direction of his eyes to that of the paper before him, he occupied them in the perusal of a few lines seemingly traced out by a delicate female's hand which by the bye had a great influence over his powers of aquiescence. The purpose of the note was as follows:-

> Mrs G.....s will esteem it a favour if Monsieur Bourdic will allow her son to pass unexamined this morning, as his severe indisposition since yesterday has utterly disqualified him from attending to his duties.
>
> Fort George, Wednesday morning, September 12th 1835
>
> Maria Ann G.....s

Whilst these few lines had been reading, the author of them had been watching with no small degree of intensity, the change of features in the reader's physiognomy and had joyfully perceived the traits of success on his part, which he imperceptibly made known to his contemporaries who were eagerly watching him, by a squint of the eye accompanied with a protrusion of the tongue from the left corner of his mouth. Monsieur Bourdic having concluded the perusal of the note and carefully folded it up again, placed it in his memorandum book, then turning to the subject of it, regarded him with all the sympathy he seemed possessed of, and thus addressed him.

'Vous direz à votre mère que j'accède a son désir avec bien du respect, et que je la conseille de vous tenir chez elle èn attendant que votre mal se soit pârfaitement guèri, de peur que n'arriverez à un etât encore pis, et en mème temps dites lui de ma part qui l'application d'un oignon roti en forme de cataplasm sur la joue est un bon remède dans une occasion pareille, entendez vous?'

'Oui, Monsieur, merci, moi beaucoup obligé!'

Thus freely aquitted and nearly choking with joy, our friend retraced his steps towards his seat, which having arrived at, he abstracted the concealed chestnut from his jaw which he replaced into his pocket and thereby of course removing the cause of his necessity of applying the prescribed onion. Everybody could not help gazing upon this extraordinary character with astonishment, and whilst lost in wonder could not help admiring his perfect adroitness in the carrying out of his deceitful schemes. School hours over and he was unanimously congratulated, and indeed had drawn nearer the affection of many through the artfulness he had displayed in working so successfully over our worthy Monsieur's credulous propensities.

These and many other 'clean tricks' did he practise whilst at this university and generally did so with impunity, but as there is an end to all thing, they say, 'except a ring', so there was an end to his fun at last, for having one day carried it too far, he met with obstruction from the party played upon who would instantly have reported him to the 'Butcher' but that he was in a particular engagement at the time, being about teaching one of the Latinists of his department the habit of the eels before mentioned, who nevertheless seemed to evince a great degree of unpleasant feelings about it, and gave everyone reason to believe that he would require a great many lessons before he was properly habituated. Our friend had been sent to his seat until the opportunity arrived for reporting his conduct, during this interval he was much tantalized by the others with all kinds of remarks, such as, 'Ah, you have left yourself entrapped at last', 'Oh you'll catch it' and so on. For my part I told him to look upon the poor sufferer now getting punished, and read in his suffering the fate that awaited him. He looked upon me with such a countenance that made me shudder whilst in a voice and manner that bespoke his feelings, he protested that he would never bear the infliction of such punishment whilst he had a pair of arms to his body and breath to give them animation. We all chaffed him on the subject, telling him he could never muster sufficient spirit to resist it, but he replied by saying that we did not know what he was capable of doing when excited, and as for old 'Butcher', he said he did not care if he had a pint of Jamaica in him, or a quart, but that any day he was able to floor him — and by the powers! if he attempted to flay him he would find his mistake, he would, he said, stand a just punishment, half a dozen or so, but any more than that would meet with decided resistance; he would teach Wadeson that the Latin *'Nemo me impune lacessit'*[1] which he had been taught by him, implied the first person singular in the present case.

These and such like were the threats he made, but each doubted if he would prove courageous at the dreaded time. Howbeit the opportunity presented itself, the report was made, and the culprit arraigned. He heard in silence the accusation and did not even attempt to deny it, but with downcast look and motionless features, awaited in silence the result of the judge. At length Mr Wadeson put to him the question, 'What do you mean, Sir, by such conduct?'

No answer. The question was re-asked. 'What do you mean I say, Sir, by such diabolical conduct?'

'No harm, Sir.'

'Oh you mean no harm is it you say. Well (straightening his cane) I am going to give you what will cause you to remember that "no harm" begets "a great deal of harm". G...s drew back a

[1] 'No one attacks me with impunity'.

step or two and changing his downcast look to that of a fixed gaze on the punisher, placed himself in an attitude of defence and exclaimed, 'You are not going to give me more than I deserve and that is just half a dozen cuts of that cane over my hands. If you attempt more than that *"Nemo me impune lacessit"*.'

Mr Wadeson, thunderstruck at such resistance and feeling himself grossly insulted by the latter words, could not keep his rage within bounds, but flew upon him with his uplifted cane about to lay into him an unmerciful thrashing, but our friend, ever dexterous, soon wrenched the cane from the owner's hands and flinging it as far as he could from him, collared him with such a degree of force that made everyone wonder where he attained it from, and the 'Butcher' feel his weakness greater than he had hitherto done. A dreadful scuffle ensued, which terminated only when Mr Wadeson found his head unpleasantly situated under the fire stove, and when an assistant had come to his rescue, and another to capture the victor. This did not end here, but however I must end my detail of this character as I think he has had his full share of representation. Suffice it to say that he was no longer a sojourner at this college after the affray but was directly taken from it by his father after matters came to light and I believe a very mutual feeling existed between both parties, Mr Wadeson and his pupil each being glad of being rid of the other.

Barter is cruelly punished

I remember of having hinted in a preceding page of an act of the 'Butcher's' cruelly exercised over myself, I will then before I have done with him, recall to mind the said instance. Amongst other rules of this college was one which strictly prohibited the selling or bartering of any articles amongst us. Now though this, like many other rules in a school, was seldom adhered to very particularly, yet we never intended the masters should be cognizant when it was broken. It was in an instance of this kind, and under the same intention that I impinged upon the precepts of the school and was punished for it. Punished did I say? Nay, maltreated.

One of my classmates, a son of Colonel Gardner of V...t, had brought with him one day an instrument for making and mending of pens, and being the first one of that kind I had ever seen, it is no wonder that it struck my fancy. I admired its qualification with no small degree of astonishment, placing a quill within a small aperture opened by means of a spring, and merely drawing it out again I had a ready made pen in an instant. To make this excellent piece of workmanship mine were my next thoughts, consequently a barter was immediately agitated by me. My friend Gardner, who was less taken up with its beauty or value than myself, did not evince an insurmountable degree of opposition, and after having pleaded upon the beauty and merit of a small pictured book in my possession, showing out the different pictures in all their glowing colours and as much to my advantage as laid in my power, I offered to give it him in exchange, besides the promise of doing his French lessons for him for a whole week. That the first part of my offer was more or less inconsiderable he clearly manifested in the visible disdain he regarded it with, but that the latter part was fraught with a twofold power over his bartering inclinations was not unperceived by myself. So after a very little more persuasion on my part, a bargain was struck and I was possessor of the much esteemed machine.

On my arrival at home that evening I made a display of it — agreeing with the pleasure I felt in possessing such a novelty one of my sisters, after admiring the object of my exultations and questioning me as to how I had become possessed of it, which several questions were answered in a manner that left no doubt upon her mind that all was quite correct, asked me to give it to her, signifying that to me it was of very little use, whilst to her it would prove of the utmost value, a truth which established itself in the fact that she had much writing to do, and which will not be wondered at when it is explained that she held unlimited correspondence with an absent lover. Now this sister of mine, it must be observed, was one for whom I had ever entertained a great degree of fondness and affection, nor has that feeling at all been mitigated since through the influence of time, for although years have rolled away since the period in which the fact I am now describing transpired, yet is our mutual affection unaltered. It is not to be wondered at then if at her earnest request of obtaining the pen machine I showed immediate compliance; having it in her possession she found upon examination that through ill-usage it had become quite blunt, and thereby unable to perform the duty it had been so ingeniously intended to do with any degree of perfection. Consequently, the next day she sent it to a silversmith to have it set. Meanwhile the knowledge of my exchange with Gardner had reached the 'Butcher's' ears at school, through I presume, the length of some of our enemies' tongues (for we were not without them), and therefore on the morning of the third day of our bargain I was summoned up, in company with my friend, to the tribunal, where we both pleaded guilty.

Gardner was less blamed than myself for having impinged the rules of the university, but myself being his senior in years, and of an age sufficiently sensible to have known better (so Mr Wadeson said it), he could not but be surprised at my conduct. Besides I had acted badly in taking advantage of his ignorance, for the book which he produced was not worth in comparison the instrument. To this I could reply nothing although I forcibly felt the injustice of the accusation in reflecting upon the promise I had also made besides the book, but of this, of course, he knew nothing and it would not have been at all conducive to our welfare if I had disclosed it, no, in justice to myself I will say that I in preference bore the imputation by which I seriously felt myself insulted at thus having my honour questioned to making a disclosure that would have served me but very little whilst it would have involved a friend in danger. I bore it all in silence and afterwards bore more; but fortunately for us however, it happened that forenoon he was not over-heated by the rays of a tropical sun. 'Jamaica' had not, through some unknown cause, made great impression over his European constitution, so that we were a great deal less subject to 'violent shocks', nevertheless we did not come off 'Scot free'. My friend, after making oft repeated vows of repentance and myself after faithfully promising to reproduce the instrument on the morrow, each received a half a dozen in the hands, which made us try how high we could jump off the floor with both legs at once, and how effectively we could conceal our pained fingers under our armpits, This pain over, we congratulated ourselves at our easy escape, but although I felt in a measure also happy at having escaped so easy, yet distressing fears worked in my brain. I had made a promise which it was not likely I could accomplish on the morrow, besides instead of confessing the truth, I had involved myself in greater danger by saying that I had it at home, which would make it difficult for me to find an excuse on the morrow for not having brought it. However, 'a dying man will catch at a straw', so with me I caught at every little hope that would present itself to my mind, perhaps he might be unwell (the 'Butcher') and would not attend college that day, perhaps he might have 'taken occasionally' and consequently forgotten all about the pen machine, or finally, perhaps my sister might have had it returned from the silversmith and I should be able to bring it back. Such were my hopes until I returned home when I found that my most sanguine was frustrated, which consequently left me in sole dependence on my former ones.

The next morning, however, arrived and I scarcely knew how it had arrived so soon. It seemed to me that night had been shorter by hours than any other, eight o'clock struck when it was time to prepare for school, why surely that clock must be fast thought I, it ought not to be eight o'clock yet. I walked to college, dear me how short the distance was, why it only seemed I had just left my home door when I arrived at that schoolroom. I was again seated at my respective place, my friend Gardner at his, close by my side. We had already exchanged a host of communication and still we had not been summoned, my hopes might yet prove founded, that it was evident that he (Mr Wadeson) was as I trusted he should be the phial 'To be taken occasionally' proved, there it lay as it was wont, with its large label fastened to its neck and he (Mr Wadeson) seemed influenced enough by its contents. Our Latin and French exercises we had already gone through, with the latter without the symptoms of a mistake, much to the satisfaction of Monsieur Bourdic who declared that Gardner 'Faisant beaucoup de progrès' and that I was 'un jeune homme d'esprit', whilst our Latin master, surprised at our faultless exercises, asked each if they were completed *'Seco marte'*.[1]

In fact everything seemed to wear the smile of favour upon us. Lost in ecstasy of joy we had nearly forgotten the danger on the brink of which we were treading, when Lo! at an instant the least prepared, our names were thundered out from the judgement seat of 'the Butcher.' Oh *bonos mores*!, how did that sound reverberate through our ears? as an omen of approaching calamity! how did our poor hearts beat within us striking against our breasts as though warned of the danger that threatened their tenement, were seeking emancipation to fly for security from the approaching storm. With trembling limbs and our heaving breasts, we approached the dreaded summoner of our names and stood before him much after the similitude of two reeds violently shaken by the wind. I was addressed first, thus, 'You are not ignorant, I presume, of the purpose you are called for?'

'No, Sir.'

'Well, have you brought back that instrument you had from your friend there (pointing to him) and which you told me you had left at home?'

'No, Sir.'

'No! And pray for what reason?'

Silence. 'And pray, I ask you, for what reason?' (with a cut over the shoulder with the cane which reached right down to the hip).

'Oh, oh, oh', writhing with pain, 'I–I–I couldn't find it, Sir.'

'And why could you not find it?' and a thousand other questions were asked me, and to as many I told a lie, and in fact to some I told perhaps twenty, for fear and agitation had so bewildered me that I knew not what I said half of the time. He also, being greatly excited, though not through fear I suppose, unless it was fear that his bottle would not last out the forenoon, 'laid it into me' most unmercifully, so much so that many in the school were crying vengeance. After he had pretty well tattooed me with his cane, he had a chair placed in the centre of the schoolroom and made me mount upon it, when he placed a card

[1] 'By his own ability'. [HM]

before and one behind me, fastened by means of a piece of tape over my neck and shoulders, on which was written in large characters 'LIAR' then ordered all the boys as they passed by me to hiss and scoff at me, repeating the word with which I was decorated. This last act of his cruelty was certainly the worst for it affected my feelings the most. That my body had been shamefully lacerated is true, but yet it was in a measure able to bear it, compared with the power of my heart to bear being made the derision of a host of unfeeling wretches, who found no greater pleasure than in taking advantage of the liberty that was shamefully allowed them, and even often encroaching upon that by spitting in my face. Some there were at this university who though they could boast a high degree of parentage, and in having been brought up in high life, were entirely destitute of the least degree of respectability in their manners, much less the smallest symptoms of the common feelings of humanity, and who would have been guilty of any crime for the sake of satisfying their own senseless pleasures heedless at the shrine of whom they were gratified. These, regarding my situation as a novelty in the school, did not lose an opportunity to enjoy themselves at my expense and the more with unrestrained feelings when they felt their superiority over me in bodily strength, little regarding the heart they were piercing, or the spirit they were breaking.

Oh had they but had a heart or a spirit of their own, as virtuous and as noble as his that formed their laughing stock, they could never have disgraced them by such mean, lowlife, degrading actions; but no, they were of that number whose name and purse substitute the place of virtue and a heart. Among these savages in the garb of Christians was one who as an example to my preceding statement, I will mention was the son of a colonel, whose name has ever been fraught with a great degree of honour and respect and who has also filled a very eminent office in the court of law during a period of his lifetime. This honoured squire was the father of him I am about to speak, and very little credit I think could he reap through the revelation. This young man was my superior in years of I presume four, and consequently was among the number of those who thought they could exercise their unbounded malice with impunity — passing by me purposely at a moment when no eye of the teachers was watching him, he added to his scoffs a blow with his hand on my cheek accomplished with words that my rage made unintelligible. Oh! what were my feelings then? had I dared I could have jumped down and challenged him to single combat, but no I dare not move. As it was however, I looked upon him with clenched teeth and told him that a day would be mine yet when I should be revenged of my wrongs. But of this he only laughed the more, believing himself my superior in strength and agility, and though I myself upon mature consideration could not but coincide with that same opinion, he having been one of the pupils of the boxing master for already eight or nine months, yet I felt determined so great was the insult to chastise him at all risks, or lose my life in the attempt, and accordingly the day of retribution at length arrived, though not so soon as my wounded spirit could have wished when I openly challenged him to a fair fight.

This challenge made no small consternation throughout the school inasmuch as the inequality of the two combatants was so great, but nevertheless caused also a great degree of pleasure, as any novelty of this kind was always looked upon as 'glorious fun'. At four o'clock then, after our dismissal from school, it was appointed the fight should take place, and I am sure my unworthy antagonist found the hours tedious until that time, so overjoyed was he at having an opportunity of displaying the advancement he had made in the art of boxing, and at the same time so confident of success. Four o'clock at length arrived, and every one adjourned to the play ground, which was to be the scene of action, two divisions were formed, the strongest party by all means on his side, but at this I took little notice so long as there was no imposition put upon me which a few able friends on my side promised to guard against. A few minutes concluded our preparation, which on my side was not great, since I made no other than buttoning my jacket and ridding myself of my cap, whilst he on his side added to this the bracing of his body tightly with his belt. This however concluded and we stood face to face, when I addressed him as follows:

'I now stand before you an injured person, and with the intention of chastising you for the wrongs I have received at your hands, and if fortune should favour me this afternoon, I promise you the chastisement will be severe. I shall not quit you until I have satisfied every feeling within me that calls for revenge. So now you are acquainted with my feelings towards you, it behoves you to act accordingly.'

'All right, my fine fellow, I am prepared to meet your chastisement. So now just strike the first blow that I may judge of the second.'

But I did not give him time for judgement between the first and second, even before he had concluded his ironical sentence I had fallen upon him like a tiger upon his prey and had dealt him two such successive blows as all his skill at fencing could not avoid; another instant and he lay prostrate at my feet. I begged of him to keep his feet and not thus to lay down for I was not yet satisfied. My friends derided him by telling him to call his boxing master to his aid, others told him he was bound too tight about the waist etc. However, amidst all this he was again seeking his perpendicular but in such a slothful manner that evinced his dislike at my too near situation with him. This, however, I endured with perfect patience and composure, and at the same time with perfect preparation. No sooner had the last angle of his body been formed into a perpendicular than without scarcely moving a foot I dealt him another two blows in such quick succession that again he lost his balance and resumed his horizontal position. Again were the 'Bravos' re-echoed on my side (I felt all the glory of them too) and once again the encouragements on his 'Get up, Bill, take courage, "my cock", you'll down him presently', but with this latter test of their faith in him I did not agree, for I could easily perceive the effect of my last two blows had done wonders. However, at their first encouragement I added mine, and begged of him to get up, which request he was certainly in the act of complying with, but as before with much seeming reluctance. At last, seeing his forlorn situation, having no chance of keeping his perpendicular when gained, he found his proud spirit to bend under the necessity of the moment, and asked me the favour of allowing him to rise fairly upon his legs. To this I replied I would as far as was consistent with my security in maintaining my situation, but no more; he had, I told him, the advantage of me in all instances; in years, in station, in art, in everything; therefore with so many advantages I could allow him no more, and just then perceiving he was about clinging hold of me in an unguarded moment as he supposed, stepped evasively on one side, thereby disappointing his hopes of overthrowing me, as well as allowing him just sufficient time to rise, which he no sooner had done than I was at him again with redoubled courage and unabated force, but did not however succeed this time in throwing him so perfectly as I had done before. The consequence of it was that many blows were exchanged, and finally staggering we both fell to the ground, encircled in each others arms as warmly as if we had been as great friends as we were decided enemies. In this situation, and panting for breathe, I thought of the danger I was now enveloped in, if he unfortunately got the ascendancy this time, he would never allow me to rise again. If this should prove the case I was literally speaking 'done for', so before I had allowed him time to regain his breath I made one desperate effort and that effort at once settled matters. I was on top of him, and after the manner of a baker thumping his dough, I thumped away right and left on his face, until at last perceiving, I suppose, his sight getting dim, my antagonist found just sufficient breath to vociferate 'Enough'.

Though I did not feel inclined to think I had yet given him enough, I was obliged to desist through the interference of his seconds, who coming to his aid, pushed me on one side and picked him up more dead than alive. Now the victory was complete! and if I had not known it otherwise, I must through the repeated congratulations of my friends, who kept up an incessant cry of 'Bravo our side'. 'Well done, Hilary, you've licked him fairly and completely' etc. And I was indeed satisfied with myself, not that I was vain of having gained a victory over an enemy, no, I was satisfied I had punished him as he justly merited. After his friends had attended to him, and in a measure put him to rights again that he was able to stand, I approached him, and addressed him with:

'I hope you are satisfied with the thrashing you have had, and as I plainly see you have had "enough" as you have been forced to own yourself, I am satisfied for the insult I had received from you, and therefore offer you my hand as a pledge of my future friendship towards you, but before you accept this pledge, I must have you observe that after this day you must be much guarded in your manners and behaviour towards me, for I will never suffer the shadow of aggression from you without the reward of an immediate punishment; if you think you can comply with these here is my hand and heart, the first to be your defender in any case of need, the last to cherish you as a friend.'

Seeing he did not attempt to accept the proffered hand I continued, 'But should you sooner continue as you are, a "vanquished enemy" it is immaterial to me. I shall ever be prudent enough to remember you as such.' To this he made no answer, and I left him to proceed homeward, whilst he no doubt found it necessary to do the same, in quest of a mother or nurse's remedies to bring relief to his sore bones, made sorer still by a crushed pride. Such was I revenged of the insult received through this 'fellow' but there yet remained one who deserved a greater share of punishment than this, it was Mr Wadeson alias 'The Butcher'. He it was that committed the greatest insult, the greatest cruelty. Was it not enough to maim the body? without also maiming the heart! Giving the shameful liberty he did to the unprincipled scholars was like letting a poor hare loose in a dog-kennel, and sitting over watching them exultingly tear the poor creature to pieces. For although I have just about said enough to form an idea by, of the treatment I received that day, yet I can vouch that the idea formed must come far short of the reality.

The consequence that followed, added in brief to this, may perhaps serve to facilitate conjecture; that consequence is that I was after this, and entirely owing to it, three months under medical care without remission of attendance, and indeed during a portion of that period, such was the nature of my ailment that it baffled all the exertions of the worthy man that attended me, and induced him to believe the symptoms of a premature decline already engendered. This was the result of a schoolmaster's barbarity towards one of perhaps his least offending pupils. And why was I treated in this shameful manner? Did I deserve it? No, I had broken the laws of the school by making an exchange with a schoolmate, that is true, but was this law a just one? Admitting it was, surely an infringement of it did not call for such inhumanity. I had also been guilty of many falsehoods, but what was the reason of this? Was it not through fear and the austerity of the judge by whom I was examined? Yes, this was enough to bewilder my brain, and cause the instability with which I answered his questions, and would not a principled man have read this cause which must have been legible in my deportment. But, alas, he was not a man of principle. Why should I expect the grape to grow on the briar, or the fig on the thistle. But enough of this, I have already gone beyond the proverb *'De mortuis nil nisi bonum'*.[1]

After the event I have just related, and my convalescence had become quite perfect, I again resumed my former situation at college, to conclude the quarter that then was nearly half-expired, for at that time it was my father's intention to withdraw us from it, and had given Mr Wadeson notice to that effect. But an event took place which would have caused our dismissal even if it had not been intended. This was the death of the above, which took place on his way to school one morning in quite a sudden manner. He had left his home and proceeded as far as within two minutes of the academy, when he felt himself taken ill, consequently thought it expedient to return and had reached the threshold of his home door when death put a stop to his further ingress. And thus closed the career of a man in the prime of life, at a moment perhaps least expected, which verifies the proverb that reminds us that 'In the midst of life we are in death'. Though I cannot now recollect with an exact degree of certainty the number of years that formed the sum total of Mr Wadeson's age, yet without being in very great error I may presume he was about forty when he died. He left a wife to deplore his loss but I believe no children and I make no doubt her loss she seriously felt, for although in his public character as I have shown he had nothing very loveable about him, yet in his private, I make no doubt he was all that is consistent with an affectionate husband. It is true that he was not a disciple of 'Father Mathews'[2] but that may have been no obstacle to their happiness, besides, I do not mean to surmise that the discovery made by us in school was ever made by Mrs

[1] 'Of the dead say nothing but what is favourable'. [HM]

[2] i.e. Theobald Mathews (1790–1856), an Irish priest and 'the apostle of temperance'.

Wadeson at home, and perhaps indeed may she always deeply have sympathized with her husband at his delicate constitution, which obliged him to have continual recourse to a medicine which had 'To be taken occasionally'. However, be this as it may, it is not my intention to write about the private character of any, neither to dwell upon supposition anywhere, my sole intention is to recall to mind facts that I have either experienced or witnessed. Therefore in conclusion with Mr Wadeson's biography I will merely state this fact, that regardless of the sorrow his death may have caused at home, with us at school the news were received as the most happy and welcome that had ever reached our ears. They were certainly unexpected, unlooked for, thereby could not be received otherwise than with no small degree of wonder.

Yet there was no sorrow mingled with it, wonder soon wore away, and exulting joy took full possession. The schoolroom, after the teachers had left it who immediately repaired to the scene of the accident, was converted into a play house. Three hurrahs were re-echoed through the room, every ruler was substituted for a flag staff, and as many handkerchiefs for flags. One was seated at the deceased's desk where he exhibited his skill in mimicry, but albeit he was perfect enough in the art and had the much dreaded cane in his hand, yet he was utterly incapable of maintaining any degree of order amongst us, and not unfrequently did a book whizz about his head to show our disregard for his threats or his cane, and many were the feats completed that day, amongst others was that of his death caused by an incessant obligation of swallowing the bitter draught of a medicine which promised no relief unless taken occasionally, the party acting as the sufferer having a phial of water decorated with the well known label as a substitute for the medicine. Finally, after having played his part with no small degree of dexterity, and with much amusement to us all, he suddenly dropped down dead. When he was taken up, carried home, laid out, and ultimately buried, the funeral procession evincing through their woeful countenances and repeated wailings, the great loss they had sustained. In fact, much may be added to this day's diversion among us, but however these will serve to give the reader an idea of the particulars, and as the whole can reflect no great credit on the parties concerned, myself of the number, perhaps enough has been said already. It only remains now for me to add that after this event, this university was dissolved altogether, and after the lapse of a few weeks which were enjoyed as holidays I was again under the tuition of one of its branches.

His last school

Mr Burman, of whom I have already made mention, having set up for himself at only a short distance from the former school, had gained through his high reputation a great degree of favour amongst the parents of the several scholars, and therefore with very little solicitation obtained the care of most of them. Under his care I was for about a twelvemonth, and indeed made exceeding great progress in all branches of literature, I was so well treated by him, but in fact not by him alone, but by his amiable wife with whom I seemed to be a pet. I know not, or at least I do not like to say, for fear of being thought vain, how it was, but I was in unparalleled favour with them both, and received such kind treatment by them, as well in the schoolroom as in the parlour, that if to push myself forward had been to prove my gratitude, I would willingly have studied day and night regardless of rest or toil, but not so, a fair portion of study satisfied Mr Burman, whilst my person, manners and character seemed quite sufficient to interest his good lady in my behalf. Thus beloved of my teacher I could not fail to make visible progress as any opportunity was never left unattended on my side to give him entire satisfaction. Consequently in the course of a twelvemonth I had gained such a degree of perfection as left no doubt in my parents mind that further schooling was dispensable.

Determined to go to sea

Now as I have previously mentioned that my father was a man decidedly averse to idleness, it follows that immediately after the terms of my scholarship were completed, he turned his mind after my future employment in life and would fain have now taken me under his charge to train me up in the rudiments of his own vocation, but however to this I was decidedly opposed, and gave him such unquestionable proofs of my utter dislike to a farmer's life, that he was soon obliged to relinquish all hopes of having a second in the person of myself. Therefore what was to be done? To remain idle he would not allow me, nor indeed had I any great desire to do so, having it at my heart to be off at sea at once and to become a sailor, but to this profession both himself and my mother showed a strong objection, made stronger still through the deplorable loss of already one of the family, an elder brother of mine following the same profession. My father invariably remonstrated with me on the subject, showing me the many hardships, dangers and privations a sailor's life was fraught with, besides the great uneasiness I would cause them as my parents, already bereaved of one of their beloved sons, in fact earnestly soliciting my forgetfulness of such an employment. But although I would fain have wished to harken with due consideration to these remonstrances meant entirely for my good, and given by a parent whose chief case was the providing for the future welfare of his children, yet the predominant wish of my heart prevailed and forced me to reject all good counsels of my father, and to regard them in a light more as if meant to thwart me in my views, than to promote my happiness.

It is true that my brother had met in the course of his travels with a watery grave, but to me that was no criterion why I should share the same fate. I recollected the day when he arrived from his first voyage, I went to meet him on the roads, with what enthusiasm I looked upon him returning from a West India voyage. How I envied his lot, habited in a blue shirt and smart pair of tight fitting canvas inexpressibles,[1] and his lower extremities decorated with a tiny pair of pumps partially concealed by the broad and fluttering canvas that hung over them, which at every step seemed to draw back instinctively for the purpose of disclosing the well trimmed bow of black ribbon placed as well for ornament as use on the upper part of a neatly polished shoe. Besides this and to

[1] i.e. breeches or trousers.

complete his garb the collar of his blue shirt which was loosely thrown back over his shoulders was kept from further receding by a black silk neckerchief carelessly tied around his neck with a 'sailor's knot', the ends of which gracefully fluttered in the breeze in conjunction with a yard of blue ribbon protruding over the right shoulder from the neat and glistening tarpaulin hat which was placed nearly on the back of his head and with a little inclination to the right, adding beauty and grace to the countenance beneath it.

I recollected this and with what earnestness did I hearken to the recital of the many wonders he had seen! How he had crossed the tropic of Cancer! How in the beautiful clear blue waters of the Atlantic he had gazed with delight on the myriads of its inhabitants, the beautiful dolphin with its varied golden hues, the fearful shark with its capacious jaws and numberless teeth, the monstrous whale with its wondrous tail and blowing powers, and last, but not least, the beautiful nautilus gliding with majesty over the surface of the deep as if its department was watching over the security of those beneath it. How he had seen several of the English colonial islands, amongst them Jamaica with its lofty peaks and mountains, how the land in general was decorated with the beautiful cocoa nut and palm trees, rising their lofty heads in majesty in the clouds. How he had eaten of the splendid fruit common in these climates, the orange unequalled in size and flavour, the banana whose deliciousness is beyond description, and the bread fruit so much spoken of in history. How he had seen the black slaves in numberless quantities, both male and female, and how he had himself spoken to some of them, and bought fruit from many. How the Spaniards at Havana were a savage looking set, how they wore a large knife always concealed about their body and principally in their sleeve.

I remembered all this, and even much more, which would only tire myself to recite, and is it to be wondered at, if I could not pay due regard to my father's remonstrances against a seafaring life. Aye the desire to witness all this, and to see myself attired in the enchanting garb already described, would have buried with my father's counsels the admonitions of a priest against purgatory in utter negligence. No wonder then I say that I treated all my father's expostulations with indifference and persisted to be a sailor.

However, my father was not to be trifled with, consequently he insisted that if I was determined to go to sea, that I should go one year more at school, as I was too young to face the hardships of my ill-fated desire, but to this I did not agree, stating as a reason that I knew many boys younger than myself who were, and had been, at sea, besides my brother was not any thing older than I was then, when he commenced. However this could not dissuade him from his purpose, he had said it, and it was a law. But the idea of going to school another year was to me like being bound for an eternity. What could I do? What plan could I suggest to persuade him to alter his mind? I knew not. However, fortune smiled over me just in the nick of time, for whilst I was purporting how I should act, he also was changing his mind, and shortly afterwards told me that if I wished instead of going to school for a year, he should obtain a situation for me as minor clerk in a lawyer's office. To this I readily consented as it was something new to me, and would be far less irksome to be a clerk of the law than to be a schoolboy beginning again at the bottom of a class.

Accordingly and without loss of time, a situation was found me at one of the most eminent of our lawyers, and on the Monday of the following week I commenced my new profession. Now I may as well observe the motive my father had for placing me here in preference to school; he was in hopes that time which it is said works miracles would alter my mind, and after becoming acquainted with the rudiments of my profession would peradventure become enamoured with it, a situation which by the bye if I had followed up till now, would perhaps have enabled me to earn a livelihood with far less danger and anxiety than my present one. But however I am deviating from my narrative. I have since learned, like St Paul, in whatever situation I am in, therewith to be content.[1] I had not been there above six months when an accident

[1] This allusion is to St Paul's Epistle to the Philippians (chapter 4, verse 11): 'Not that I speak in respect of want: for I have learned, in whatsoever state I am, therewith to be content'. St Paul's First Epistle to Timothy, ch. 6, verses 7–11, and

happened to me which kept me at home for three months or nearly. This was the fracturing of my right leg, a little above the ankle. However, when this was totally well again, I resumed my former attendance until another incident took place which took me away from it altogether and at once brought me to the summit of all my desires.

This was the arrival of one of my uncle's ships from the West Indies one fine afternoon between the hours of three and four just as I had finished my daily business and was about to turn my steps homewards. But it was very seldom I did so before having first taken a turn around the harbour to make myself aquainted with the transactions of the day, and in fact so much did the navigation of our port interest me, that on my return home, had I been questioned on the subject, I could have told any one how many ships had arrived, who they were, where they came from, and what their cargoes, and with the same accuracy how many ships had sailed, and wither bound. Indeed more than that, I could also tell by whom they were commanded, and what kind of a reputation each commander bore.

It was on one of these philosophical excursions that I perceived a strange sail in our roadstead, and that she had not long cast anchor was only the work of a glance of the eye to perceive. But what was she? Where was she from? What was her destination? etc. All these questions came instinctively crowding to my mind, and to have them solved was my immediate task. But at that moment when I was in search of my informer (a pilot) I perceived my uncle with hasty steps proceeding toward the landing place. A thought struck me directly, but could it be? Yes, I remember that he expected her about this time. So to my uncle I ran without any more delay.

'Is that the *Nancy* in the roads, Uncle?'

'Yes, my boy.'

'Oh, where is she bound pray?'

Hebrews, ch. 13, verse 5, are further references to being content and the latter was commonly (but wrongly) attributed to St Paul until this century. For help with this, and other Biblical references, I am indebted to the Revd Simon Morgan.

'To Antwerp, my boy.'

'Indeed, and is she going directly?'

'No, she will not sail until tomorrow.'

'Oh, may I go in her, Uncle? You know you have always promised me I should when she was arrived. Now realize your promise and tell me I may go.'

'Well, but you are not prepared, you have no clothes ready. How therefore can you think of going.'

'Oh, I will manage that, it is only a short trip, only tell me I can go, and I will run home and get a bundle of my old clothes which will do very well for the voyage.'

'Well that may be all very well so far, but are your parents of the same mind?'

'Oh as for that they must be. Father has always told me if I persisted in going to sea, that I should have to look after a ship myself as he would not for me, so now I have done so. Consequently he cannot make any objection.'

'Well then, you have my sanction. Go you at once at home and tell your father the *Nancy* is arrived and that your uncle has given you permission to go with her to Antwerp and back to Guernsey, providing always that he consents.'

I scarcely took time to thank him, but I was off at full speed and was not many minutes before I was home enquiring in a breathless manner where my father was. The folks at home when they witnessed my great excitement did not know what to make of it, they loaded me with a host of questions instead of answering mine, which made me little less than mad. At last, however, having satisfied them that nothing else was the matter but that I was going off to sea in the morning and that I wished to see my father to apprise him of it, they laughed in their sleeve and told me where I could find him. With this satisfactory information, away I ran to the spot that engaged his presence and addressed him as follows:

'Now Father, the moment has at length arrived when all my anticipations are fulfilled. The *Nancy* has arrived from Havana and sails again tomorrow morning for Antwerp. I have asked Uncle to give me a berth on board and he has kindly acceded to my demands. I therefore have hastened to inform you of it, in order that you may not be surprised at my unexpected departure in the morning. Of course you will not think of raising any impediment towards it. You know I can go with what clothes I have now, and when I return I can get a complete "fit out" made for a future voyage.'

To this my father had been a silent listener, and no doubt thought my apology very well dictated. Consequently his silence gave me hopes of meeting with no impediment from him. But alas, what were my feelings when gently raising himself from the task that occupied all his attention and from which he had not deviated one single instant during my harangue, he leisurely took his snuff box out of his waistcoat pocket, and whilst applying his finger and thumb to its contents cast a meaning glance at me while a smile which to me spoke volumes was visible on his countenance. I knew directly by his deportment that his views did not coincide with mine but still he kept silence, and still kept meaningfully glancing at me, and this silence was certainly cruel to me at such a moment, but such were my father's ways that he generally gave everyone an opportunity of guessing by his actions what he was about to decide by his words. At last having replenished his finger and thumb with a fresh pinch be broke silence in words to this effect:

'It seems then that you are determined to act contrary to my wishes, you still persist in going to sea. Well, since that is the case I shall no longer offer any opposition. I shall leave you to follow your own wayward fancies, but depend upon it, the day will come when you will hate yourself for having despised a father's counsel that studied nothing but your welfare and happiness.'

'Then you have no objection of my going aboard the *Nancy* tomorrow?'

'Rash boy. My words seem to you as idle tales. I have not yet spoken of the *Nancy* at all.'

'But you have said you no longer presented any opposition to my going to sea, so I have taken it for granted that you were willing I should avail myself of the opportunity I have now.'

'Not so, but harken to what I have to say. Since your uncle (who seems as thoughtless as yourself) has promised you a berth on board his vessel I will go and consult with him on the subject some of these days and whilst she is performing her Antwerp voyage you shall be got in readiness so that you may join her on her return, but as to going now to Antwerp in her, you must not even think upon it, for I will not allow it. You have neither clothes suitable nor any thing that is necessary for a seafaring life. So now satisfy yourself with that, and wait patiently till she returns.'

But oh, how much easier was this injunction given than obeyed. Satisfy myself and wait patiently! Me who has been disappointed in the dearest hopes I had ever entertained! Me whose fondest wish was blighted! Whose only earthly desire was crushed! How could I satisfy myself and wait patiently? No, to me the thing seemed impossible. I therefore gave my grief vent in a full flow of tears whilst the idea was passing through my brain of absconding. But yet upon further consideration I knew my uncle, as obliging as he was, would never receive me without having my father's consent viva voce. So what was to be done? It was a painful time for me until the vessel had sailed, but after that event, I of course made a virtue of necessity and bore my trials with as much fortitude as indeed could be expected under the circumstances I was placed.

The time soon slipped by, and I heard of her safe arrival. What joy this was for me. A short time longer I heard of her sailing. O how much did I pray that a pleasant gale might expand her milk white canvas and bear her to our shores with speed and in safety. Every day I was on the pier watching every sail that floated by in anxious expectation of my favourite *Nancy*. During all this time it must be noticed that my wardrobe was not being neglected. No, my entreaties were too prevalent to allow any procrastination at home. The tailor was busy making blue flannel shirts, pea coat, monkey jacket, pantaloons etc. The carpenter had received an order for a sea chest, the shoemaker for several pairs of shoes and for a pair of sea boots, in fact all was getting on entirely to my satisfaction. I had already procured myself a tarpaulin hat, and was only waiting until I had commenced my new profession to wear it.

At length one day from an elevated position on my father's estate I perceived on the signal staff of Fort George a brig to the northward was signalised. Of course it could not be any other than the *Nancy*. Away I went to town and just as I was on the pier I perceived the signalised vessel making her appearance round the point of Vale Castle, that she was a South Spainer[1] and not a collier I could easily perceive by the colour of her canvas. So I had but to wait a very short time and I should be able to discern by her flying colours to what nation as well as to what owner she belonged. Whilst I was impatiently awaiting for this discovery that was to give me either joy or disappointment, I could not but admire her graceful appearance as she was bounding over the waters which were curling under her fore foot, and every now and then separating in a volume of milk white spray which she sent forth many yards under her lee, as if defying the power of the ocean to stain her spotless suit, her mast seemed gracefully bending over her side impelled by the billowing sails that crowded them, her tout ensemble forming a picture matchless for its majesty and grace. I could not but recall the words of Byron to my mind and thought the occasion a very suitable one for their application: 'She walks the waters like a thing of life.'[2] Oh how I envied the lot of them that formed her gallant crew, what would I not have given to be able to call myself one of them. I wondered how it was that everyone did not wish to be a sailor, indeed I fancied it could be no other than a proof of little mindedness in them who could not appreciate the majesty with which I was so taken up. In the midst of my reverie however, I had not taken notice that she had approached near enough to discern her bunting, so much was I lost in the ecstasy of admiration, but upon awaking out of my dream of pleasure I plainly made out at her peak the ensign that was waving in the breeze to be an English one, and upon closer inspection read by the aid of a borrowed glass in her burgee[3] at the main the word *NANCY*.

Then was my joy complete. I danced, I skipped, I jumped, in

[1] A vessel trading to the southward. [HM]

[2] Cf. *The Corsair*, Canto I, Stanza III: 'She walks the waters like a thing of life / And seems to dare the elements to strife'.

[3] A square flag with a swallow-tail cut in the fly. An early instance of a term which the *SOED* dates only from 1848 and supposes to be an abbreviation of 'burgee's flag', i.e. owner's flag, the first element being derived from the French *bourgeois*.

fact I scarcely know how I behaved myself in the presence of the public but sure I am that some set me down as crazy. Others who were familiar enough with me, asked me if it was that I had a brother, or some near relation on board the vessel that was arriving, but to them I replied that no, better than that I was going to join her on her arrival, that I had determined to devote my life to the mercantile service and that sooner or later I hoped to command as stately a ship as that myself. Of course they laughed at my seeming presumption, but even at this moment which is many years since that date, I could tell those same parties that I felt all the force of my words. Yes, I did not begin a seafaring life in a thoughtless manner. I knew enough, though in a literal sense I knew nothing, to be aware that I should have to experience many hardships, dangers and privations, but all these I was fully prepared to meet, I was determined to battle my way through thick and thin, to brave anything and everything, neither to be discouraged by one or the other in order to, in the course of time, attain my ambition, that is the command of a stately ship. And thanks be to God I have done the former with His help, and I trust to my credit. And the latter I have ultimately attained with much satisfaction to myself, and although I do not find so much honour, or pleasure, in commanding a ship as I formerly thought there was, yet I am certain there are many occupations in life where there is far less.

But I perceive I am deviating from my chapter and stealing from one that must be far astern of this, as I see that I have made myself a captain just at the moment when I am but a cabinboy, about to enter my apprenticeship. Now although I admire the maxim of Jonathan to 'Go Ahead',[1] yet I rather think I have overdone that, by going too fast. Therefore I have no other alternative but that of turning right round short, and leaping slap down into the *Nancy*'s cabin at once before any of the knowing folk are about, where I am busy sweeping it out, polishing the mahogany and brass and making it look like the saloon of one of

[1] Hilary is using the name Jonathan to mean a typical citizen of the United States and thus identifying the phrase quoted as American.

our first rate coffee houses, and in a state fit to receive the owner or any lord of the land. Such was my employment for about three weeks that she stayed in port, besides now and then exercising my abilities in going aloft to train myself in the way I should have to go. At last the day of departure came at hand, a day I was longing for, but a day which when it arrived proved a cruel one to me. However, come it must and come it did. All my traps[1] were on board, my bed was already into my berth and made up, everything with me was in perfect readiness for quitting my paternal home and I believe the same with all the rest of the crew.

Consequently on the evening of the 20th November 1839 our captain gave the order that everyone should be at an early hour on board the next morning to get the ship under way and launch out to sea. Now was my joy full, I repaired at home with speed and made known our captain's orders to my parents, and begged them to be sure and rouse me up in good time the following morning, as I did not wish to be the last on board, but on the contrary if possible the first. This promise having been made and after having taken my evening's repast, Alas! I thought, the last perhaps for a long long time, I took a parting farewell from my sisters who I was not likely to see at the very early hour the next day, each wishing me a pleasant voyage and a safe return etc, etc. But from my mother and father I could not yet part. No, I merely wished them the usual goodnight, with the intention of saying 'goodbye' the next morning, but in truth this delay I was glad to avail myself of, as my already throbbing heart was too much excited to undergo the painful task.

Alas! only a few days before I thought I could have parted from every one without any painful feelings, indeed I would have deemed it but weakness on the part of any whom I should have seen evincing the same feelings as were predominant with me then, so great is the difference between feelings for yourself, or feelings for others. And who has experienced the painful duty of the first long farewell from home, happiness and all that is kind, and has

[1] i.e. baggage, belongings, perhaps shortened from trappings; the *SOED* dates the form only from 1813.

not felt like me that pain which none but he that feels it knows. I own there may be hearts so much estranged from filial affection that they may brave a parting moment with seeming indifference, but they alone can do so. None who feel the full force of the ties that bind them together can quit their parents without the sensation of bitter anguish. True some may go through the trial of the parting moment and maintain their appearance of fortitude better than others while in the presence of company they are quitting, but still the anguish of the heart is there, and though kept in control for a time, yet at length it must have its course and when that subdued heart feels itself alone then is its pain greater. Mine on the morning of this eventful day was a mixture of both cases, for whilst I did not manifest all the weakness that my heart then did feel, yet I could not control it sufficient to make it wear the aspect of indifference.

First Voyage

21st November 1839 – October 1840

Bound for Havana

At the early hour of five on this memorable morning I was aroused by my father who had himself risen to see that breakfast was got ready in time that I might partake of it before I left, and brought me the news that a fair breeze was blowing for my vessel, at which news I was up in an instant, and recalling every thought to my mind afresh which had been buried in oblivion for at least a few hours, whilst indulging in the sweet sensation of undisturbed slumber, I feared I had laid in bed too long and imagined I ought to be on board, my ship being already under sail. With these thoughts I hurried on through the process of sitting at table and rising from it again, for in truth I could not partake of the meal it had cost my father so much uneasiness to provide, my heart being so full and my mind so much taken up with the business of the day.

At last the moment came when I had but one more duty to perform, and then I was freed from home for at least some months, perhaps for years! This was taking my leave of an anxious mother who still lay in bed. Oh, how I could have wished to have avoided that parting, I lingered, and stayed, and knew not how to command strength enough to approach the bedside, but at last being reminded by my old faithful friend the time piece that six was on the eve of striking, I found it was no use to tarry any longer, so up stairs I went and knocking at mother's bedroom door demanded admittance. She lay awake in anxious suspense for the arrived moment; another moment and I was at her bedside. Need I describe the scene which followed? She saw in me an affectionate child, a dutiful son about to be torn from her care, the image of her lately lost one, the bereaved of her heart, she looked upon me and seemed to read upon my countenance the same fate of him she still bewailed. Bathing me with her tears she seemed to say with Jacob of old, 'My son shall not go down with you, for his brother is dead, and he is left alone. If mischief befall him by the way in which ye go, then shall ye bring down my gray hairs with sorrow to the grave.'[1]

Tearing, however, myself from her embrace I bid her remember time was fast slipping by, and that I was in danger of losing my passage. But alas it was not so much the fear of that that hurried me on, but the great desire of absenting myself from the cruel scene. I felt not only my share of sorrow, but deeply sympathized with her in hers, for I well understood her grief at her late bereavement. I knew I was the image of my lost brother, I knew that in me she saw him, that in me every past painful feeling came fresh to her memory. I knew that my presence only tended to disturb the wounds that time had already partly healed, therefore I sought the more earnestly to absent myself as soon as possible. I need not add to this, let it suffice that ultimately with heaps of blessings I parted from her, and subsequently from my father, who lacked not in blessing me also. Accompanied by a brother I then made my way towards the town and the harbour, now and then uttering a deep drawn sigh as I passed some familiar spot which stood as a memento of my childhood's sport, but without giving utterance to scarcely one word throughout the walk.

At last I arrived at the harbour and on board I found that the crew had already been engaged some time under the direction of the pilot in unmooring and that in all appearances another hour would bring us at sea. I immediately, after changing my suit, set to work in company with the others, whom I found bore also the appearance of regret, and indeed much more so than I expected would have been visible in the countenance of an old weather beaten sailor, but alas! I had it not in my thoughts then, that sailor had perhaps just taken his last farewell of a beloved wife and

[1] Genesis, ch. 42, v. 38.

family of babes. I did not think that parting could be attended with any sorrow unless it was from an endeared father and beloved mother. Alas for the innocent, happy ignorance of youth! Experience has since made me wiser.

Our ship was now hauled between the pier-heads and only stationed there by a small cable over her stern fastened on the shore, while her sail was being made which in quick succession was sheeted home and hoisted up, the jibs were also loosed but not yet hoisted, their service not being required until the command of 'ease away, 'let go' had been given. All her square sails being set, and main sail peaked, her yards were braced just a shivering, and there she lay like an impatient steed trembling as it were with anxiety to be let loose. At length the pilot, after casting his glance first aloft, then ahead, then alongside, to satisfy himself that all was right and clear, called out 'Now are all hands on board?' and being answered in the affirmative ordered every man to take his station, 'a couple of hands here to the stern line', 'one more to the bow-fast' and 'the rest to the braces'. 'Aye, Aye, Sir' being re-echoed throughout the ship's company, and as instantly every man had resumed his station. Another look around him and then 'Are you ready, my lads?'

'All ready, Sir.'

'Haul in your starboard fore and larboard main braces. So well of all. Ease away the bow line. Ease away the stern line. Ease away, my lads. Ease, let go. Hoist away the jib, up with them smart my lads. Well done, my lads, now she's ours.'

I cast a glance astern and with indescribable astonishment perceived the pier and the whole town fast receding from us, each friend stood waving his handkerchief as a token of farewell, but at each moment becoming more and more distant, could it be? I glanced over the side of the ship and all wonder was explained. Yes, she was off! She was bounding noiselessly over the smooth green sea at the rate of perhaps four or five knots. A short time more and having cleared all dangers, the main yard was laid aback, the pilot's boat was hauled alongside, and after shaking hands with the captain and wishing all hands 'Good bye' he jumped into his boat and left us to proceed on our way. No sooner was his boat clear of the ship's side than our captain gave the order 'Fill away the Main Yard'. That being done and the rest of the sails trimmed she was bounding over the water with all her wonted majesty — but what were the feelings of those on board? Who can tell?

Home-sick and seasick

Mine alone I might attempt to describe, and yet I could not with any degree of accuracy, for words would prove but feeble agents in the case. Yet it may be conceived, when casting another look at the fast receding shore where dwelt all that was near and dear, I perceived that each moment added to the distance that separated us. I remembered my last parting adieu from her that perhaps was now deploring my absence. I remembered also that I had torn myself away from them against their wills. I could no longer expect the tender care of a mother, no longer the sound counsels of a father, the fond caress of sister or brother. Alas, I felt that I was all alone! To add to all this and while yet my heart was swelling almost to breaking, I felt the uneasy motion of the ship, which already was out of the track of smooth water, becoming more and more uneasy, creating a sensation that added to my torture. Oh could I at that moment have taken wing and flown back to the bosom of them I had just quitted I think I should have never attempted to leave them again. But no, that was impossible and that very impossibility seemed to make every thing around me wear a darker aspect. Already the words of my father came fresh to my memory in all their force. 'Rest assured the time will come when you will hate yourself for having disregarded my counsels.' Oh that I had perceived the truth that prophecy contained in time. Now it was too late, remorse was doing its work, and I felt I could have exchanged time for eternity with thankfulness.

By this time I was fairly seasick and vomiting and reaching[1] had already commenced to a fearful degree. I had lost all energy, my poor frame was become entirely helpless. I entreated of the chief mate to allow me to lay down as I could no longer keep my

[1] i.e. retching.

legs and he very considerately reported my state to the captain who immediately ordered my conveyance to my berth. A wash hand basin was given me as a receptacle for nauseous excretions and certain it is that I found the necessity of it for the whole day and night following, which so much weakened my system and not being able to take any thing in the way of sustenance I became a mere skeleton. In this state I lay for the long period of three weeks, an uncommon period for a seasick person. Both the captain and the mate (which by the bye were very kind to me) at last became alarmed at my situation and viewing me daily loosing strength, as well as flesh, entertained anxious doubts for my recovery. Every day they pressed upon me to partake of food, assuring me if I continued to refuse it I must surely die, but even these threats could not induce me to taste of any thing in the form of eatables. I had become so careless of myself that 'Death had lost its terrors'. There was a sickly smell about me of bilge water, tar, and a host of combustibles all of which my nasal organs were strangers to, which acted in dire opposition to my convalescence. In fact everything that reached those organs was detestful, even the victuals themselves when brought to the table.

Oh who has ever been at sea and seasick, and will not understand the unfortunate, the pitiable situation I was placed in. Perhaps this curtailed description of myself may reach the eyes of some who have at some time or other shared an equal fate. They alone will understand my case, but quite impossible it is for any other to do so.

During the time I have mentioned in which I lay more inanimate than otherwise, the ship had ploughed through many a mile of foaming billow. Now labouring under the force of a severe gale, every thing creaking and cracking in conformity with her labour, the huge seas sometimes striking her broadside, causing her to lurch over in such a manner that every inanimate object in the cabin seemed to have taken life except myself. Then bounding over a smoother sea with a fair breeze every stitch of canvas crowded upon her, and she as though proud of her decorated apparel gliding along with a swiftness adapted to meet the wishes of her commander.

At length having run out of the bad weather latitudes and

entered into that climate where the sun never ceases to shine during the day in all its splendour, and by night the moon and stars seem to glisten with uncommon brightness, where the perpetual trade wind blows its constant cooling breezes keeping a temperature of the atmosphere at once healthy and delightful, our captain insisted one unusual fine day that I should go on deck to inhale the fresh air. Consequently I put together all my remaining strength and endeavoured to crawl on deck in compliance to his command but no sooner had I put feet on the cabin floor than I found they had refused their wonted duty, and not all that I could do would compel them to bear my weight. No, as fast as I endeavoured to place my body erect as fast would they bend under its weight and compel it to resume its wonted prostrate position. At the same time everything seemed to me to be moving round and round, in fact, I felt an altogether very unpleasant sensation. However the chief mate after witnessing my extreme weakness and understanding the cause, took compassion upon me, and helped me up on deck, where he place me in a good position to benefit from the fresh air and the fine weather.

I had not been on deck more than an hour before I felt a slight change had already taken place in me for the better, and when noon had arrived, and the dinner served up, I felt an inclination to taste of something. Perhaps then if I had had a kind mother to prepare me some dainty morsel I might have recruited my appetite, but no, my only nurse in that department was the cook, who by the bye was but ill calculated to substitute a mother. Dinner having been served up and the captain and mate partaken of theirs, I was ordered by them to go down with the second mate to take mine, and with strict injunctions to the second mate to see that I did eat, they left me to enjoy their pipes. Down the cabin I therefore crawled but what was my astonishment when arrived at table to find instead of some nice broth and chicken as I had anticipated, a mess of 'Lob Scouse'.[1] Ah me!, that was but ill fit for a weak

[1] A mess of salt beef and potatoes mashed and boiled up together. [HM] The *SOED* spells the name as one word (a nautical term of unknown origin, dating from 1706), and defines it as a sailor's dish of meat stewed with vegetables and ship's

stomach. I turned away with disgust from it, the second officer insisted that I should eat some, said he had orders to make me eat, and that knowing well I was in want of food he was determined to make me eat. I replied that I was equally well aware of my want of nourishment, but that he had to offer me could not merit that appellation.

At last he seemed to be angry and told me I was 'nasty nice' but that I must remember I was at sea now, and not in parlours attended by servants. Alas I needed not his insinuations to remember it! I remembered it but too well! However, placing a plateful of the composition before me he insisted that I should eat it, assuring me when I had once began it I would not wish to leave the plate until it was empty. I begged of him not to force me, for I felt assured if I attempted it my stomach would refuse it and that I might be forced to act with impropriety whilst he was at table, or at least if I must eat it to let me go on deck and do so, where upon the first notice of sickness I might put my head over the side. But no, to nothing of this would he hearken, and concluded by saying if I did not at once commence, he would call the captain who decidedly would soon make me swallow it. Now not wishing if possible to give the captain cause to be angry with me, I took the spoon and commenced polishing my allotment.

I went on very well indeed, much to my surprise, until I had reached about the half, but at that moment I felt my stomach was crying enough and therefore laid my spoon down again. But again were the threats of my guardian vociferated. I assured him I had taken quite enough, that he must take in consideration the weakness of my stomach which had been without food for three long weeks but, bah to that, was his reply. He was sure that such *light* food could not hurt me. Light food! O ye judges of truth, decide between arrow root and salt beef and potatoes! Well, force put is no choice, to work I went a second time, each spoonful making my poor stomach to creak under its weight. At last, having reached nearly the end of my set task all at once and without a moment's notice and before I could stir one step, like a shot out of a gun, my

biscuit, or the like.

vexed stomach discharged its load into the very receptacle it had been taken from, and in such a well directed manner that not one particle overreached its circumference.

Mr second mate, momentarily alarmed at so sudden an ebullition of my system, instinctively drew back a few paces in his chair, fearing I presume, that our proximity threatened his person with a sprinkling. The moment I had regained my vocal powers I looked up to him, exclaiming, 'There now, I told you what would happen. I knew my stomach was too weak to bear such an enormous load as you have forced me to take. You see the consequences of your cruelty; had you permitted me to know when I had enough, it might have been well with me and you would besides have avoided me the disgrace I feel at acting in a manner I certainly could not help, as well at table as in your presence.' But however, I soon found out I had no very great occasion to be alarmed at my indecency with reference to him, as in answer to my remonstrance and apology he merely remarked as praise to myself that I had done well in not strewing it about the cabin floor and now said he, 'If you will take my advice you will go to work again and eat another plateful and you may depend it will stop down with you.'

But at these refined manners of his I felt quite disgusted, and without thinking of asking leave, or licence, I left the table and proceeded on deck where I resumed my former station. The captain soon after came near me to enquire if I had eaten a hearty meal. I replied I had done my utmost towards doing so, but that my stomach was yet too weak to bear the victuals to which I was quite a stranger but I hoped at tea time I should be able to enjoy a cup of tea and bread and butter. Tea time arrived and I did really enjoy a cup or two of it with a nice piece of sweetcake my kind mother had provided me with on my departure, and I may date my convalescence since that day; for ever afterwards I grew better and better until I became indeed both heartier and healthier then ever I had been. My appetite became so voracious that I believe, like the African ostrich I could have swallowed a stone and digested it. Having everything in the provision way under my care I never suffered hunger to gnaw at my stomach long — besides having entered into an arrangement with the cook that he would provide me with all sorts of little niceties cooked after his own fashion which he promised would be palatable, and that I would provide him with a drop o'the creature every now and then, but that it should remain a profound secret between us. I may say I might have gone further and faced worse.

Complete recovery

In short, five weeks after we had been at sea I was perfectly recovered and quite myself again and began already with my renewed health, and the beautiful weather of the tropics, accompanied with the occasional novelties with which my eye was delighted, to entertain a relish to my new profession, and to forget the sorrow my absence from home had caused me. One thing was in my favour which greatly added to my comfort, that was the extreme kindness of my rulers. Both the captain and the mate treated me indeed with all the affection of parents; the former especially though quite a stranger to me seemed to have centred an affection in me which amounted almost to veneration; the latter, a fine young man of about three and twenty of a character quite irreproachable and a disposition at once amiable and prepossessing, though not a perfect stranger to me was neither any relative, but owing to a particular intimacy that existed between a sister of mine and himself, promised to be one in due course of time,[1] also looked upon me with seeming affection and treated me less as a servant than an equal, so that with comfort on that side and the satisfaction of being generally beloved by all, everything proved fair for rendering my first voyage at sea replete with happiness.

[1] This was Henry Cohu, who later married Hilary's younger sister Rachel.

Porpoises and dolphins and the agents of the Devil

Until the time I have spoken of we had travelled over the surface of the deep blue sea without the least obstruction on our way or having seen any thing to engage the attention more than now and then a school of playful porpoises, which would come under the ship's bows exhibiting to our wandering eyes all their skill at play and indeed amusing mine to a degree bordering upon delight, or perhaps at another time the majestic dolphin would be seen gliding through its element around the ship with a beauty and grace that baffles all description, the transparent blue of the Atlantic adding perfection to the picture. It is seldom, if ever, this beautiful fish, the prince of the water, can come around the ship unmolested. No, at the first cry of 'Dolphin O' every eye is upon him and every hand engaged at its capture, some with hooks and lines upon the jib-boom, other over the taffrail playing their tempting baits to induce the hungry tempter of an eager crew to become himself tempted and ultimately captured.

Whilst the crew are thus employed with the playing baits, the captain is generally armed with a pair of grains,[1] for striking the fish if he shows the least disinclination of taking the hook, and the moment he appears near the surface of the water, if the captain's eye is good, and his aim sure, the fish's doom is that moment sealed. Thus if a school of dolphins come round the ship it is seldom their number is not thinned before they take their departure again, though I must say they are very cute fish, and it will happen sometimes that notwithstanding the many preparations which are ever ready for their siezure, as well as the unabated exertions which are made, they will maintain their amusements around the ship for hours together in defiance of molestation, and will go away again after a satisfactory stay quite unharmed, much to the mortification of their would-be captors, whilst at other times again it so happens that a number of them are caught. If, for instance,

[1] A grain was a fish-spear or harpoon with two or more prongs (*SOED*, first noted 1815).

they prove to be hungry and the line is well played, they will seem to battle with each other at who shall catch himself first and on such occasions as these I know of no finer sport than Dolphin fishing.

I have myself hauled in board eight and twenty from one school in the short space of two hours, the smallest of which did not weigh less than 10lb but many far exceeding that weight. There is also among the fishing excursions on board ship one that creates no small degree of excitement, that is the capture of some monstrous shark. It will often happen that these are caught of such a size that not all the force of a ship's crew combined can haul them on board. On such occasions they are generally left to hang in the water with the head downwards until they drown, then by means of tackles they are boused[1] on deck where they have then to undergo the process of a post mortem examination after which a verdict is generally returned of 'Died through having swallowed a piece of pork with a hook concealed in it'. The carcass is then quartered and perhaps the jaw and backbone are kept as curiosities by some of the crew, and the rest is then committed to the deep without the least symptoms of funeral rites, though I must say a short prayer generally accompanies the body such as 'May the rest of your tribe, you ugly monster, share an equal fate, and may your race be extinct tomorrow.'

I recollect of having myself only a short time since greatly aided to extirpate the tribe of sharks in a manner very surprising to myself as well as to all who witnessed it. Although it is well known that the strength of this fish is very great, so much so that it is never attempted to capture one without a hook of a tremendous size and a good line of proportionate strength, yet strange as it may appear I can vouch of having caught twelve at one time upon the same hook and line, which was only a small cord used for catching dolphins, the largest of which measured nine feet three inches from the end of his tail to the snout. Now this may appear incredibly strange, but so strange so true. Yet as the prejudiced mind of many may be apt to believe this statement exaggerated

[1] To bouse is to haul with tackle (*SOED*).

and desiring to convince them of the contrary as well as to assure them that throughout the whole of this reminiscence of earlier days I have strictly adhered to the rules of truth. I feel myself obliged to disclose this seeming impossibility in terms easily understood.

The monstrous shark here spoken of was a *she* one and just happened to be in that noble state of multiplicity which it cannot be denied is the glory of the whole creation, therefore having hauled her with her multitudinous progeny on deck, she as others was at once doomed to have her maw[1] strictly investigated and scarcely had she been unfastened from the line that had secured her than two or three large sheath knives were embedded in her flanks and soon an aperture was made whereby to extricate the said maw, the receptacle of stolen property, but what was the astonishment of the murderers as well as of the bystanders their accomplices when after a thrust of the knife in the region of the genitals out jumps a young fish with all the sprightliness of youth, and the vivacity of life, and after it ten others not less agile followed. A scream of wonder from some, a laugh from others, and amongst all a general run from the scene at once proved that a mystery was extant which the wonder stricken spectators could not explain. This mystery, however, was of short duration, and the whole was soon explained as only a natural cause by one or two of the oldest members of the crew, and I dare say the most experienced in phenomenons of generations! No sooner, therefore, were the rest satisfied of the truth and reassured that the animal was not a monster from the lower regions of satanic relation, and her offspring as many imps, as they at first were ready to believe, than the arm of one made bare was thrust into the aperture as far as the elbow to ascertain if any more young devils lay concealed there, and during all this time it must be noticed the old animal still full of life, writhing with pain, and making such movements with her tail as threatened destruction to any thing that might have come within its reach, the young also imitating the mother in every direction about the decks.

Now I have been explicit enough I believe to convince the

[1] Stomach.

doubtful, but not only for that one reason, but for two, for whilst I have been describing a scene which I gladly would have passed unnoticed, and which my own discretion prompted me so to do, yet to serve my second purpose I could not well over-look it, which is to show the unparalleled animosity with which sailors in general regard the race of sharks, and the unjustifiable cruelty with which they glory in treating them, whensoever fortune brings it within their power. Superstition, that great bane of the ancient world, has not yet found excision in the modern one and sailors are yet in these our enlightened days fain to believe that their greatest enemy after the devil, is his agent the shark, and that if they should peradventure meet with a watery grave, a shark is sure to find itself to feast upon their bodies. In fact some there are who believe that there is a shark constantly following the ship ready to devour the first whose misfortune may be to fall overboard. That there have been instances where human beings have been mangled by these sea monsters I will allow, but that they thus mangle the human being through a natural enmity, or that they prefer human flesh to any other is far wide of the truth. They, like all other animals of prey, are fain to devour the first morsel of food that they may happen to fall in with, and whether it be man or beast when these huge monsters which starvation makes voracious fall in with a morsel in their element, it is but natural they should at once devour it without consulting of what species it is, and as a further proof that they are not the enemies of man, but man their enemies, they like most of the creation fear the sight of man and dare not to approach him, and if even in the water surrounded by them man may scare them all by attempting to face them.

An instance I have read of and which I believe, relative to this subject, a young man, mate of a ship, who, wishing to convince his master of the truth of what I have just now explained but failing entirely owing to the superstition that existed in his breast, called him up one calm day when one of these monsters of unusual size was playing about the ship and told him he was about to give him demonstration of his former assertions by jumping overboard in pursuit of the shark. The captain, who the very sight of the fish had scared, could not find words to dissuade his friend of his rash purpose but was panic struck on perceiving him bare himself of his clothes in order to jump overboard. The young man waited until the shark was close to the ship's side, that everybody might view without conjecture his enormous shape. A small piece of pork was thrown at him to prove his hunger, but scarcely had it reached the water when it was precipitately gulped down the monster's throat. 'He's hungry, boys', cries the mate, 'here goes to feed him!' and with one bound he jumped close at his side. The poor creature, alarmed at so unexpected a shock, with one bound was off at more than thirty yards distance, but upon second consideration returned to ascertain what it was that had so disturbed him. The young man who perceived him coming towards him, and who the cries of those on board almost deafened of 'Here he comes, save yourself, take hold of this rope etc', made directly for him swimming at his maximum speed. No sooner had Mr Shark ascertained that it was a live being who pursued him, than turning round made off as fast as his fins and tail could carry him. The mate returned on board amidst the wonder-stricken crew, contemplated by them as one gifted with supernatural power but laughing at their weakness ultimately succeeded in convincing them. The captain, however, older than the rest and I suppose more hardened in superstition still remained undecided but whether he has since been convinced or no, I cannot tell. Certain I am, however, that he must have been more obdurate even than Thomas[1] for seeing he could not believe and feeling he still remained in doubt.

Now I think I have dwelt sufficiently upon this sharkish topic and if I have failed to convince my readers (which I do not intend will be many) of the harmlessness of the lion of the sea I trust that at least their opinion is established more in favour of it than it has hitherto been. And in order to continue what I have attempted to begin, I shall have to retrograde a little to follow up where I had left off.

[1] i.e. St Thomas, the Apostle who doubted the truth of the Resurrection (John ch. 20, v. 25).

Land O!

Nothing had obstructed our way more than I have here noticed until the 38th day after leaving Old England, the cry of 'Land O!' reverberated through the ship. Every eye was instantaneously directed to that point of the horizon from whence issued the object of our attraction. Far to the west, and right ahead of the ship rose in majesty above the clear blue sea, the well delineated hills of Antigua.

Now was a subject for contemplation. Here was a source of joy for everybody. First for the master in being assured of his situation after so long and tedious a journey over the trackless main, then for the crew in feeling how much nearer they had got to their destined port, and the likelihood of soon again enjoying their pot and pipe. And last but not least for your humble servant whose joy though not occasioned on any of these accounts, only differed from theirs by being greater. Well do I remember the effects the first cry of 'Land O!' then produced, effects that can be better conceived than described, and even then, only by those who like me have launched upon the mighty deep exiling themselves from home and the comforts thereof, willing to undergo the main hardships and privations attending a sea voyage, as much for the sake of gratifying a curiosity which like the young mouse who had been born under a tub, mounted on its summit one day and after casting a glance around her with indescribable astonishment exclaimed, 'I did not think the world was half so large!' and whose enthusiasm would then immediately have led her to launch out in contemplation of its surrounding beauties, as much as I say for this reason as for a secret desire of, like the famous 'Cook',[1] becoming a circumnavigator of the vast expanse and wide range of our terrestrial globe which philosophy had then already taught me was not only practicable but fraught with new beauties here and there issuing out as it was from the bowels of the surrounding waters.

A few hours with the pleasant and steady trade wind served to

[1] i.e. James Cook (1728–79), circumnavigator of the globe.

bring us on the meridian of this beautiful island, well known as an English colony, and edging close to its shores we had every opportunity of feasting our eyes on the variegated beauties that offered themselves to view, though perhaps indeed few if any besides myself found subject for admiration, as most of the crew being old sailors had more than once passed on the same course, but every object new to me was deemed worthy of admiration. Hither and thither rose in seeming sublimity the towering heads of the cocoa nut tree, at their base extended in vast plains floated in the breeze the beautiful sugar cane, whilst at another view amongst the young hills resplendent with their verdure lay interspersed the shingle huts of the negro, thatched over with the leaves of the banana and cocoa nut, forming to the eyes of the distant observer the appearance of the wild rabbit's burrow on our English farmer's plains. These and numerous objects besides arrested my attention and I must allow filled me with a sort of Antiguarian passion.

Having passed this island but long ere it had receded below the horizon rose others ahead which again promised subject for contemplation. The remarkable Redonda Island with its hay-rick appearance,[1] the notable Mount Serrat named after its mountainous appearance etc and all of which to the eye of a young navigator proved objects of admiration, and in short, though I still well remember the preceding novelties that arrested my attention until our arrival at Havana, yet I will dispense recapitulating them for the reason that the trifles which I then deemed wonderfully admirable, have since through a wider extended philosophy become almost ridiculous. Yet the numerous scattered islands of the West Indies each with its share of natural embellishments must not be thought amongst the objects of my present ridicule, far from that, where nature is concerned its minutest gift find a place in my mind for veneration. And the passage from England to Havana by the southern route commencing at the aforementioned island of Antigua is diversified with new beauties towering above the horizon, every now and then attracting the eye of a lover of nature which cannot fail to remind him of nature's god!

[1] A small island to the NW of Montserrat and W of Antigua.

To mine at least it has proved the case; and many a time whilst pouring over the contemplative scenery and leaving imagination to run on in an unobstructed course, has the vain desire arisen within my perhaps enthusiastic breast of having been born a Columbus. After having left in the distance the group of the Virgin Islands and those already mentioned, rises with continued progress to the westward the beautiful island of Porto Rico, then St Domingo,[1] both larger and richer than the former, then Jamaica, exceeding them both, then comes the Cayman Islands, then the Isle of Pines[2] abounding with its renowned turtle, then comes rich Cuba rising in majesty seeming to challenge all the others as to their inferiority together in extent and wealth and produce.

Arrival in Havana Bay

Thus after having passed all these scenes of admiration, our gallant ship at length found a temporary rest and shelter in the smooth and motionless waters of the beautiful bay of Havana where under a display of her many colours together with her stately appearance she seemed to enjoy the tranquillity with which she was then surrounded, and to evince a certain degree of joy, but greater pride of having so long contended with the boisterous elements and at last after overcoming all the dangers safely achieved her course.

Nothing material occurred during my stay in this port although I might fill volumes with the many trifling matters that arrested my attention. Being for the first time in my life in a strange land everything was quite new to me, consequently quite as wonderful.

[1] At this date the two halves of the island of Hispaniola (the former French colony of Haiti, which became independent in 1804, and the Spanish colony of Santo Domingo) were united under Haitian control; Hilary is presumably using the name to refer to the entire island, or alternatively to the town of Santo Domingo, which in 1844 became the capital of the newly independent Dominican Republic.

[2] An island 60 miles off the SW coast of Cuba; renamed Isla de la Juventud ('Isle of Youth') in 1958 in recognition of the contribution made by young people to its development.

The Market

The splendid city with its so lofty buildings, the extensive market every day heaped up with a profusion of the richest fruits, the splendid flavoured orange heaped up in piles as our cider apples are at home, each person heedlessly passing by not even deigning to favour them with a glance. The rich and exquisite banana in all directions hanging in bunches of inconceivable weight offering their peculiar delicacy to each passer by. The incomparable pine apple freshly culled from the field with the morning dew yet fresh upon its outspread coronet of leaves, tempting even the most heedless to pause awhile and if not to purchase at least to admire. The mash and water-melon, the mamey-apple, the bread fruit, the mango and these productions of nature are here to be found in abundance. Indeed the Havana market in my humble opinion can vie with any of the West Indies. Poultry are here also in abundance; geese and turkeys may be had cheaper than fowls; the Guinea hen, the pea-cock, the Muscovy duck all are here in profusion, while here and there may be seen a school of parrots and macaws creating their everlasting deafening noise amongst the multitude of not much less noiseless dispositions, for the vendors in this market are all negro-women (or with very few exceptions) who with perhaps a couple of babes tied upon their backs, and their breasts *in puris naturalibus*[1] for the convenience of the little ebony infidels who have the instinct, if I may use the word, to reach over the mother's shoulder without even troubling her for a moment in her most busy occupations and to draw up to their puny mouths the pulp from which they derive their sustenance.

The natural appearance of the Spaniards under (then to me) their eccentric garb at first created in me a certain degree of apprehension, and I would not have ventured on shore alone for a world, believing always according to the various reports that they were never unarmed although secretly, and that where ever they saw an Englishman they thirsted for his blood; but in process of

[1] i.e. naked.

time this fear of, and antipathy against them, wore away and after a stay of three weeks amongst them instead of shunning I actually sought their company; and amongst the few which duty compelled me to associate with, they being on board every day whilst loading, I so perfectly ingratiated myself that had it been necessary they would have risked life and limb for my protection. And that their affection when once placed is durable I have proved, for the same men although of the lower class or class of labourers, on a return port after an absence of a twelvemonth recognised me instantly and greeted me with a more than brotherly affection.

I had more reasons than one, although perhaps not above two for securing to myself a few friends here. The first was a consciousness that by winning the affection of a few I should be protected from the ire of many, and that unmolested I might stray about the wharves or adjacent streets of the town of an evening whither my boyish propensities led me. The second was that I had an insurmountable desire of being acquainted with the Spanish language, I took an early fancy to it, and to this day it has not left me; to accomplish my purpose then, not an opportunity was lost to have a few words of chat with some Spaniard or other, and by this means in an incredibly short time I had picked up the rudiments of this beautiful, elegant, language, and on my second return with a redoubled perseverance I became acquainted with the language sufficiently to converse with any of the natives without being at a loss either to understand them or to make myself understood. In fact they universally agreed and protested, although perhaps meant as a flattering complement, 'Aunque es Ingles, habla tan bien Español, que los Españoles le creén Español'.[1] But to proceed with my narrative in order to accomplish as near as I can my intentions I shall have to crack on all sail to make up for the lee-way I have sustained.

[1] 'Although he is English, his Spanish is so good that Spaniards would take him for one of them'.

Bound for Trieste

With a rich cargo of sugar and coffee we left the Havana bound for Trieste, and although it is by no means my intention to follow up the every day transactions of my life, yet I shall have to follow up some of them on each voyage that will bear with my present work, in order to arrive at something near to what I intended when I first started out. These few days then on this present voyage which here become worthy of note may be considered to commence about a fortnight after we had sailed. The usual inconveniences, impediments, or obstructions attending a sea voyage had hitherto of course prevailed, but are here passed unnoticed for the reason afore stated, but on this day began something more than the usualities. Dangers 'tis true which those whose lot it is to go down to the sea in ships and to do business in great waters may expect, but yet through the kind dispensations of a gracious providence not so often meet.

A Storm

We had attained as well as I can now remember the parallel and only a few degrees from the meridian of the Bermuda Islands when a storm of wind from the western quarter arose, and in so short a time that with all the activity that could be displayed when occasion required it by a not misnamed smart crew, we had as much as we could do to gather in our canvas in time. However not without difficulty it was gathered in and the ship brought under a close reefed main top sail and reefed fore sail and being steered at that point directly opposite to the wind, she bounded through the foaming surge, each successive wave rolling after her with an appearance and noise that struck dismay into every heart, and which seemed as if the angry billow had long meditated the destruction of our gallant little bark, but onward she moved for a long time outdoing the enemy in chase, or when a swifter one approached so near that nothing now seemed able to avoid it, she would gently rise her stern allowing the mountain of sea to roll beneath her, whilst with a majesty and grace which even conception cannot equal she rode upon its crest, thus, and thus did she pursue her course unmolested for eight or nine hours gliding along at a speed of nine and nine and a half miles an hour amidst the praise of everyone on board, the oldest tar exclaiming with an oath to strengthen his assertion that 'he had seen many a ship and many a sea, but that he had never seen one to match the *Nancy* in point of behaviour'.

At length however we were sorrowfully taught that however majestically a ship may brave the resistless wave for a time, yet there comes a moment when its anger may arrive to that pitch of power when nothing ever made to ride upon its bosom can contend with it. One mighty swell arose and came curling along after us, each moment gaining a greater strength and height when as she had done before the gallant ship attempted to ride in defiance of it but the proud floury white wave had marked her for its prey. Onward it came with a dreadful roar! a voice was heard, 'hold yourselves on my lads, hold! hold on for life!' It was our chief mate who stood conning the ship, and plainly saw that this one was not to be avoided. His last words were lost amidst the dreadful crash that followed, the sea had struck us, and for a time completely swallowed us up. I can however recollect nothing more than having a confused idea of the drowning sensation I then experienced. Unconsciousness for a time had overpowered me, and when that sensation vanished and I began to feel the effects of returning animation, opening my eyes and staring around me I found myself prostrate on the deck surrounded by the rest of the watch who were shaking their feathers and regaining breath. I was told afterwards that everyone was afloat about the decks and that I, having less muscular strength could not hold fast of any thing, consequently had been washed to and fro obeying the impulse of the water till ultimately with a lurch of the ship to leeward I was seen following the rapid torrent through an aperture in the bulwark which the sea had forced away, and was fortunately rescued by the man at the helm, the only one who had not been forced from his hold, who declared that he had just been quick enough to lay hold of my left foot when all the rest of my body was overboard. This was certainly a narrow escape, but I will, ere I have attained the end of my task, have occasion to comment on many others which I have experienced.

As soon as we had got over this unexpected severe visitation, everyone was immediately employed in looking round to ascertain the extent of the damage, when to our grief we found first the jolly boat[1] which had hung on the stern davits shattered all to pieces, nothing remaining but a small part of her gunwale yet attached to the ring-bolts, next the round-house had been started from its fastenings, then the starboard bulwark from the after part of the main rigging to the after part of the fore was completely washed away, one or two solitary stanchions only remaining. The other or larboard side was yet in a more awful state and may be said to have been swept away altogether, as only a small patch remained here and there; thus in the short space of less than five minutes was more damage done than could have been repaired in twice as many days, but however, as it is said by some, 'There is no grief unbacked by joy', so in the present instance was the case with us, our grief at the loss was sufficiently great but we were lightened with a corresponding degree of joy to think that not one of us had followed the fragments.

Hove to

This over, and everything temporarily secured, the captain bethought himself of heaving her to and conferring with the chief mate on the subject, it was decided between them that at eight bells p.m. when the watch would be on deck she should accordingly be hove to. In course of time eight bells were struck and the watch called in the usual manner with the additional words to their bemoaning tune of 'Heave ship to', another five minutes and the watch stood at their stations waiting the commands of the master and intimating their readiness by the cry of 'All ready forward'. The captain then taking his station on the skylight, supporting

[1] A clinker-built ship's boat, smaller than a cutter, used chiefly as a hack-boat for small work.

himself by the main boom to watch a lull of the sea, gave out the orders to 'Haul the fore sail up' that being done almost as soon as said, the next order was 'Stand by your main braces. Brace the main yard foreward. Luff, luff (to the helmsman), Down helm. Belay the main braces, now brace forward the head yards a bit', but just as this manoeuvre was being performed and every heart began to rejoice she had hove to so prettily, up comes another sea curling mountains high and strikes the ship on her broadside, throws her on her beam ends and fairly passed over her. Soon, however, she righted again and after giving herself one shake or two deprived herself of the encumbering water yet sweeping her decks. Now, of course, it was thought that nothing would have been left remaining upon the decks after such an intrusion but to the utter amazement of everybody everything seemed to have stood the shock with impunity except the caboose,[1] which had deserted its post and stood trembling at an angle of 30 degrees midway from its original place and the fore rigging. A sauce pan or fish kettle had sustained some damage also by changing at once its dimensions from an oval to an octagon, the frying pan was nowhere to be found, consequently must have gone to furnish Davy Jones's locker. This was of course a sore trial to the cook who did not pretend the sea had any business to interfere or disturb his part of the ship, and who stood contemplating the disaster and cursing the caboose for having removed itself, and wishing another sea to come and wash it away altogether since it could not face a spray and stand its ground like a Briton.

Nancy *springs a leak*

A few trifling losses similar to this was all the damage it was concluded this sea had done and consequently everyone rejoiced, but there were others of a far more serious nature which the eye had not detected and which it was feared the eye would never

[1] The cook-room.

detect. At ten of the clock when the pump was tried as was usual every two hours, the watch found that after pumping the usual spell the pump showed yet no signs of sticking. The sounding rod was had, the pump sounded and lo! three feet of water yet remained in the hold. It was evident the ship had sprung a leak. Here was a new disaster! Here was cause for fear, in the middle of the Western Ocean with a tempest of wind and a sinking ship!

All hands to the pumps

To the pumps therefore all hands were immediately set, and it was soon joyfully perceived we were fast gaining on the leak but almost as soon proved that the leak was of that extent which would not admit of a moment's respite from the already much fatigued crew. The morning, that dawn of day, that cheering hour which is hailed with a welcome by every sailor, at length came, but alas with it no moderation in the gale, rather an increase.

Lighten ship

On that morning the sea making a fair breach over the ship, the order was given by the captain for lightening her. One hundred bags of coffee were, therefore got out of the fore and after holds through the companion hatchways and thrown overboard, after which the ship seemed like the fatigued camel when disburdened of its load, in plain words quite differently behaved, and to the master's as well as the crew's satisfaction, it was evident that comparatively small weight of which she was lightened had made a great difference for the better, but still she rolled, and plunged and laboured desperately. The captain not believing otherwise than this heavy rolling and plunging increased her leaks ordered the top-gallant masts[1] and yards to be sent down, and for reasons best

[1] i.e. those above the topmasts, the second section of a mast above the deck.

known to himself and which I have never questioned, to be thrown overboard. This done she laboured somewhat less, but still the hideous clink clank of the pump met the ear amidst the howling roar of the tempest, a noise which, bye the bye, none but those who have heard it in alike circumstances can conceive with what dismal forebodings it meets the ear.

A sail on the horizon

Shortly after the top gallant masts had been sent down and whilst the men were still aloft, a sail was decried at the horizon. This was tidings of great joy to us who only a few moments before thought ourselves alone in the world, and who expected a few moments more would see us out of it unseen, unregretted! Half an hour served to satisfy us that this ship was steering towards us, therefore no time was lost to signalize to the ship our distressing situation. The ensign, that glorious standard of Britain's glory beneath the shadow of which every true British heart receives animation, was hoisted up union downwards, and for a time gazing at this invulnerable drapery floating in the breeze every heart seemed reanimated, the danger that threatened us was for a time forgotten, and the fiendish power of the billows was defied, in fact so great was the enthusiasm existing among us, that we deemed it impossible for harm to befall us whilst the standard of glory waived above our heads. The strange ship soon making out our signal was not long ere she bore down upon us, at the same time displaying her national bunting in token of her perception of ours.

A French ship

The captain by the aid of his spy glass soon made her out to be French and bark rigged, apparently bound on the same course as we but running whilst we still remained hove dead to. Soon she came up to us, when our captain, who was as fluent in Johnny Petite's lingo as with English, took the opportunity of hailing him first. The captain of the bark, who no doubt had amassed all his philology together for the occasion, seemed highly delighted to find it was not necessary to make use of it, ours speaking his language, and answered his first enquiry of 'Ou allez vous?' immediately by the short response of 'Au Havre'. A host of communications were then exchanged and finally our captain asked him if he would be considerate enough to keep company with us for a few days, in case the existing leak should overpower us and thereby oblige us to leave the ship. The Frenchman, whose philanthropy did not seem limited, readily consented, and promised to keep as close to us as possible intimating his proximity by night through the aid of a lantern light.

Thus far were our fears assuaged of meeting with a watery grave. The helm was put 'hard a weather' and once more the ship glided along in close pursuit of her French protector, but this friend in need, as we looked upon him to be, soon found that to comply with his promise it would be necessary to shorten sail for though our little ship sailed by no means bad, yet his sailed somewhat better. This however he did without seeming hesitation and before the night closed in upon us we had the satisfaction to see that we could cleverly keep up with him. At two o'clock p.m., not being able to distinguish him, we put up our light and was almost immediately answered by his, though at a greater distance than he ought to have been according to the rules prescribed during the day. All went on well during the first watch of the night, the continued howling of the tempest's noise only broken by the yet more hideous clink, clank of the pump. Midnight and the watch was relieved, fatigued and spirit broken of having been four hours at the pumps, they went below to seek a temporary rest in their water logged cabins. Not long, however, were they to enjoy that repose which is sweet to the tempest tossed sailor even on a bed which often is as wet as the clothes which he has taken off to retire to it. No, at about two o'clock the alarm was given, 'All hands on deck, the ship is sinking!' The captain, who whilst meditating in the cabin on the misfortunes of the moment, had fancied he heard the water gushing in at a rapid rate in the lazaret[1] and calling myself, who lay also in a happy state of unconsciousness on my pillow, bade me get a light and clear away the lazaret hatch that he might convince himself of the truth or fiction of his supposition. This done we both repaired in the lazaret when sure enough it became but too evident that his fears were not ill-founded, the clear streams were seen rushing down the ceiling at a rapid rate. Now the captain in the fear of the moment did not give himself time to consider this might be the identical leak that had kept the pumps agoing all the time previous, but immediately set it down as a fresh one just broke out.

Sinking!

Hence arose the alarm throughout the ship of ship is going down! Directly, as many hands as could be spared from the pumps were sent down the cabin and in a short time every thing was hauled up out of the lazaret upon the cabin floor, and never shall I forget the confusion of that night. Barrels of provisions, kegs of butter, barrels of flour and vinegar, jars of oil, kegs of paint, crow bars, coils of rope, in fact a host of other objects not necessary to mention, were strewed about the cabin floor all topsy turvy, the hurry of the moment not allowing time to secure anything, and with a ship running before a gale and high sea, rolling side for side, I ask who cannot conceive the splendid mess we were in. Once a thing took a start we ran to secure it,[2] and whilst in that act half a dozen others came tumbling about our legs which made us jump and frisk about like as many wounded hares in a furze-break. After all the attempts that were made to come at the leak the searchers were at length obliged to give up the chase as unsuccessful. Consequently no alternative was now left but pump or sink.

[1] A space between decks, used as a store-room.

[2] Emended from 'One thing took ... ' in the MS.

Where is the Frenchman? – Gone!

In the midst of this awful conclusion the captain ordered a light to be immediately put up as a signal for the Frenchman to approach and had he done so I am confident that under the mental distraction the captain then laboured, being a man that soon gave way and withered under the heavy hand of misfortune, we should all have left the ship and repaired on board our rescuer. But however, fortune without the title of *mis* did not will it should be so. Mr Johnny Crapeau was no where to be seen, in vain did we show our lantern lights, in vain did we exhibit a burning tar barrel. The philanthropy that had warmed the Frenchman's breast during the day had been cooled by the shadows of night, and under cover of it had he pressed on all sail and absconded leaving his faithful charge to perish in the waves if (as no doubt he thought) fortune would prove as benevolent, and concluding of course by what he had seen that little chance of escape was left to us, he reported us as lost on his arrival home.

But not yet however were we doomed to be numbered with the waves of the sea. The omnipotent eye was watching over our safety and the omnipresent hand defending us. The return of another day was soon announced by the beautiful twilight in the east and soon the glorious sun, though obscured by heavy massive clouds, came forth to banish the gloom of the night and to hail the new born day and with it came a perceptible moderation in the gale, in short that day at noon we lay like a log upon the waters only tossed about by the yet agitated element, but no longer with that dangerous velocity we were wont to be. The agitated sea soon, however, after the cessation of the wind found its level, and for many successive days afterwards we were favoured with beautiful weather.

It was on the second fine day, the ocean being comparatively speaking smooth as a mill dam, our captain ordered the carpenter to rig himself a stage and to go over the stern and with minute examination endeavour to detect the leak which he had every reason to conjecture was not far under water, if not above it. The carpenter accordingly rigged himself, and was soon with his pricker trying every seam and butt, which proved all sound enough until he came to one just above the water mark which had not the power of resistance the others had evinced. Pitch, oakum and caulking tools were soon under way to arrest the current of the stream, but lo! the first blow of the mallet decided at once that all the oakum in the ship would not fill the excavation, it was a piece of new wood that was required, and a piece of new wood was put and then securely caulked, after which the ship left off her tippling propensities and kept on a sober tack ever afterwards to the great joy of every one on board, more especially the sailors, who could have kissed the carpenter every time they looked upon the pump and thought how likely the bolt was to become rusty again. Thus were we rescued from a premature grave through the kind dispensations of a gracious providence whose mercy is boundless and power infinite. And after a passage of no more than the usual number of days we reached our destination port in safety.

Arrival in Trieste – Heavy repair work

The arrival of the *Nancy* this voyage in the port of Trieste was a phenomenon that very soon became a subject of town talk, and for the first few days multitudes came down upon the Mole to contemplate the shattered appearance of the newly arrived ship. Soon, however, she presented a different appearance, for after being discharged she was immediately put under the hands of some forty or more carpenters, who doing their duty under the eye of a competent but strict master soon brought her to the semblance of her former self.

Leaves for London – Captain becomes insane

Everything righted again we left this port after a prolonged stay of above two months with a cargo of beans for London. We were then emphatically speaking ‘Homeward Bound’. How sweet the word to the long exiled mariner! But alas, home we did not reach with the usual monotony attending a lengthened passage. This voyage seemed to be destined to be a voyage of incidents. We had not left Trieste above a few days when we perceived the mental faculties of our commander, to our consternation, in a state of disturbance. This was a dilemma for which we were not prepared. Indeed it was one which aroused the sympathy of every man on board, for much to his credit be it said, every man was affectionately attached to the good natured and affable Captain Le Cheminant.

At the first overture, however, it was looked on as a passing indisposition owing to the many severe shocks the poor man's mind had sustained, for previous to joining the *Nancy* he had lost a splendid yacht-built ship of which he had command, figuratively speaking, in the door of his own home, besides other calamities which had yet previous to that befallen him, all of which in fact had tended to obtain for him the popular name of 'The unfortunate good man'. All the dangers he had experienced, the consequent uneasiness that followed, and the misfortunes that had befallen him, were brought together and established as a reason for his present state of mind; and it was hoped that its former soundness would soon again return, but unfortunately, however, our hopes were vain, ere we reached Gibraltar he had become completely insane.

One night whilst still in the Gulph of Venice, at about an hour before midnight, he alarmed the whole ship's company by repeated cries of 'They come, they come. We're taken! We're taken!' etc. The chief mate, whose watch it was below, aroused by the cries, hastened out of his berth, when the first thing that caught his view was the cabin floor strewed all over with papers, the ship's being among their number. The captain, who just was in the act of precipitating himself in the hold through an aperture in the bulk head commonly called the nor'wester, was arrested by him and asked from whence arose the reason of his alarm, to which the captain only answered by supplicating him not to tell *them* that he was on board, but to keep him concealed in the pump well whither he was about to stow himself by telling them he had been left in Trieste. But who, the mate wished to know, did he wish to conceal himself from?

'From those pirates that are about to board us. Go on deck', said he, 'and you will see them rapidly overhauling us, they will be alongside in five minutes and then I am a doomed man. I have no papers to show them, I have left them all in Trieste, and by that I am condemned.'

The mate endeavoured in as passive a manner as possible to undeceive him, assuring him he had no grounds for his strange conceptions. No pirates were chasing us but two vessels like ourselves who had been in company all day, and as for his papers he felt assured they were all there and quite conformable. This, however, failed to satisfy him and it was only after repeated and peremptory refusals on the mate's part to allow him to conceal himself that he at length became somewhat conscious of the absurdity of his suspicions.

Globe and Bible navigation

At another time in one of these fits of insanity (which varied greatly in strength) after having been up all night long, now with his quadrant on deck taking altitudes of the stars, and then in the cabin pouring over a small globe of his suspended by a thread to his left thumb which he kept at about parallel with his eyes, then touching it with his right hand in order to make it whirl round, after which when it ceased moving he compared something off the globe which he attentively marked down at the moment of cessation with a passage or passages in the Bible and thus went on studying no one knew what (himself included) for hours together and so deeply buried in study at times was he that my appearance before him repeating the same question over and over again caused no relaxation.

After being thus engaged all night long at about six o'clock a.m. he went to the mate's state-room and roused him up, telling him to be smart if he wished to save his life. The mate, yet half asleep, had not understood his words but in order to make sure whether he had been called or not, got up when lo!, what was his wonder to perceive the poor lunatic *in puris naturalibus*[1] with one razor in hand and the other on the table, trying to make an incision in his left side. The mate, horror struck, begged of him to withhold his hand asking him at the same time what it was he wished to do. He replied it was indispensable he should be wounded there in order to save his life. The mate yet trembling to see him in such a state with a naked weapon in his hand at the same time knowing how imprudent it would be to attempt to take it from him by force, had recourse to a stratagem for which he deserved great credit, this was seeming to agree with him in his idea of phlebotomy but at the same time assuring him he could not practise it himself without danger; and if he wished he would undertake the task and perform it to his satisfaction.

The captain, nothing doubting, immediately agreed and whilst giving him orders how large and deep he wished to have the incision made, handed him the razor. The mate no sooner had this one in his hand than with a motion as quick as thought secured the other which lay upon the table and carefully locking them up, proceeded to expostulate with the unfortunate man and ultimately succeeded in convincing him of the danger he had been trifling with and concluded by bringing him to a temporary state of consciousness.

At another interval being off the island of Sicily after having again indulged in the practice of his globe and Bible, he called the mate's attention to a remarkable gap on the land (which no doubt has been seen by everyone who has passed that road).

'Do you see that opening yonder?' says he.

'Yes, Sir.'

'Well I presume you'll be surprised when I tell you that is the Gut of Gibraltar and the only outlet which we have to pass from the Mediterranean to the Atlantic ocean.'

'Indeed I am surprised', replied the mate, 'if such is the case, and still more grieved, for as the chances are 10 to 1 that we'll never get the old *Nancy* to leap up that height it follows as a consequence that we shall have to remain penned up in this sea.'

[1] i.e. naked.

'Well be that as it may, but I declare to you that such is the case, I have just now found it out by my globe with the aid of the Bible.'

The mate, knowing how to humour him, did not contradict him too strenuously, but rather let him enjoy his opinion on the subject for the time being, knowing well that by the morrow's dawn Sicily and the Gut of Gibraltar would both be buried in oblivion.

Some few days after this, being on the Barbary Coast and plying to windward with a westerly wind, at the dawn of day we found ourselves within about five miles of Cape Bon, a proximity which prudence teaches every one who is aware of the piratical propensities of the savage race of the natives, is great enough. The wind at that moment dying away with the opening of the day, the second officer who had the watch thought it highly essential to heave about, knowing himself by unhappy experience how intent upon plunder the natives were upon the whole line of this coast, consequently went below and intimated to the master the situation of the ship as well as his opinion of going about.[1] The captain answered him by saying he was coming on deck, but instead of doing so immediately procrastinated for near two hours, so that at half past seven when he did make his appearance, a fort which is situated on Cape Bon bore from us south west only 2½ miles. The captain stood looking at this scenery before him through the telescope of his sextant as a substitute for a spy-glass, apparently heedless of the imprudence of keeping on that tack any longer. The second mate, trembling at the danger that might ensue, but yet not wishing to thwart him in any manner, politely hinted to him that everything was ready for tacking ship to which he gave the answer of 'Very well'.

By this time eight bells were struck and the chief mate appeared on deck; after rubbing his eyes a little and looking round himself, saw the line of coast immediately under the ship's bows, turned himself to the captain and politely remarked we were very near the shore, to which he received the reply of 'Yes, but unfortunately it is near calm'.

[1] Tacking ship. [HM]

'One reason the more for going about before it is altogether calm', replied the mate.

But now the captain, who the two previous days had been in an apparent sound state of mind and who it was thought had become the better of his weakness, was yet this morning looked upon to be in that state for which reason the mate did not wish, much less dare, to oppose him. But here was a critical moment, we could not much longer stand in without going on shore, and the master showed no intention of standing out. At last, however, the mate thought it was high time to know the captain's intention, therefore asked him if he intended to run the vessel ashore, to which he replied very gravely, 'No'.

'Well then, you had better put her on the other tack, else she will find herself there whether or not. Besides', said he, 'standing in as close as this to the shore with only a faint air of wind is actually courting danger in a two-fold sense, for besides the danger of it falling calm and being driven ashore by the long existing swell, there is the danger of the natives putting off to us, as they have before done to others, and plundering if not murdering us'.

'Why you talk like a madman', quoth the captain. 'Do you not see on yonder point that magnificent establishment? Well then in that self-same establishment is the Seventh Golden Candlestick which indicates the approaching end of the world![1] We must wait here till it is sent off to us, and then the great, the awful end of time is come! Aye and in which you can prepare yourself to tremble, for depend upon it, you are one to whom it will not be welcome.'

Pirates

Just as this risible speech was being concluded one of the crew, who was intently watching the shore, sang out 'A boat, Sir, a boat, coming off to us'. Instantly all eyes were directed towards the dark

[1] An allusion to the Book of Revelations, ch. 1–2, where the seven churches of Asia Minor are described as the Seven Golden Candlesticks.

speck just receding from the shore. Sure enough a boat, which seemed a large one,[1] was being rowed towards us. That it was a piratical band under the intent of plundering and murdering us was immediately decided amongst the crew, whose alarm was greatly increased by the various tales recited amongst them of the awful destruction of life and property which had already taken place on this coast.

Accordingly, one and all of them, as soon as they were quite satisfied that the said boat was steering toward us, animated through fear and a sense of the danger that threatened them, came aft and begged of the captain to heave about, but seeing that the chief mate was already doing his utmost to persuade him retired again forward, trusting that soon an order would be given. A few minutes more elapsed, during which the mate and master were arguing at a few keys higher tune than they were wont, and the boat, still taking advantage of our position, was gliding through the mirror-like water at a rate that each minute made her appear to our troubled minds one good mile nearer.

This was the boat that was bringing off the Seventh Golden Candlestick for the master after which the end of time was come! Prepare yourselves to answer the Judge severe, ye rebellious men, the seventh trumpet speaks him near. But although Jack heard the warning, he had by no means the desire of being examined yet that day. Not, as some of them said, 'but what I am just as fit for examination now as I was yesterday, or will be tomorrow, but as how I thinks my time is not yet come by at least 20 good long years, I don't see the use in meeting it before hand', so according to this impression, came aft again and told the mate that if he did not take charge and put the ship about, seeing the master was mad, or had a devil, they most assuredly would themselves. They were extremely hurt to be under such a disagreeable necessity of speaking in such authoritative language to their superiors, quoth they, but instant death, or eternal slavery was left for them to choose if they permitted these ruffians coming off to take charge

[1] The MS has 'and which seemed a large one' here, which has been modified to read more easily.

of them. Therefore in self-defence they had determined to put the ship about if he, the mate, did not do it himself.

The mate, who found it a trying moment for him, but who foresaw the imminent danger threatening us as well as the more superstitious crew, and having nothing in the shape of arms wherewith to defend us, or to depend upon, except an old blunderbuss which had lain in the old iron locker for many years, and which was scarcely worth troubling about, seeing that there was no powder or shot on board, once more remonstrated with the captain, making him at the same time acquainted with the feelings of the crew, but no persuasions could turn him. They were not pirates, but holy men from the Holy Land with holy intentions, coming to present him with a holier gift; at the same moment jumping down the cabin, fetched the ensign and hoisted it up himself at the peak.

This was enough, the mate (evidently labouring under disagreeable feelings) gave out the order 'About ship there'. 'Aye, aye, Sir', was the hearty response that met his ear, echoing throughout the ship with a dismal sound occasioned by the stillness of the air and sea, and perhaps a little more by the awkward predicament that fear had placed us in. The helm was put 'hard a lee' and the little ship, who it had been feared would not obey her governor, came round like a top, seeming to join herself in our precipitations. Tacks were boarded, sheets were hauled, braces were tautened, and then a general whistle for wind was heard throughout the ship. By this time the boat which had perceived our retrograding motion acted accordingly and plying their sweeps with renewed vigour were approaching us at that rate in which it was perceptible enough they would soon overtake us, unless indeed our continued whistling could reach the ear of the worshipped deity in time, and thereby persuade him to favour us with even half a sigh, but Aeolus, this mighty god of the winds, if not asleep seemed at least heedless of our calamity, for after repeated whistlings and invocations not the slightest air of wind was felt the now. Here was a trying moment, a moment when life and death seemed to hang upon a breeze, and yet that breeze did not come! All through the inconstancy of that deceitful god upon whom, as some of the oldest tars averred, they had placed their trust for more than forty years. Alas for the superstitious ignorance of the age!

One of our crew, who for the purpose of extending his eyesight better had jumped in the rigging, and now hailed us below with the nonconsolatory affirmation that he could count 32 sweeps[1] at work and that he believed by the bulk of men that each sweep was double manned, so in that case there would be no less than 64 men plus the sitters and coxswain, and the mate, by the aid of the telescope of his sextant, confirmed the disclosure.[2] Dear, oh dear! What was to be done! could be read on every horror stricken countenance in the ship (except two). One poor fellow spoke of his wife, another of his babes, and a third thought with a long drawn sigh of one perhaps not so near by sanguinary ties as a wife, or child, but to him equally as dear. 'Oh, my poor Betty! Thou mayst look out for another now, but never will thou find one so true as your poor Will!' I have mentioned two amongst the crew who seemed not to participate in the general dismay, these will be as well named to prevent a mistake although the one has already been, I dare say, rightly guessed at. This was the captain and indeed instead of fear, his was an expression of joy, every succeeding length the boat gained upon us seemed to animate him with greater pleasure, indeed at one time in the ecstasy which prevailed within him, and forgetting that his command had become less imperative than it was wont to be, ordered the main yards to be thrown aback. But to this order no one on board seemed to listen and for the first time perhaps had he the mortification to perceive that he was in the ship like a cypher which describes nothing.

The second individual upon whom fear had not yet lavished her favours was the young cabin-boy, alias your humble servant, and though neither stimulated by the hopes of a Golden Candlestick or by the more noble principal of courage, yet true it is that I looked upon the danger threatening us more as a 'glorious lark' than in any other light, of course although I could not at that time have known through whose agency I was kept from sharing in the general dread that excited more experienced heads, and by far

[1] Very long oars, commonly called sweeps. [HM]

[2] The ship's spy glass had been lost previously. [HM]

stouter hearts than mine, yet now I can easily explain that youthful unconsciousness was the only cause. Be it as it may I kept on the laughing side of my ship-mates when our safety was reassured and danger had winged its flight with the piratical band in a direction opposite to us. Aeolus being found insensible to the prayers of a distressed crew, it was thought expedient to invoke some other powerful god. Consequently as with one accord, every one fell to worshipping at the shrine of St Antonio,[1] the idol so much esteemed and respected by the Austrian, Portugese and Spanish sailors, and indeed this deity, perhaps proud of having gained the esteem of another nation added to the already long list of its worshippers, at once attended to their prayers and just in the nick of time, when another twenty minutes calm would have sufficed to our pursuers for making sure of their booty, sent us a pleasant breeze, which filling the lazy canvas that had hitherto lain as it were dormant, enabled our gallant little bark to launch over the undulated waters, dividing spray beneath her bows, every now and then one of which would top over the bulwark as if to remind the awe stricken crew to dispel their now needless fears. By this time, although only what is termed at sea a light breeze of wind was blowing, the little *Nancy* taking the advantage of smooth water or otherwise only different from that by the lazy motion of the long undulated swell which to her was no impediment, glided along at a rate of about $6^1/_2$ knots.

Our pursuers still kept in our wake, who during the prolonged calm had gained such a proximity that even now they seemed unwilling to give up the chase, but plied their oars with correspon-ding swiftness and force to the breeze, trusting no doubt to favourable lulls of the wind, for a long time owing to their energy no decline in their approach was perceptible, and indeed the shaken imagination of our crew led them to affirm that they were yet gaining upon us. But if so was the case, this case soon underwent an alteration visible enough to every eye on board, and more especially to that of the poor insane captain, who stood on the taffrail deploring his fortune in the loss of his golden assurance

[1] Probably St Anthony of Padua (1195–1231).

of a future immortality. To effect this once successful change to our safety, a nautical expedient was had recourse to, which to an inexperienced eye would not have been observable, but to those whose long acquaintance with a ship have enabled them to ascertain the exact point at which her maximum speed is enhanced, this feat of nautical experience is no enigma.

The ship's head was kept away two points from the wind, the lee main and weather fore braces checked accordingly, the fore main and jib sheet eased off so as the pressure of the wind upon the bellying sails might have a simultaneous effect, and by this in itself trifling manoeuvre the ship's progress was increased to $7^1/_2$ knots. Now were our pursuers visibly falling astern, now was exulting joy depicted on every countenance of the latterly dread-stricken crew. Now was St Antonio blessed above all other whistle to gods, whilst Aeolus was without hesitation cast in the shade, nay more buried in insignificance and oblivion! The manoeuvre alluded to had not escaped detection from the piratical band whose hope and joy decreased at each stoke of their sweeps, but who nevertheless maintained their determination of pursuing us for full half an hour more, but by this time they found themselves so much in the rear, that the hopes of coming up with the advanced guard was at once abolished and at about eleven o'clock we had the satisfaction of witnessing their retrogression. Thus were we once more upon the wide blue field of ocean's vast expanse in perfect freedom and safety, the living monuments of a gracious God's mercy, who had he dealt with us according to our sins, or then rewarded us after our transgressions, might justly have withdrawn his interference and suffered us to meet the reward of our depraved life in a cruel death, where many of our fellow sailors have gone before us, perhaps less deserving than we.

And how many of this wonderful rescued crew, I ask myself now, did lift a grateful heart heavenwards? Alas! I fear not one. The breeze had just sprung up in time to save us from perhaps a cruel death; this was acknowledged to be fortunate! and whilst we now manifested our thankfulness at the shrine of fortune, we forgot the author of it. Without anything in the shape of a useful weapon on board for our defence, nature had supplied us with a powerful one, that not even all the forces of our pursuers combined could overpower; and whilst we could not but view nature as our supplier yet so great alas the depravity of man, we were heedless of its God. Here, as well as in many other instances during a perilous life on the sea, do I accuse myself of having accepted the proffered hand of God as a shield and protector, and in return only made use of base ingratitude. But enough of this, my present work is not intended as a public confession, fain will I obey the precept which commands us to pray in secret, that our Father which seeeth in secret may reward us openly.

It will, of course, be remembered that the mate had now charge of the ship, so after all doubts had vanished and our safety once more perfectly established, he the mate, ordered the helms-man to luff to the wind again and having yards and sails trimmed accordingly, onward went the gallant little bark towards her destination, apparently conscious herself of the dangers she had emancipated her gallant crew from.

Everything went progressively for the following few days, the captain interfering but seldom and when he did so, his commands were always received and obeyed by both the officers and the crew with pretended earnestness, so that he was thereby spared the mortification of being disobeyed. But in reality no notice at all was taken of his orders. Had it been otherwise indeed, the ship would have been lost amongst the several islands that abounded in our track long before we could have reached Gibraltar.

It was as near as I can recollect about six or seven days after the incidents related in the previous chapter that we sighted land at last, the long looked for rock of Gibraltar. It was a beautiful morning, the sun was shining in all its glory, the sea of transparent blue beneath, variegated by the curl of every little foaming wave which rolled on hither and thither adding still to the grandeur of the scene. Every heart seemed animated with joyous feelings, the prospect before us added to the pleasure of having a fair wind for the first time for some weeks, heralding to us a speedy exit out of the Mediterranean Sea and to our beloved home.

It was on this gay morning that Captain Le Cheminant, who had been indulging for an hour after breakfast in the perusal of some fancied book of his, came upon deck with an air of as much sanity as a judge, and with seeming equal joy blended in his countenance, called the mate to him and addressing him first by passing a remark about the beautiful weather that was then predominating, asked him if he did not think we had better put in at Gibraltar for a few hours to obtain a few refreshments, adding that we were short of a few necessaries owing to our prolonged passage from Trieste and therefore we might replenish our stock and so proceed on our way comfortably. Mr Cohu, the mate, answered by observing that in his opinion, after having consulted with the steward, there was a plenty of provisions on board to last more than for an average passage home, and that for the sake of obtaining fruit and such like, he did not think they would stand justified in loosing a fine fair wind that had just set in, and which might only last to take us out of the Straits. He added 'You must recollect, Captain, that it is now near two months since we left our port and we have wished and prayed for a fair wind many times, now that we have it fast in the nick of time, I just think it is our bounden duty to avail ourselves of it to the best advantage. You have asked my advice, Captain Le Cheminant, and I have given it you without circumlocution but with all due reverence to you I am prepared to submit to your orders which you may direct and rest assured they will be obeyed both by myself and the crew whilst you are in a state of sanity. Let me add whilst I have the opportunity that I wish to remind you if your orders for the last few days have been disregarded by the crew, as well as by myself, it has been because you have been labouring under the influence of insanity, giving orders both as to the steering and otherwise endangering the safety of the ship and lives of her crew. Now I hope you are convinced of the truth of my statement, you seem to be perfectly sane at present, and must own to the prudence I have used in acting as I have done, for you well know that whilst necessity compelled me to act thus for the safety of your life, of mine, and the lives of all concerned, I would rather have been exempt from such a necessity.'

Captain Le Cheminant, who had been a silent listener to the mate's argument now replied with apparently feelings much softened, 'Yes, Henry, I know and feel that you would not harm me in any way, and certain I am that the way you have acted has not been through motives of hatred against me, but on the contrary, you have valued my life more than I have myself, and whilst you have so done you have valued and preserved the lives of the crew. I know that I have sometimes been rather beside myself and scarcely knew what I was about but at any rate you must feel for me, knowing well that dreadful circumstances have been the cause.'

'I admit', replied the mate, 'that dire circumstances may have preyed upon your mind and I would at any time rather pity than blame you, but on your part you should study to treat me in a manner more becoming friends and relations such as we really are; you have hitherto been very ill-disposed towards me, and thereby made me lead a very unhappy life, whereas had I retaliated and cared for you less than I have done, long ere this would you have been where there is no return from. Are you aware that my own hands have arrested the knife with which you would have committed suicide on several occasions? Know you not that but for the incessant watch I have kept over you, that you might have added murder also!'

'Well, well, Henry, I thank you for all your care but let it be all forgotten. It is time that we should bear away for the Bay of Gibraltar.'

'Then you are decided on going in?' asked the mate.

'Oh certainly, why not? I want some refreshments, you know I have not been well and require some.'

'Well, Sir, you are the master, you will act as you think proper but once more I add it is a great pity to lose this fine fair breeze.'

The captain then ordered the helmsman to put the helm up, and the crew to square the yards, whilst he sent the mate to see the anchors all ready. This being done half an hour or more and we commenced shortening sail by that time, having neared the shipping in the bay to one or one and half miles, another few minutes and the main top sail was clued up, then the fore one, then the jib was hauled down and the ship rounded to, when the anchor was dropped.

Gibraltar – Mutiny

There she was then our gallant little bark, once more fastened by the bows, resting herself as it were after the toils of a tedious passage. Hitherto the ensign had been floating in the breeze hoisted at the main gaff end, a compliment which must be attended to on nearing Europa Point where stands a fort of immense power which would open fire upon you otherwise, but once round the point, no one on board, so much were we engaged contemplating the beautiful scenery around, had observed the captain to lower the ensign about half-mast high. Nevertheless this he had done and the consequences of this manoeuvre of his may readily be imagined.

In the harbour there lay three or four men-of-war ships and these failed not to observe at once our colour in distress, so that to our utter amazement, as soon as the anchor was let go, three boats were immediately alongside, the boats coming from the men-of-war and at such a speed with so many hands in them. All this tended to excite the mate's suspicion, so walking abaft to consult the captain on the subject he happened to cast his eyes aloft, and at once solved the enigma, but not for a moment thinking the flag had been lowered purposely he rushed to the halyards and exclaiming 'Why there's a shameful mistake', he hoisted it up at once to the peak end.

But in the meantime what was Captain Le Cheminant about while laying over the bulwark of the vessel, impatiently awaiting the arrival alongside of the boats that were now so near that words could have been exchanged? Other boats from the shore had by this time put off so that plenty of company was promised us on our recent arrival. In a few short minutes they all were alongside and after the usual questions had been asked, answered and noted down, 'Where are you from? Where bound etc?', the more particular one of, 'What is the nature of your distress?' was put to the captain, but imagine our consternation, imagine the mate's bewilderment, to hear the answer given 'Mutiny, Sir! Mutiny. My life is in danger and I have been forced to put the ship in this port to save it, where I now place her and myself under your protection.'

The several functionaries in their boats stood as paralysed, they looked upon each other in amazement, each look seeming to imply the question of what was the best course they had better pursue? The first lieutenant of the *Vanguard*,[1] looking up, spoke thus: 'This is a serious case, Captain, a case in which proper measures must be taken at once so I shall at once send by this boat', pointing to the reporters, 'an intimation on shore to the effect, whilst I myself will at once proceed on board HMS *Vanguard* to report the case to the commander. Meanwhile I will leave these two other boats alongside for your protection, and if during my absence your crew should show the least sign of mutiny, you have but to give the alarm and the boat's crew will at once jump to your assistance, unless', he added further, 'you would rather leave the ship at once, then in that case I will take you away with me?'

But the captain replied that with the assistance of the two boats alongside he entertained no fear and therefore would content himself by remaining.

I must here break the thread of my narrative for a moment by stating that we had been placed in quarantine in consequence of having been boarded by a vessel in the Mediterranean which was from South America where the yellow fever then greatly prevailed, so the reader will cease to wonder why the officials remained alongside in their boats without coming on deck. It was only half an hour after the despatches sent to the shore and to the man-of-war that several other boats were again alongside, each containing two or three functionaries which I did then not recognise, that is with the exception of the commanders of two, of HMS the *Vanguard* and the ... .[2] After a consultation among them (that is the sea officers and the shore ones) which lasted for about twenty minutes, the captain was called and afterwards the mate and crew to the gangway. A strict investigation of this very important and

[1] See the Introduction, pp. xxx–xxxi, where it is shown that HMS *Vanguard*, although in the Mediterranean at about the time the episode described here took place, was not moored in the harbour at Gibraltar and so cannot be the warship referred to here.

[2] The name is left blank in the MS.

serious case then took place, the whole of the captain's depositions being taken down in writing by an individual apparently summoned there for the purpose.

It will be as well here to glance at an outline of the captain's statement for the benefit of the reader. He commenced by stating that on the day of ... we had left Trieste bound to London, that suspicions during his stay in port had on several occasions preyed on his mind that some underhand work was going on between the chief officer and the steward, but that nothing more than base suspicion could be entertained until the first evening of our sailing when about eight o'clock the two individuals above mentioned having been below for some time together, he, the captain, went down to procure himself a cigar when to his utter amazement he found his writing desk laying on the table wide open and all his papers strewed about the cabin floor. He immediately selected the scattered papers to examine if any were missing. When he perceived that all the ship's papers were gone, there was no hesitation in his mind as to what had become of them, the cabin-boy (alias myself), had stolen them, this conclusion he at once came to, and he could have sworn to its truth. 'The vessel, you see gentlemen, belongs to his uncles', quoth he, 'and he I presume thought he had a better right to the papers than I had, but for this fault I can scarcely attach any great degree of blame to him, for he being but a youth can easily be led astray. The mate there', pointing to him, 'is the person that instigated him to do this and it is to him I look for reparation! But although, gentlemen, I am led to screen the youth for this one fault owing to circumstances mentioned, yet I wish to remind you that I do not hold him guiltless altogether, for on other occasions has he compromised himself, nay more, he has even suffered himself to be subject to the utmost rigours of the law. One particular instance of his atrocious guilt I will mention, and that is in the attempt at poisoning me.'

'What!' exclaimed the authorities with amazement, 'Do you mean us to understand that that youth' (pointing to me) 'has dared to attempt to poison you?'

'I do, gentlemen, mean all that I have said.'

'And how, or in what manner did he practice his diabolical

intent?'

'By placing the poison in my coffee cup one morning at breakfast time, but fortunately before his evil intentions were fully accomplished, I had detected the poisonous powder in the cup.'

These gentlemen, astonished at what they heard, that such an innocent looking youth as I then appeared to be, *and indeed was, nor have I altered in that respect for indeed innocence is a predominant part of my nature,*[1] could be guilty of such villainy, looked towards me and surveying me with eyes flashing with indignation said 'Do you hear what your Captain says of you?'

'I do, Sirs', was my reply, 'but I am prepared to answer to all his false accusations.'

'False indeed, you will have to prove their falsity.'

'I am able to do so, Gentlemen, thank Heaven.'

'Well enough from you now, we shall hear your proofs by and bye.'

'I don't think you will give yourselves that trouble.'

'Silence, Sir', was the rejoinder, but myself like all other *innocent* youths would have the last word, therefore to this command I answered, 'I'm silent, Sir.'

These gentlemen then turned their attention once more to the captain who went on stating and heaping falsehoods together until he had made his case a distressing one, and every man (but one) a decided mutineer. The mate had tried to take his life also, he had taken charge of the ship on two or three different occasions, the second mate had once attempted to throw him overboard and would have carried his intention into execution but for the timely rescue by that one exception above named. The crew all combined in playing all kind of cruelties upon him, and he could not help himself. One of the crew, Nicholas Le Lacheur by name, being a sorcerer and had the means of playing many kinds of satanic tricks upon him with whom all the rest of the crew joined. In fact he continued for near one hour as I have stated above, devising and heaping the most unwarranted falsehoods together, but all the time wearing the most serious countenance possible, and all the

[1] Emphasis as in original MS.

appearance of perfect sanity, so that indeed the officials mentioned looked upon his statements as correct and believed this to be a most appalling and unheard of case of mutiny.

The mate, who like ourselves had been a silent listener to this unexpected behaviour of our captain, now at the conclusion of his statement attempted at saying a few words in justification to himself as well as to the crew but was most grossly answered by the commander of the ship already figured in my narrative.

'Hold your tongue, you mutinous rascal. You shall be taken from your ship and put on board my ship in irons, and be taken to England where you shall be hung as an example to all sea-faring men. As for you men', addressing himself to the crew, 'you see that large building there', pointing to the goal, 'that shall be your domicile for some weeks to come until you have the strictest examination'.

What could we say to all this? We, it is true, felt ourselves innocent of all crimes laid against us but yet if they would not allow us to justify ourselves, but placed all confidence in what the captain told them, what would be the consequence?

By this time it was near four o'clock of the afternoon and our gents, feeling their dinner hour near, made preparations to retire, but did not do so until they had placed a guard for the night of two boats around the ship, and given instructions to the captain that if he wanted assistance during the night it would always be at hand, etc, etc. They now bid the captain good night, assuring him that they would see him early the next morning and that something would be done. Once more left to ourselves each began to reflect upon the strange incidents of the day, and I must add that the last address of the powdered headed old veteran to us all had made no unmistakable impression on some of the crew. The chief mate for one, who had been so cruelly rebuffed by him, went down the cabin to contemplate over the strangeness of the day's proceedings, when in a deep reverie his feelings owing to the captain's behaviour to whom he was much attached overpowered him and he gave vent in a full flow of tears. Captain Le Cheminant just at the time stepped down the cabin also, the mate who had buried his face in his hands, his elbows resting on the table, looked up to see who it was that had thus come down, and seeing it was the captain addressed him thus.

'Captain Le Cheminant, do you know what you have this day done? Do you know how much may be the consequence of all this?'

'Aye', replied the captain, 'I do know both what I have done and what may be the consequence. And I joy over it. It is my turn now to be cruel, I will be as much as I can.'

'But what mean you by saying it is your turn to be cruel? Surely you do not mean to infer that I have been cruel towards you on any former occasion?'

'Never mind whether or not, you shall see how I can be vindictive when I like.'

'Well that is very wrong of you, Captain Le Cheminant, to act ... '. But here the mate's remark was interrupted by the captain, who with a cigar in his hand was rushing on deck exclaiming 'It may be wrong or it may not be, but it suits me to act thus.' And thus did he act and thus did things remain till the morning. The crew for best part of the night talking the matter over and wondering how it would all end, the boats always plying abreast of the gangway on each side keeping us more in awe still.

The morning however, in its natural course of time, returned and with it the troubled crew of the *Nancy* arose, but there was one of the ship's company who did not rise much refreshed, or I mean less than the others, for none could be very much refreshed. And who was this upon whose mind the incidents of the previous day had so much worked during the night that a total abstraction had taken place? It was no less a personage than Captain Le Cheminant. His actions he had ruminated over, and all put together had brought on insanity again! so that by the time the powdered heads came alongside he was just fit to undo all his work of yesterday. The chief mate as well as all the rest of the crew witnessed this with no small degree of satisfaction for had he still kept in a state of temporary sanity for a few days, and persisted in his vengeance against us all, the consequences might have proved very seriously disagreeable to us, at least for a time, for although the premature course of punishment which might have been accepted by the several functionaries at Gibraltar might have lasted for a time, yet when we weighed the matter thoroughly in our minds we all cheered each other up by the assurance that in the long run our innocence must be established.

However, it was greater pleasure for us to avoid if possible any such disagreeable courses, and we agreed together that we should all with one accord demand it as a right, to be heard in our own defence that day, when the officers should come alongside, but we were not pushed to that necessity. As soon as the said officers came alongside which was about nine o'clock, the captain was asked how he was, and how he had passed the night, etc, etc, to which he replied that he felt very unwell that morning, and had had a very restless night, adding that he had seriously thought through the night of the absolute necessity of having a conference with some medical man to whom he wished to impart a circumstance relating to himself which he thought had a tendency to keep him in continual pain, on the chest, in the head, and sometimes in the abdomen! ' Well', replied the commander of the *Vanguard*, 'When I return I can send my doctor to you. He is a very eminent man and no doubt will thoroughly understand your case'. The captain thanked him exceedingly and went on to observe that he would fain impart to them (the officials) this circumstance, but that he wished to impart it in private, and not in the presence of the crew and his officers, who were all of course, looking over the side of the vessel.

'Well but', replied the aforementioned gentleman, 'I have no doubt your men will all retire if you tell them. Nay, I will tell them myself'. And accordingly we were politely asked by the old gent (who by the bye had much changed in his disposition towards us) if we would retire whilst Captain Le Cheminant wished to hold his conversation private. Of course we could not refuse and our answer was at once given by our retrogression.

But a feeling of deep curiosity gnawed within us, it was very strange thought we, that the nature of what the captain had to impart could not permit us to overhear it, whilst at the same time there were three boats' crews alongside for whom he did not seem to evince the slightest diffidence. Now was this not a fresh act of deep duplicity on his part? Was this not a stratagem used for the purpose of disclosing some dreadful untruth against us which perhaps he had fabricated in his mind during the night and which he could not find courage enough to speak before us? These and many suggestions arose in our minds. Something was wrong. The captain in his state was capable of any atrocity; was it right that he should be permitted to speak privately? Whether or not, it was decided to let the project have its course, but at the same time if it was possible to play the part of eaves-droppers we were well decided to do it.

The chief mate accordingly placed himself on the cabin table and looking through the skylight had his ears on a level with the deck, and consequently could over hear all that was said in the Gangway. The second officer, Mr D.L.P., placed himself in the companion where not many words could be lost to him. The crew forward were all dispersed as best they could, three or four in the caboose-house listening through the side door which was purposely left ajar and exchanging sidelong glances and smiles with the boats' crews through one of the gun ports which was open, the latter having turned their heads forward for decency's sake. But there was yet one of *Nancy*'s crew which I cannot pass unnoticed, this was the young cabin-boy who equally excited as the rest, not perhaps through the same cause, for it was very little he cared if the captain spoke against him or not, in fact all this was to him a novelty which of itself was glorious fun, and if the truth was said of his then predominant feelings, it would be that his hopes were that all hands should have to be put in irons, taken away to goal, and subsequently tried for mutiny! Oh, what a glorious lark that would be, he himself would have to be tried for attempt at poisoning the captain. Oh, would that not raise an éclat that would be long remembered.

The captain's confession

But to return, I have said his curiosity was as piquant as that of any member of the crew, I think we can admit to that it was more when we make allowance for his age, his innocence and what has been stated. However, be that as it may, he was determined to overhear this secret information the captain was about to impart.

Consequently, stealing from the caboose where he had first taken his post, he crept under the longboat towards the stern until he came directly under the quarter, and there ensconced himself between a water cask and the boat where he was directly behind the captain and at not more than a couple of yards from him, at the same time hidden from his gaze by a tarpaulin that hung to the boat's side used to protect the studding sails from the wet. Here in this situation he could not lose one word of what was said by the captain and with breathless expectation did he await for the first words that were about to reveal this hidden mystery; in fact all was suspense on board, all were concerned, and therefore all were impatient.

At last the captain, having surveyed the deck with his gaze on two or three different occasions to assure himself that there were no listeners, commenced by addressing his hearers thus. 'Well, gentlemen, what I am about to tell you you may think strange. In fact so do I, but nevertheless so strange so true. The fact is this. About seven years ago I was in a ship called the *Albion* and we went to Hamburg to discharge. Well, during our stay there', and here he turned round again to observe if quietness still prevailed, then being satisfied on that point he continued with a rather lower tone than before and stooping over the side of the vessel rather more also, so as to bring his mouth in closer proximity to the ears of the gents who by the bye commenced eying him very differently from what they had done yesterday. This change of position in him called for a change of position in the young man's attitude behind the tarpaulin, accordingly, popping his head out from beneath the curtain that so effectively concealed him, extended it as far as possible and thereby brought himself in closer contact to the speaker than he had hitherto been. The captain, having by this time resumed his statement, continued, 'During the ship's stay in that port I felt many temptations to go on shore to satisfy my passions in the indulgence of a woman! but always resisted, until at last only a few days before we sailed I grew weaker and my passions stronger, so I had to succumb! Well, gentlemen, I went on shore and had a woman, but in the morning when I awoke I perceived she had a very offensive breath, so since that time I have not been well at all, on the chest, the head and sometimes elsewhere!'

Here was a disclosure! Well might he require privacy indeed to disclose this great secret. Ah, ah, ah! How the cabin-boy did laugh to the splitting of his sides behind his curtain of rude drapery. How the crew were glad that their former fears were premature. How the chief and second mates were pleased to perceive the captain's insanity established in the official's eyes and last but not least how these officers, with suppressed laughter, stared at the captain and then at each other and then at the captain again, not knowing what to make of him or his statement at all. At length they consulted with each other for a minute or so, merely in whispers, then turned round to the captain and asked him if he would be kind enough to send the chief mate to the gangway, whilst he himself remained aside. This he at once assented to, so calling the mate to take his place, he walked abaft on the quarter deck. One of these officers (the same that had spoken so very roughly to the mate the day before, threatening him with ignominious death as an example to others), now addressed him with much courtesy, enquiring from him if the captain was in the habit of drinking freely. To this the mate responded that he was not, indeed he was and had always been a strictly sober man.

'But is there not something the matter with him just now, he seems to us so strange?'

'I have no doubt of it', quoth the mate, 'but I am only surprised that you have been so long in discovering this strangeness. The captain, Sir, is insane, perfectly insane, and has been so during the whole passage from Trieste, and it has been with difficulty that we have prevented him from committing suicide on several occasions, and where he has accused us of having attempted to take his life, it has been on the contrary, when he has himself attempted to take that life and prevented by us. But I would have fain made you aware of his state of mind yesterday, and would have saved you a great deal of trouble, and myself, in fact I will speak in the plural, for there are here those who have feelings as well as those whose privilege it is to hold higher stations in life, and ourselves, I repeat, a great deal of disgrace.'

This remark was so beautifully put together and delivered with such coolness and in such decided a manner at once implying contempt for those who were before him, and a severe rebuke for their behaviour that these gentlemen who now saw the sad mistake they had made by placing confidence in the captain's statement too hurriedly as well as by using unjustifiable threats against the mate and crew, and moreover denying these the right of saying a word in their own defence, began to cool down somewhat, and indeed it was visible enough in their deportment that they felt the mate's censure keenly and knew within themselves that he was quite justified in speaking as he did, in as much as they had greatly surpassed the bounds of justice in taking it upon themselves to use the threats they had done to him the day previous.

The powdered wigged old veteran, as soon as the mate had done speaking, made a somewhat short apology and then said, 'I will retire, Mr Cohu, for the present and on my arrival on board will immediately dispatch my doctor, who will examine the captain and report his case to me, after which you may rely on seeing me again.'

A very polite bow was made by each party and they retired. Shortly afterwards the doctor was alongside and summoning the captain, commenced questioning him relative to the state of his health, to all which questions he answered in the most ridiculous manner, leaving after a very short examination no room for doubt in the doctor's mind that his patient was a lunatic! He, the doctor, therefore did not tarry alongside but at once repaired on board his respective ship where he made known to the commander the result of his examination; the latter person being now satisfied on this point, repaired on shore to consult with his contemporaries as to the best mode of acting in the case, but before they could come to any decision they deemed it necessary to hear the chief mate's argument. Accordingly once more the boats were manned and once more did the gangway of the *Nancy* lined with her crew, grace their presence.

The aforementioned officer now addressed the mate by stating that they were (speaking for the others) perfectly satisfied that the captain was as he had reported him to be and that it was therefore urgent on their part to look into the matter but before they would go any further into the case, they had decided on hearing what the mate had to say. The mate replied that since the captain's insanity was established he had nothing more to say unless it was once more to refute the captain's statement of the previous day, but that if they would condescend to take this small manuscript, presenting it at the same time, they would learn through the medium of its contents the several incidents of the captain's behaviour on the passage. This said manuscript, I may as well here observe, was a journal the mate had kept of all the principal incidents of the voyage relative to this sad affair. They accepted the document, as is customary in cases of quarantine, with a long pair of tongues, much after the similitude of those used inside the fender at home, and the mate, concluding his statement by calling their attention to the deep duplicity the captain had been guilty of, lastly of running the ship into the Bay, they replied that they had heard quite enough to assure them they had altogether misunderstood the case at first, they would now repair on shore and on the morrow pay us another visit, hinting to the mate at the same time that if he should require assistance of any kind, or in any case wish to communicate with HMS or the shore, he had but to hoist the ensign at the main and his signal should meet with immediate attention.

Thus were the appearance of things in the course of 24 hours greatly changed, the mate rejoiced at the thoughts of going home without the inconvenience of wearing those rude bracelets he had been promised the day before, the crew rejoiced also because the large heap of stones they had figured themselves cracking daily were now vanishing from their mind. But there was one who did not join in their glee, it was the young cabin-boy, who being disappointed in his highest hopes of having a 'glorious lark', could have knocked the captain down if he had dared, for not keeping an equanimity of mind for a few days longer.

On the morrow, we were again visited by our friends with the powdered heads, who came this time to transact some business, and commenced by calling all the crew to the immediate vicinity of the boats, then bidding us all to pay attention to what was about to be read to us as we should require to be put upon our oath *pro* or *con* at the conclusion. The manuscript before referred to was then opened and leisurely read by one of the officials, stopping every now and then to ask if we understood. When the contents had been read over to us, we were then told that we were required to take our oath that all that had just been read to us was the truth, the whole truth, and nothing but the truth, but that if we believed it was not, or that there was any exaggeration, we could decline. Each answered that it was but an abridged statement of the truth but that the truth it certainly was. Consequently, the usual formalities of taking an oath were gone through, and thus this part of the business was ended.

The mate is appointed master

The next was to inform the mate that after consulting together it was decided that the captain was not in a fit state to retain command of the ship, consequently if he, the mate, thought himself qualified to take the charge in company with the second mate, that charge would be given him. To this end the mate responded that he felt himself thoroughly qualified, and that he knew the second officer's qualifications were equal to his own. Then at that rate, what was to be done with the captain? They thought they had better take him out of the ship and send him home by the first conveyance. The captain himself, who had been a silent listener to all the proceedings, now gave vent to his feelings, beseeching the authorities not to take him out of the ship. They might take away his command, they might put him in irons, if they chose, 'But do not take me out of the ship', quoth he. 'I will not interfere in any thing, the mate shall be master and I shall be as a passenger, but I do not wish to leave the vessel, I wish to go home in her.'

The mate was then asked if he had any objections to present against the captain's stay on board, for if he had, he would at once be removed, but to this Mr Cohu made answer that if the captain promised faithfully he would not interfere on the passage, he had no objection, he should be allowed to remain. Moreover, his particular regard for him prompted him to see him home himself. Accordingly it was decided in favour of the captain's desire, and having promised once more not to interfere, and also to allow the mate the use of whatever books, charts or other implements he might require for the voyage to London, he was discharged in form, and the mate installed to replace him.

Documents were then handed the mate certifying his authority as master of the vessel, and the cause of such a change of mastership, for it will be understood that owing to the master's name not being changed on the ship's papers, which was not deemed necessary, such a document was of the highest importance, for had any caprice of Captain Le Cheminant taken place in the event of falling in with any of HM ships, the greatest inconvenience would have resulted to the mate. Orders, when all this part of the business was settled, were given to the new captain, that he must consider himself and ship for the remainder of her stay in port under the immediate superintendence of HM ship the *Vanguard*, that the former signal referred to would at once meet with attention, and that he was not to weigh or attempt to sail until ordered by him (the commander).

To all these several injunctions the new master promised strict compliance. A 'Good night' was mutually exchanged and the boats with their charge pushed off from the ship, and once more were we left to ourselves and freed from any further intrusion now that all was settled and the *Nancy* once more properly commanded, each heart's desire was for a fair wind that we might pursue our way on to that home for which every loyal subject of Albion yearns. But alas, we had suffered a fair wind to blow itself out, and who could tell how long ere it returned again?

Three weeks passed thus in anxious expectation during which we had an occasional visit from our guardians. At last, one fine day, after a calm which had lasted for the whole of the forenoon, a light breeze from the east sprung up. Immediately the well known sound of 'Yo heave ho' was distinctly heard on board of the several ships in the bay (for we were upwards of 200 ships windbound), the windlass of each ship answering chorus to the tune of the light hearted seamen who hove it round, every countenance on board the *Nancy* now wore the expression of impatient anxiety to join in song with our brother sailors. Yet we were under restriction, the orders had been imperative not to attempt to weigh until ordered, all we could do then was to wait as patiently as we could for some short time longer, the captain felt assured that orders would soon be sent to us, for assuredly our guardian chief would not allow us to lose a fair wind which in this part of the world is so valuable. Half an hour more, half an hour which seemed to us an age had elapsed during which time upwards of one hundred and fifty anchors had left their submarine beds of clay and passed at once into another element, and hung to the bows of each ship dangled about in the air seemingly with joy at being emancipated from a long cold entombment.

The ships themselves had been gaudily arrayed with the fluttering canvas which now properly set, swelled majestically before the breeze impelling onwards the floating homes it decorated. We gazed upon this sight of near 200 ships under sail at once, each trying to outdo the other in swiftness with a feeling of enthusiasm, and wished our little bark was also there. I cannot forget this sight or my feelings at the time, it is a sight which to every nautical man appears awfully grand. Oh why did not the order come from the man-of-war? Why were we not under weigh as well as our companions? Was it that our keepers were ignorant of our anxiety to proceed? Or was it that carelessness among them was the ruling cause? This latter conjecture we thought was the most probable. Suddenly a thought struck the mate, why should he not manifest his desire to communicate by means of the signal agreed to? Of course he would, so up went the blood red pavilion to the mast head demanding at once attendance from those it was intended to signal. If we had branded the officers of the *Vanguard* with carelessness a few minutes before, we now at once perceived the erroneous conjecture we had formed, for scarcely had the ensign waved at the mast head for one minute when a boat with six oars pushed off from the *Vanguard*'s side, in a few minutes she was alongside our vessel and this time it was a lieutenant that graced her stern-sheets.

'What is the nature of your request, Captain, the signal of which is conveyed through that flag?'

'Why, Sir, I wish to know if I may be allowed to get under weigh, and why this unnecessary delay in permitting me to do so. Here all the ships in the bay are under sail and taking advantage of the fine fair wind blowing, and I am anxious to join them.'

'Well, Sir', the lieutenant replied (who by the bye was a well spoken and seemingly very affable young man), 'I do not doubt your anxiety, neither do I wonder at it, in fact it was anticipated on board, and I have orders to inform you that you are not to sorrow at losing a fair wind until some more propitious occasion, for the easterly wind which is now blowing in the bay does not extend out of it. A strong westerly wind is blowing outside and before night you will prove the truth of this statement by witnessing the return of all these vessels who will be glad to regain their anchorage. You will then be able', he added with a smile, 'to laugh at them for their untimely precipitation. You may rely upon it, Captain Cohu, your interest is in good keeping and as soon as a favourable opportunity presents itself you will be permitted to avail yourself of it.'

The captain, who saw the truth of this statement, allowed his mind to regain composure, assuring himself that after all no loss of time had occurred. Of course, we all followed his example and were thankful we had not had the trouble to weigh our anchor in vain. A sociable chat then ensued between this officer of Her Majesty and our captain which lasted for a quarter of an hour or so, then with extreme civility he wished him a very good day. The evening was drawing on, and remembering that we had been assured each ship which was now out of sight would return, we determined to keep a good look out, and it began to seem more likely to us that such would be the case, for the east wind was dying away fast, so that a doubt was removed from our minds as to its probable durability. At six o'clock it was perfectly calm, and ere the sun went down in the western horizon, the clouds were visibly arising from that quarter and indeed so progressively that before seven o'clock the atmosphere was entirely changed, being densely clouded all over head and wearing a dismal appearance. At eight o'clock a light breeze was felt from the west which gradually freshened until at nine it was blowing a strong breeze. At this time we commenced seeing the concluding fulfilment of the naval officer's prognostications. The ships were returning! Helter skelter did they run in, chased by the opposing enemy, the west wind, seeking in the dark their former anchorages.

We rejoiced now that we had stayed! Good was it, the barometers of the *Vanguard* were enlisted to our special service. The west wind continued to blow the whole of the night and the following day until about seven or eight o'clock in the evening, when it was succeeded by a calm of the same period of time. Then again did a light favourable air set in, this time thought we, we shall have a start.

They sail for London
Three weeks in St Katherine's Dock

It was not, however, till the following afternoon that the weather showed any temptation to move, but at this time a boat from the ship oft named was sent off to us with instructions to weigh anchor and proceed to sea in company with a brig-of-war (I forget her name) that was ordered to escort us out. Our eagerness to be at home made each and all of us turn to our work with a zeal that must have conferred a deal of credit on us from the men-of-war that we felt assured were watching our movements. In the short space of half an hour our anchor was up and the gallant little bark was winding her way through the unruffled waters decorated with her snow white suit which swelling to the gentle breeze fitted upon her as though pencilled by an artist.

Our escorting companion had preceded us only of some few short minutes and therefore kept of the advanced guard just sufficiently to enable us to follow close in her rear. Were we not honoured to be thus escorted by one of Her Majesty's ships? Aye, not any of our friends who had also got under weigh could boast of such honour. The brig kept company until we had reached near Trafalgar. Dusk was then just setting in, at which time she rounded to us, and having neared her sufficiently to speak, the captain hailed ours and asked him if he was now in want of further company or in fact any thing else. To this our captain answered, thanking him, that he was in want of nothing, neither of his company. A good bye, pleasant passage to you, was re-echoed between the two vessels and the next minute we were going both in opposite directions.

We were now left once more upon the bosom of ocean's vast

expanse to ourselves to push our way onward to our destination as best we could. I should not say that we were alone for all the ships I have before mentioned as being wind-bound with us were now following close in our rear, but then each was dispersing from the other more or less, and as night closed in and buried each object in its sombre veil of pitchy darkness, it seemed as though we had actually been alone.

The passage from Gibraltar to London was rather tedious owing to successive contrary winds and was only achieved in 30 days, during which time everything went on in the usual routine of a sea life. At any rate I have no incidents connected with this passage that are worth my remarks upon, unless it is that Captain Le Cheminant strictly observed the promise he had made by not interfering in any way relative to the ship, indeed he behaved in a manner truly astonishingly quiet and peaceably inclined always, during the day he amused himself at some new discovery he had made (when the end of the world was to come) and this was done by study with the globe and the Bible referred to in a preceding page; sometimes he would spend the whole day and part of the night at this study. At other times he would study the celestial objects with his sextant and work up on his slate a mass of cyphering that would have puzzled a Philadelphia lawyer to sum up, in fact he amused himself in various ways, but always very innocently and not once did a word of what had taken place escape his lips, he seemed not to recollect any thing of the past or if he did his silence was truly wonderful. He seemed neither to recollect that he had once had charge of the vessel for his actions were those of a very disinterested passenger.

Ultimately we had reached London and an uncle of his had repaired thither to receive him on his arrival, the owner of the ship (my uncle) was also there, and present at the dock entrance when we entered. Captain Le Cheminant, who had made every necessary change in his toilet previous to reaching the docks, as soon as he could get his feet to bear on the sod, stepped from the ship in the most precipitate manner, and passing by the owner that was standing there at the time without even exchanging a glance of recognition, hurried away toward the city. He was fortunately confronted by his uncle who was hastening to the docks at the time, and by him he was taken care of.

He was placed shortly afterwards in an asylum, I believe, but here I lost sight of him and saw no more of him for many years. I often enquired about him on my return from a voyage, and indeed was only too happy when I heard of his welfare. He has partially recovered his intellect, sufficient to enable him to pass through the maze of society, but there are yet moments when his vacant gaze denote the abstracted mind. I shall now take my leave of him who has taken up so large a share of my time and space, but not without imploring the Almighty to watch over him, to bless him with all the use of perfect sanity, granting him a long life to enjoy it, and hereafter peace everlasting.

Home to Guernsey – Joy

To return to the St Katherine's Dock in London where the *Nancy* was entering, I will observe that after the usual stay of about three weeks, we left in ballast for Guernsey, which place we reached on the fifth day after our exit from London. And now how shall I describe the unequalled raptures that filled my breast on my return to my native home from my first voyage at sea? Words would prove but feeble agents in the case. I cannot, no I dare not, attempt to describe the ecstatic feelings that were mine. Suffice it to say that they were so great that each object I recognised on my way home that evening which I remembered as a momento of my childhood's sport brought a tear to my eye. Arriving at home I flew into my mother's arms who had perceived me through the window and had approached the door to receive me first. No words were exchanged but the telling kisses told but too plainly what words could not have expressed.

My father afterwards, my brothers and sisters, were all embraced in their turn, but far less warmth was manifested in these embraces than in that of the first, not but that sincerity, deep sincerity was there, but so it is, the mother has always, I think I can venture to say, the greatest share of affection from the child.

It was now that I was questioned by all concerning my voyage, each question succeeding the other faster than I could properly answer them. To see me that evening seated in the centre of the group of eight or nine brothers and sisters[1] besides the father and mother, relating to them the wonderful accounts of my voyage, how we had battled against the fury of the tempest in the Western Ocean and once had given ourselves up for lost! and how *I* had done this thing, and that thing, and the other thing besides. In fact, often placing myself foremost in the greatest dilemmas but at any rate never forgetting to place the sufficient stress on the word *I*. I'm certain that Captain Cook on his return from the voyage round the world had not more to disclose than I had that evening, or at any rate, he never thought himself a greater man.

The next morning I was up betimes and having taken an early breakfast I bade good morning to the members of the family that were up and wound my way towards town again to resume my avocations on board. Oh, it was on this memorable morning that I wish to dwell for a moment, the first morning I had been up at such an early hour surrounded by the beauties that nature at a country residence can supply, the first time for eleven long months I say did I enjoy a salubrious morning in the country, and oh, how I did enjoy it. I learnt a lesson that morning that I have not known before, that is that we never value blessings until we have been parted from them for some time. I had often been up and rambling about the fields and orchards on previous occasions before I went to sea, but being an every day occurrence and having been brought up among this sublime scenery, I had never known how to value it, but this morning, one of our fine sunshiny October mornings, how shall I describe it to convey to the reader a faint idea of my vast admiration of nature? The sun had risen perhaps about half an hour; light had broken with gradual step upon the earth, and breathed the breath of life into the hitherto pulseless veins of slumber-locked creation. The orb of day, said I to myself whilst contemplating around me the myriads of objects to arrest the attention of a lover of nature, the orb of the day breaks out in glory upon the world — nature is awakening from her trance, but

[1] In fact, after John's death at sea, Hilary had eight brothers and sisters.

all the night dews remain upon her breast, like sparkling gems on the bosom of an oriental sultana aroused by the break of morning from the voluptuous cushions whereon she has reposed. The loveliness of the scene, the freshness of the morn, the gay carolling of the birds, the myriad tiny voices in which the insect world was speaking all, all had the effect of elevating my spirits to the highest point, and riveted to the spot I indulged to that degree that it was only when the distant sound of the town clock striking seven aroused me from my trance and taught me that I had lingered a full half hour and consequently would be that half an hour later than I ought to have been at my duty. I hurried away from the enchanting scene, and soon was on board again, it being the first morning after arrival it was not thought anything of that I should be rather after time.

I had occasion to enjoy these salubrious mornings many times afterwards; for upwards of three weeks I was every day on board on duty, and consequently up at an early hour. Oh, how many hundreds there are, aye I may say thousands, and tens of thousands, whose business seems to be never to be in bed till a very late hour, often midnight and later and then remain buried in sleep until a corresponding lateness in the morning and rise when the orb of day has performed the best half of its duties. Oh, how much of the most essential part of life is lost to these, it may well be said of them that they only have half the time they *encumber* this earth, for the other half of their existence is spent in sleep.

Oh, is this not a truth that cries vengeance against such habits as these? Does nature not feel offended when unfolding its beauties to the world to find that it has only proffered them to meet a refusal?

I have now pretty well satisfied myself of the detail I have given of my first voyage at sea. I have brought myself home again in October 1840 where I am enjoying its comforts, valued now most dearly, and made dearer still by the consciousness that in a short time I shall again be banished from them and exposed to all the privations of a sea life.

The *Nancy*'s stay in port was of sufficient duration to enable me to spend the Christmas holidays with the family, and I certainly enjoyed them much. I had many little attentions shown me, many indulgences allowed above the others of the family. I was treated in many instances more like a much revered guest than one of its members. 'Poor boy', as my dear mother was wont to say, 'he will soon be away at sea again, let us endeavour to make his short stay among us as pleasant to himself as possible'; and indeed it failed not to be pleasant, with so much love and kindness shown from a beloved mother whose only study seemed to be how to lavish it sufficiently. Is it any wonder that the thought of the parting moment which was hastening apace grew painful?

I am now about to enter on my second voyage and I trust it shall be a speedy one, that I may bring myself back again in time for Xmas, for the idea of losing that fête of plum pudding, etc, etc is cruel to entertain.

– 1841 –

Second Voyage

January – October

Havana – Trieste

It was in January that the little brig was again fitted out for another excursion on the mighty deep. My preparations were accordingly made. A new master had been appointed, Moses Reeves by name. All due and necessary items executed, the day of departure was announced. I will not dwell over the parting scene at home with my beloved parents and fond brothers and sisters; suffice it to say that it was of a corresponding nature to the first one which may be referred to in a preceding page.

We set sail from Guernsey I believe on the 8th or 10th January bound to the Havana again, and again had we a part cargo of potatoes. Nothing of any note transpired throughout the passage which was performed in the usual number of days and we reached our port in safety. Once arrived I felt myself quite at home as it were. Whither I turned my eyes I saw some face or object that was familiar to me. The houses, the streets, the shops, all, all indicated that I had seen them before, and then the well known salutation which would every now and then meet my ears of 'Como esta, um muchacho? Y de donde vienne? Cuanto tiempo hace que um esta en la cuidad? Tengo mucho gusto de ver um, etc',[1] to all of which questions and expressions I answered with as much facility as though I had been there for years. Indeed I became so fond of the

[1] 'How are you, my lad? What country have you come from? How long are you staying in this town? I am very glad to see you, etc'. (The interpolation 'um' appears to be used here to indicate pauses, as one might use 'mmm' in modern English.)

Spanish language that I lost not the slightest opportunity of having a social chat with any of the natives of Havana that circumstances brought me in contact with and so enthusiastic did I become in my notions that a quotation of the Spanish seemed to form a necessary part in my existence.

The captain and mate both perceived my ability in conversing with the Spaniards with no small degree of amazement, and not seldom did the former seek my aid in interpreting for him the business he had to contract. Also whenever either of them had any small purchase to make, such as buying fruit, or going to market for the ship's company, I was invariabley sent to effect the same and was sure to obtain the purchase for a smaller amount of money than they could have done.

Our stay was not long in this port, immediately after the cargo was out, another one of sugar and coffee was taken in for Trieste, it seemed that circumstances intended we should perform the like voyage as the former. The cargo was taken in without delay and soon we were again ready to sail. I felt a certain regret in quitting this familiar spot. It is true I had not a mother, or a father, or brothers, or sisters, or kind friends to take my farewell from, it is also true that I had neither a dark eyed senora to bewail the loss of, yet certain it is, that there existed with me some friendly attachment to this place.

Sail for Trieste

We sailed, however, notwithstanding any wish of mine to have lingered yet a little longer, and ultimately arrived at Trieste. I had often been cheered on the passage that if I was leaving one familiar place I was at any rate about to visit another, for be it remembered that the great attachment I had formed to the Spanish port owing to perhaps only a great desire of aquiring its language did not in the least mitigate the object I had in view of acquiring the Italian language also. I have remarked in a preceding page to the proficiency I had made in that art on a former stay in the port of Trieste. It will not be wondered at if I now state that ere we left this port again I was thoroughly acquainted with as much Italian as ever can be necessary to transact any mercantile or other negotiations. Captain Reeves not unfrequently manifested his astonishment at my capacities in this respect; nor do I wonder, seeing that he was an old navigator of more than forty years standing and had visited both Spanish and Italian ports perhaps more than a score of times, besides other countries, in fact all the world over, yet did he nevertheless stand in perfect ignorance of any dialect but his own. I certainly do not wish by this remark to infer that he was blamable for this want of acquisition; neither do I wish to attach to myself any praise. No, this is my argument and my belief. 'To the one it was forbid to acquire. To the other it was a gift to do so.'

Description of Captain Moses Reeves

Nothing having transpired in this port worth my remarks upon, I will precede with my narrative by calling the reader's attention (that is of course myself) to Captain Moses Reeves who I may introduce for the sake of regularity and conformity consistent with my narrative more particularly than I have hitherto done.

He was a man of about fifty two or three years, tall and of muscular form, his countenance indicated severity but he was not severe. His head was fast becoming white, at least that portion of it that still retained its hairy protection, for the crown was already bald. He wore large whiskers which also had changed their colour and were now that disagreeable mixture of dark grey which makes the bearer seem repulsive, his beard, of which he had no small coating on the lips and chin, was of the same disagreeable colour, and when left unshaven for a week or two resembled for all the world the back of an old badger. His forehead was low and protruding, his eyes large and of the same colour as his beard, and with a large pair of eyebrows coarse and long, rather darker than grey, seemed deeply-sunk into his head although in reality they were not. His nose formed a conspicuous part of his physiognomy, it could not have been less than six inches long from the lower part of the forehead, and at the base it was of an immense width, perforated by two wide opened nostrils from which a bunch of hair hung, resembling a tuft of dry hay. His cheeks were naturally hollow but his right one was kept constantly swelled out to an extraordinary size by a large lump of tobacco which for ever he was chewing. Indeed chewing seemed to form a part of his existence, for unlike other chewers of the noxious weed, he kept his quid[1] in his mouth all night, as well as all day, and not unfrequently did he in his sleep by mistake swallow it, which circumstance would make him terribly sick for many hours during the following day. Yet did he persist in his habits, nor would he desist from them for the chance of keeping his health more regularly.

The first circumstance of this kind that I was witness to I thought some serious illness had fallen upon him. Turning out of his berth earlier than usual, I perceived that he was very pale, in fact as pale as ever death can be represented and his look entirely confirmed my first suspicion that he was very ill. Interested of course, I directly became, and accosting him said 'Are you ill, Captain Reeves? You look very pale. Can I do anything to assist you?' To none of these queries did I receive an answer. Not satisfied and in reality alarmed lest he should be labouring under the influence of some severe attack, I repeated my enquiries. 'What is the matter, I bid you will tell me, Captain Reeves?'

'Oh nothing, nothing. I will be alright by and bye. I only swallowed my chaw[2] last night.'

The enigma was solved, I felt satisfied no wonder he should look pale and felt sick after swallowing at least half an ounce of tobacco besides all the decoction thereof. He had also the habit of emitting the contents of his mouth any where, no matter in what situation he stood and I must observe that each time he did emit this fluid it was a perfect stream of itself. Now that I was steward and had the care of the cleanliness of the cabin, by no means relished this habit of the captain's, it was not seldom that the lee side of the cabin floor was literally afloat, and oft have I seen in

[1] A dialect variant of 'cud', here meaning a lump of tobacco for chewing.

[2] i.e. the tobacco which he had been chewing.

his stateroom of a morning a rivulet of the nauseous fluid deep enough to float a small boat but what is yet more disgusting, when on my knees drying and washing this mess, repeatedly has he discharged his mouth at random without altering his recumbent position and I have received the contents on my head or in the neck. If there happened to be left a pair of shoes about the cabin so sure as their owner resought them, so sure was he to find them full. It was seldom we left any of our shoes astray!

Captain Reeves was not a native of Guernsey, he was from the West of England, but had been resident in the island for many long years. All that I have said of this worthy captain must not prejudice the reader's mind against him for with all his faults, if indeed faults they can be called, no, I will say with all his frailties, he had many redeeming qualities. I shall have occasion further to mark his natural character more particularly.

From Trieste bound again for Havana

Enough for the present has been said to make the reader partially acquainted with him, therefore I will continue my narrative by hurrying on the *Nancy* out of the harbour of Trieste from whence she sailed (in ballast) for the Havana again. After an ordinary passage we reached our port of destination, and of course once more I was at home again, but this time not so much hilarity existed among the crew. No, a cloud of a somewhat gloomy aspect seemed to be hanging over the countenance of each one of its members.

Yellow fever raging. Sailors dying

And why had this gloom prevailed? It was owing to the information imparted to us on our arrival by the health officer that yellow fever was raging fearfully, that it was making dreadful havoc among the shipping! Consequently he recommended us to be very careful in all our habits. This overawing intelligence it was that caused the said gloom to prevail. To make matters worse business in the mercantile line was entirely suspended, so that we had to look forward to a long stay in that now pestilential port. It was June when we arrived and September when we left.

We had not long been in port ere we perceived the fatal truth of the awful case we had learnt of. Every now and then a boat would be seen pushing off from some ship's side with occasionally one, two or three sailors sitting in the stern besides the captain. There goes a fresh prey to the fever! More food for the land crabs!! were our exclamations, and oh how sadly true they too often proved.

At this time I am speaking of (1841) seven cases out of every ten proved fatal. I have known as many as 183 deaths occur in one day. It was a very severe season indeed, the fact was pronounced and established that yellow fever had not prevailed so severely for the previous thirteen years. Each one on board was looking forward to his turn but I must remark there was no despondency existing. No, each cheered the other up as much as possible, we knew full well that hilarity was consistent with health, whilst on the contrary fear and despondency were the best and effectual agents employed in the service of the grim destroyer.

Soon we became so accustomed to see the flag at half-mast high around us, the signal of death!, that we looked upon it only as a matter of course. Three weeks had already elapsed during which time hundreds of our fellow creature and brother sailors had been consigned to the 'Lime Pit' and we were still in the full enjoyment of health. It is true that we took good care of ourselves, not exposing ourselves to the night dews, not eating or drinking any thing contrary to the system. Then our captain was also very particular in not allowing us to be exposed to the heat of the sun during the middle of the day, so that with all these precautions we were cheered with the hope of escaping the fangs of the pestilence. But alas! our hopes were doomed to be crushed, they were but evanescent; one of our men fell sick. The captain examined him for a brief minute, pronounced his case decisive, so away to the hospital at once with him, for be it remembered it was certain death to neglect an attack for a few hours.

I know not if it was now fear that struck the crew, or if it was that the destroying angel had alighted on the ship on her rounds elsewhere, but certain it is that another of the crew began to complain, and then another, and another, until in a very few days all hands with three exceptions were in the hospital. The exceptions were the captain, the chief mate, and your humble servant, but soon however, the former and the latter shared an equal fate.

Yes, ultimately everyone (the mate excluded) were sharing the attendance of Dr Bellot's establishment; of course we never expected we should all come out of this establishment alive where several hundreds were laying upon their stretchers in double rows in each ward, and at an average one every hour taken away to the grave prepared for them behind the building in a thick grove of cocoa-nut trees. This was a large square pit dug in the earth to the depth of about 20 feet and half filled with lime.

One or two coffins were in use, and when the last breath was gone out of poor Jack's nostril, the slaves of the establishment then immediately placed him in the coffin and shutting down the lid, carried him out to the lime pit where the coffin was placed on the edge, then opened, and the corpse let drop into the grave. One splash was heard, the opening gulph had closed again, all was still, poor Jack was gone never to return! The coffin was then brought back to the hospital and often ere it was returned it had become in requisition again and thus it was that four black slaves were kept in constant employment carrying out the dead and burying them.

No funeral rites were here observed, no procession attended the funeral, no prayer was offered up to heaven for the repose of poor Jack's soul! Nay, no eye to shed a tear over him. No father or mother to own him for a son. No wife to deplore the loss of a beloved husband. No children to weep over him there. No! No! Poor Jack was gone for ever, in a strange land unknown, unheeded! I witnessed many deaths on each side of me during my stay in that hospital, yes, and many an awful one too. I have known the poor dying man in his last agonies cursing and swearing, making use of imprecations dreadful to hear, because he could not obtain the desire that perhaps the whim of the moment had caused. Yes, I have seen the last dying moan of death, a curse! I have known other instances again where that latest breath was made use of with the most solemn, impressive ejaculation of 'O

God! My wife, my child!'

Gangrene and much suffering

My case was a very serious one of yellow fever followed by black vomit and gangrene, in fact it was the most serious case in the hospital, and Dr Bellot prided himself not a little at having cured it. I was thirty nine days confined to this establishment, and I can aver that I endured many sufferings during that period, the repeated cuppings on my neck, shoulders and abdomen made me a great sufferer and left me literally weltering in my own blood, my hair which had grown long became clotted with gore, so that the back of my head was one complete hardened cake of blood. My body also was crusted all over with blood, and strange as it may appear I was not allowed a drop of water to wash myself once during my illness. Wounds were inflicted on my thighs in thirty two places on one and twenty seven on the other, these wounds were about one inch in length and three eighths of an inch in breadth, and about the same depth! It caused pain enough to have them inflicted, but that was not the worst part pertaining thereto, they had been inflicted for some particular purpose and therefore were not allowed to heal but must be kept open. Consequently every morning one of the assistant doctors (Mr Hayes) came with his instrument box under his arm and placing it on a small table at my bed side, would open it, search for one particular utensil which having found and wiped it on a dirty piece of cotton he had for the purpose, he would then throw the coverings off me, and pulling up my chemise commence operations on my unfortunate thighs, just as though he was going to operate on a marble statue on whose feelings he could make no impression.

His business was to undo all the work that nature had been busy about for the previous twenty-four hours, and by picking and probing the wounds, removing the scab that had formed itself over them would lay them quite open again, then taking some ointment for the purpose he would rub it in the raw flesh with not a very light hand. Now I have never known what this ointment really was, but I can compare the effect it had upon me when rubbed into these wounds so very sore to nothing nearer than to saltpetre and vitriol poured into a new incision made in the flesh. Oh it was a cruel pain to bear, I actually writhed with pain for a full hour after the operation, and when the mornings came every sound of footsteps I heard on the stairs made me tremble with fear, thinking it might be my torturer again.

Oh, if I had been left to choose at the time whether to be left to die by not touching the wounds, or by continuing an attendance upon them be allowed to live, I really think I would have chosen the former. Yes, I believe I would have rather died than bear the tortures I endured. Nevertheless at the present moment I feel rather glad they did not allow me to choose, and I think by the bye that some one in particular, and society in general ought to be very glad of it too. But this portion of my sufferings though by no means trivial were not destined to be the last.

The gangrene I have alluded to now commenced showing itself but fortunately for me its appearance was in my right foot, had it been in any of the upper parts of my body it evidently would have carried me off, as this dreadful disease whensoever it reached any of the arteries leading to the heart baffles all the skill of the most eminent physicians, and inflicts immediate death on the patient, in spite of the most attentive remedies. My case, thank heaven, did not savour of so much anxiety, it being in the nether parts of the body but yet attention must be paid to prevent it reaching above the knee, for once there it was fatal. This gangrene I may as well here observe for the benefit of those who know not what it is, is a mortification, or in other words, a stoppage of circulation of the blood followed by putrefaction. Now this putrified blood must be emitted from the body and free circulation produced. To effect this an incision was made in my leg a little above the ankle and the disease carefully watched, but notwithstanding, it extended itself in a very short time above this incision, and promised fair for reaching the knee.

Now the learned doctors seeing this, began to grow alarmed, for after all the cures they had effected on me they were loath to let me slip out of their hands, besides another very good reason was that I was their most profitable patient in the establishment, paying them three dollars every day since the time I was removed from the sailors' ward through the kind interference of a gentle friend[1] in concert with Captain Reeves. Consequently all these reasons taken into consideration, all the skill that the establishment could boast of was devoted to me. One remedy was tried and failed, and then another, but shared the same fate, and so forth till all the means they could suggest were proved unsuccessful.

Amputation is decided upon

The head man, Dr Bellot, then decided that no alternative was left to choose but immediate amputation must ensue. Consequently, preparations were made at once, the instruments, bandages, cloths, basins and water, and even a basket full of sawdust were brought into the room, but here I must observe all this was done under cover, and all these necessaries placed on a table brought into the room for the purpose, well covered over with a table cloth to prevent detection on my part. Their intention being to place me under the influence of some narcotic, no doubt, whilst performing the operation.

Now it is a positive fact that notwithstanding the seriousness of my case, and the evident pending calamity so soon to follow I could but ill refrain from giving vent to risible propensities which I was subduing with difficulty. The reason of this was that the doctors, three in number, had been consulting together over this case of mine, and the better to keep me ignorant of their conclusions they had adopted the French language, and only varied their discourse now and then by using an occasional phrase of Spanish. A sad delusion they were under! Their patient who lay so quiet in his bed, with his right leg stretched out in the position they had placed it, and who seemed so unconscious of what was passing in the room, was all the time listening with open ears at their discourse, and failed not to catch every syllable of it, aye and

[1] This friend was Thomas Le Lièvre of the Grange. [HM]

to understand it as well. They could not have used any language with which I was more familiar, admitting they had used English. Is it to be wondered at if I laughed in my sleeve when they were so cautiously introducing the articles I have mentioned above into my room? No, for the life of me I could not help it. But I had to be very cautious in keeping my countenance so that they might not perceive the discovery I had made which for certain reasons I wished to keep from them.

After everything was in readiness, they took one more minute examination of the diseased limb, then it being about four o'clock and their dinner time, Dr Bellot advised that they should give the last remedy they had used a fair trial and in the interval go to dinner, after which quoth he (in French) 'We shall be stronger and fitter for the operation.' Accordingly placing my limb under cover again they left me to go and put their last project into execution. Now this was a moment I had wished for, my intense curiosity made me feel inclined to hurry them from the room that I might go and have a complete survey of all the utensils that lay on the table, but alas I was doomed to disappointment for on making the attempt I found that my legs refused to perform their office!

Captain Reeves pays a visit

It was a very short time after this moment of which I am speaking that Captain Reeves made his usual evening call. Entering my room with his customary salutation of 'Well, Harry, how do you get on by this time?'

'Oh, much about the same, Sir, thank you.'

'Oh, that's always the tune day after day. I wish you could alter it and tell me "Very well" instead.'

By this time he had taken a seat at my bedside as was his wont upon that article of furniture that is indispensable in a sick chamber, and continued his interrogation about my wounds etc. Having answered all his questions I remarked that perhaps the difficiency of a leg would make some alteration for the better. Now this to him was a parable, moreover having his face towards me, his back must be turned to the table that supported the articles I have already mentioned, consequently he had not yet noticed them. I ought also to observe that he had a certain twang in his pronunciation which made his observations at all times more or less risible.

'What d'ye mean by the deficiency of a leg? You are not going to throw one of them out of the window, are you?'

'No, Sir', was my response, 'but they are going to cut one of them off this evening and then perhaps it will be thrown out into the lime pit where there are already so many with the bodies attached to them.'

The poor old man had been looking at me with a gaze that I would not attempt to describe. 'What do you say they are going to do?'

'Amputate my leg, Sir.'

'Hampitate the Devil!'

'Well, Sir', I replied, 'if you are kind enough to look on that table' (pointing to it) 'you will convince yourself of the truth of my statement.'

The old man turned round in the direction I was pointing and at once stepped across the room, without any ceremony and in his rough handed way tore the cover off the table, and at once the whole paraphernalia met his gaze.

He stood amazed for a moment and motionless, then turning towards me again, asked when they were to put their intention into execution. I replied that it had been decided if no change for the better was perceptible in the limb after they had done their dinner they were to take it off.

'Take if off', replied he, 'take the devil off.' Then stamping his foot on the floor continued: 'They'll tak my head off first. Where are they, the monsters? I'll go and talk to they.'

I replied they were at dinner but — and I was about to offer a remark but before I had time to speak another word he was out of the room and proceeding at a rapid pace in quest of the doctors.

He found them at dinner and introduced himself in their presence without the slightest formality — how he blew them up, or what passed between them I would like to have known, but however did not, at any rate be that as it may, in the course of half an hour they all repaired to my chamber once more, and I had no difficulty in perceiving that the captain was a deal more pacified than when he had left it at about three quarters of an hour previous. The first thing Dr Bellot did on entering was to call the black man that was my attendant to account for having disclosed to me the secret connected with the amputation of my limb and which it had been their intention of keeping me ignorant of, for be it remembered that Captain Reeves had told them at the dinner table that it was I who had apprised him of the whole affair, and how he had subsequently discovered the infallible truth by examining the several instruments etc pointed out by me also.

The poor black man, dismayed at the accusation thrust against him by a master that perhaps was very severe over his slaves, fell upon his knees and with joined hands denied the accusation and supplicated mercy for daring to confess the truth, all with the same breath. This scene wrought upon my feelings so much that I resolved to divulge the secret and thereby save the poor slave a whipping. Consequently I spoke out to the top of my voice. 'Dr Bellot, the man is perfectly innocent, he has not spoken a word to me on the matter, neither have I questioned him, indeed I had no reason to do so, being so well informed of all your intended proceedings by YOURSELF.'

The doctor looked at me. 'By myself' (laying a stress on the first syllable), 'How do you mean? Or what do you mean? I have never spoken a word of this to you.'

'I beg your pardon, Sir.'

'When then have I done so?'

'Just before you retired to dinner.'

He was amazed, he could not make it out, this was to him an enigma, then all at once the thought flashing to his mind, he asked me if I understood French. My response at once settled all. 'Oui, Monsieur, je l'entends, et le comprends, et si ce n'etait de peur de me flatter, je vouz dirais que je le parle aussi.'

He turned himself round to his companions and with astonishment depicted in his countenance exclaimed 'Who would have thought it!' Now this last exclamation was uttered in Spanish, so understanding it well I thought I should astonish him yet more, and exclaimed in my turn, 'Why? Is there any thing strange in my understanding French?'

'Carrumba!' quoth the doctor, 'he speaks Spanish also!'

Of course this freed the black man and he was dismissed. There being now no further necessity for secrecy the conversation was held in English that Captain Reeves might benefit by it. Dr Bellot then addressed me whether I should rather run the risk of being a corpse before morning or by suffering amputation continue to live. I replied that there ought not to be a question on the subject, if it was necessary to clip me of a leg, or a wing, I was perfectly resigned. It was then decided that the operation should take place. Captain Reeves then at once took his leave, and with tears in his eyes wished me 'good bye' with the assurance he should come early in the morning to see me again. Just at the moment that the preparations were being made by the assistants Dr Bellot's partner, a Spanish gentleman, suggested that another last experiment should be tried, adding that he had sufficient faith to believe in its efficacy, but that if it came to the worst, it could only be to the same alternative they were adopting now. The experiment being explained to Dr Bellot he gave his sanction for the trial, and accordingly it was at once tried, and I am happy to say proved successful, so that every time I have the necessity of hurrying an intruder onward, I have cause to thank the Spaniard I have a right leg and foot to do it with. The reader will no doubt exhibit some anxiety to know what this experiment was.

The leg is saved

In a few brief words I will explain it. A large hole was bored in the flesh on each side of the knee, then a silver tube was passed through which extended about two inches on either side; the mouth was applied to this tube, and by means of suction the putrid blood was brought to this tube and ultimately found its way out of the limb through it.

Next morning when the good old man Captain Reeves returned to the hospital, he was surprised and delighted to see me still in the possession of both pins. He told me how he had dreamt I was walking upon crutches and how my parents at home had blamed him for allowing the doctors thus to maim me. In fact it was evident enough that he had passed a very restless night on my account. These wounds now took some time to cure, indeed they were not cured when I reached home but before I left Dr Bellot's care he assured me that they were sufficiently advanced to allow me to go to sea, of course taking care not to bruise them, or to get salt water to them, he also assured me that I need never fear the yellow fever again providing I did not stay away from Havana more than three years at a time for, said he, 'All the blood you have now in your body has been made here, the whole of your European-made blood we have taken from you.' Thank a merciful God we all hands recovered, and had the satisfaction to go home together, but I believe I may safely aver that ours was the only ship in the harbour that lost none of its crew.

Return to Guernsey

After laying in port from June to the latter end of September, we received instructions to come to Guernsey, there being no cargo to be had, we proceeded in ballast, the same we had taken at Trieste. It was indeed an unfortunate voyage for the owners. We were fortunate in having a pleasant run to Guernsey, and arrived there safely the thirty second day after leaving Havana. I was a pretty picture indeed to arrive home. My head had been closely cropped after the fever had left me, or rather after I got on board, so that the hair had not had time to grow any length which made me look very queer. Then I was scarred about the body like an old soldier returning from the wars, aye, I could show more wounds than any that have ever returned from Waterloo. I only wanted the crutches to complete my appearance.

Home again

But here was I home again and, as I had desired, in time to spend the Xmas holidays. What new joy was this: too great in fact for me to describe. My dear mother did indeed fold me in her embrace more ardently than ever, for she had expected never to see me again — like the father of the prodigal son she could indeed exclaim my son was dead, but is alive, was lost, but now is found.

Time wore on and the holidays came and passed away, then did I once more exhibit signs of anxiety to return to sea, but what was to be done? The *Nancy* had met with an accident the day after her arrival, and the owners had laid her up with the intention of disposing of her altogether.[1] Nothing was left for me now but to seek another vessel. My parents tried, but in vain, to keep me on land.

The Adelaide *and Captain Taylor*

I sought myself another ship and soon found one. This was the *Adelaide*, Captain Taylor, and of this ship and captain I would have much to say, indeed enough to fill volumes were I inclined to follow up the every day incidents of my life, but as this is not the peculiarity of my desire I will content myself to say but little, as much only as will be consistent with my present work.[2] I have yet another motive for being laconic on this subject, that is that everything I have to say of the captain is bad; nay I could not decorate a narrative however long with one good sentence in his favour, and as I remember an old proverb which I have already quoted in a preceding page, inculcated into my mind by Mr Wade-

[1] She was eventually abandoned at sea in a sinking condition on 6 Nov. 1858 during a voyage from Demerara to Cork (ex inf. Dr Alan Jamieson from Guernsey shipping registers in BT 107).

[2] The *Adelaide*, a brig of 190 tons, was built by John Vaudin of South Beach, St Peter Port, in 1830. Her original dimensions were 82ft 3in. long, 23ft 6in. broad, 14ft 10in. deep in the hold. She had a figurehead and a square stern. She was broken up at Sunderland in March 1888. (Ex inf. Dr Alan Jamieson from BT 107.)

son's rattan 'De mortuis nil nisi bonum',[1] I mean to adhere to it as much as possible.

Certainly I often think when casting a retrospective view on that past part of my life, is it possible that I could endure so much during upwards of two long years without being disgusted with a sea faring life? Our avocation must indeed be born with us. I must have been predestined for a sailor.

[1] 'Of the dead say nothing but what is favourable'. A rattan here means a piece of stem from a rattan, an East Indian climbing palm, with long, thin, jointed, pliable stems, used as a walking stick etc.

– 1842 to 1844 –

Third Voyage

It was in the month of March 1842 that we sailed from Guernsey in the said vessel, bound on a voyage to Jersey, from thence to Rio de Janiero. I was quite elated with the prospects all new before me, besides being proud of my advancement for I was now 'before the mast' and on the ship's articles as ordinary seaman, and attached to my name in the column headed 'monthly wages' was affixed the figures 1 15 decorated above with the well known sign of pounds and shillings thus: £1 15s. – . I was at this time in my opinion at least a young man and no more a boy. I may add, if I am not thought vain, I was for my age tall, stout and well made,[1] one thing only tended against my thorough sailor-like appearance which was a very delicate look owing to my complexion which was extremely fair, and which at the age I am alluding when disguised in female attire made it impossible for anyone to detect my sex. How much I have altered since that time I will leave for others to imagine. I certainly yet think myself fair to look upon, but I am digressing.

Besides my well proportioned stature I had spirit and activity in my favour, all combined raised me much in Captain Taylor's estimation but how much he knew how to value these qualities will hereafter be seen. I have before said we sailed from Guernsey for Jersey there to load cod-fish for Rio, and certainly a more gallant crew than was on board the *Adelaide* at this time never graced a ship's deck.

[1] Mr Eric Marquand recalls that his grandfather remembered Hilary as a very tall, powerful man.

Life on board hell – crew abscond

We had not arrived in Jersey 24 hours ere the Captain commenced displaying his true character, which had long sought for emancipation, for be it known that when in Guernsey he acted with greater dissimulation than I have ever known any other well-finished hypocrite capable of. All hands of us at the ungenerous treatment we were receiving at so early a period of our voyage were made discontent and unhappy, and as we very justly observed, if he commenced in this manner, what must the end be like? The consequence of this was that three of the men forming the noble crew of this ship, made a hell upon earth by her commander, absconded. Aye, before we had left home three weeks, were we minus of three hands. The captain at this discovery literally foamed with rage, his threats upon their devoted heads if he ever caught them again were boundless.

Through some then to me unknown channel, the captain was informed that I intended also to join my companions, but in truth I had no such intention, for I have always looked upon it as disgraceful to run away. No, I had made up my mind to bear anything, and everything for the sake of learning. I knew that Captain Taylor was severe when I engaged myself (of course I did not think he was cruel) but I also knew that his was a good school for learning the art of seamanship, and for that did I prefer him above any other. I always bore in mind that my future advancement depended upon my present exertions and I was determined to advance, and equally so to exert myself I did both, admidst inconceivable miseries. I do not repent it.

We boarded on shore and it was one evening whilst taking our teas that the captain received the said information respecting myself, the informant being no other than the landlady of the house, Mrs Gilmour. At this piece of information the captain raved anew, and calling the steward to his aid, immediately repaired on board whilst yet we all were at tea, and thinking to put a stop on my intended proceedings hauled up my chest which contained my clothes out of the forecastle and took them in the cabin. Now, I that was perfectly innocent of any intended wrong, on returning to the vessel after tea and finding my chest gone began to surmise none other than that a robbery had been committed the which made me very unhappy, as the whole of my sea stock (not a trifling one) was contained in that chest.

I was alone in the forecastle, and as I supposed on the ship, consequently I resolved at once to go up again to the boarding house to give the alarm to my shipmates that the forecastle had been robbed during our absence, but on reaching the deck I perceived a light was burning in the cabin – perhaps the robbers are pillaging the cabin, thought I. Thither I went on tip-toe, but instead of thieves there was but one thief, that was the steward. Calling him by his other name, I mean the one given him by his godfather and godmother, I made known to him my disaster expecting if not great surprise from him, at least a small share of sympathy, but to my amazement neither were brought forth, but on the contrary a smile lighted his countenance. Now although I am not thoroughly a physiognomist yet I have always had a share of discernment of the human countenance. Consequently at once I perceived that the expression of his eyes indicated that he in a direct or indirect manner was connected with, or knew something of the robbery. I begged, I entreated of him to ease my surcharged mind by explaining to me the mystery. The wretch only laughed and seemed to enjoy my anxiety, but I would not leave him thus, I felt still more convinced that he knew something about the affair. I begged, I entreated anew, I promised, I threatened, at last he bid me be at ease for my chest was not stolen but only temporarily abstracted from the forecastle to the cabin. I asked him why in the name of all that was good, those measures had been had recourse to. He replied 'You had better ask the captain', but the captain was not on board, therefore my only alternative was to bear my anxiety till the morrow, which I did with all the resignation that I possibly could command, thereby making a virtue of necessity.

On the following morning we had been aroused as usual by the mate at an early hour when on opening my eyes from slumber and perceiving the vacant place in the row of chests that bounded my side of the forecastle, all the incidents of the previous evening hurried up to my memory. On reaching the deck I was glad to perceive that Captain Taylor was already pacing the quarter deck.

The Captain strikes Hilary

I hurried up to him at once, and in the blandest manner possible begged of him to explain his reasons for having taken my chest of clothes in the cabin. Any person worthy of the name of man could not have refused to answer a question put in such a polite manner, but he was a brute. Instead of replying, first he flew at me with the rage of a tiger, and giving me such a blow on the face with his clenched fist as I have not forgotten to this day, sent me reeling backwards some eight or ten paces until I fell almost senseless to the deck.

'I'll teach you to run away', quoth he, 'you young blackguard.'

Now let the reader imagine for a moment what kind of reception this was for me, that knew no reason for it whatever. I knew not what his teaching me to run away meant, certainly it was in my opinion a very efficacious plan of teaching anyone to run away and had I had any inclination previously this would have decided the case. I rose from the deck feeling my head to ascertain it was yet on my shoulders, the blood boiling in my veins, my rage at this brutal treatment overpowering me, heightened yet by having been called a blackguard. What should I do? Should I not resent it? Alas I was not able. Oh for strength at this present moment. Oh that I had been a few years older, but never mind thought I, one day will yet be mine and will I not repay with interest?

I looked at the captain directly in the face when I had reached my perpendicular. I'm sure he must have seen the workings of my rage, but feeling that I could do no more, I only spoke, assuring him that he had been mis-informed or that some private enemy had been at work against me for I had no intention of quitting the ship nor had it ever entered my mind.

'You mistake me very much, Captain Taylor', continued I, 'if you think that I would run away, no, I abhor the very words. Were I inclined to leave the ship I would do so in a respectable manner as I have always been taught to act, I would repay you your month's advance, and further you are very mistaken if you believe that my chest of clothes would keep me back. No, Sir, I thank God I have a father who can give me another, and if I wished to leave the ship I would do so in spite of you and make you a present of my clothes, perhaps you have more need of them than I.'

These last words literally inflamed him, but I cared not; I had vented my rage and I felt somewhat satisfied, and perceiving an advancing movement of his I hurried forward out of his reach, the next minute I had a job of work given me to tar the stays down, as a punishment for having dared to receive his brutal treatment otherwise than like a dumb animal.

Things went on in this manner during our stay in port, and many will perhaps wonder that I was foolish enough to trust my future peace with a man of his character upon the wide ocean, but I have ere now given my reasons. I know that few would be found of equal zeal, but such I was, and did not wish to remodel myself. Meanwhile a strict search was being made by several constables for the absconded party before mentioned, and on one or two different occasions did these functionaries enter an ale house in the country by the front door, whilst my shipmates retired by the back, thus were all traces of them lost and ultimately the chase given up.

Our captain, finding this to be the case, engaged another three men, and we made sail from Jersey pier for our destination. An incident occurred just at the moment we were hauling in the stern rope and sailing out, which I must not leave unnoticed. At this critical moment I say it was that voices reached the captain's ears wishing him good bye and a pleasant voyage, amidst the crowd of spectators assembled as is invariably the case on the occasion of a ship's sailing. The captain looked up to see which of his friends it was that interested themselves so much in his behalf, and also to return the compliment, when to his utter amazement he beheld the three identical men for whose capture he had laid out so many expenses. What his pent up feelings were at this moment I will not attempt to describe, let them be imagined.

Arrival at Rio de Janeiro

We sailed down channel with a fair fine breeze which we kept for a considerable time and arrived at our destined port on the 42nd day of our sailing from Jersey. Many incidents happened during this interval which I might relate, but which would occupy too much space. Suffice it to say concerning myself that I was worked up like a slave, and not treated half so well, but I was not the only one of the crew who received such treatment: with the captain there was no respect of persons. Old and young, all were the objects of his ire.

Whilst in the port of Rio de Janeiro several of our crew again ran away, others were shipped to replace them, then after a short stay on board ran away also. In fact few could put up with the harsh treatment which it was Captain Taylor's character to exercise and not unfrequently was some poor fellow goaded to that pitch that made him insolent, which was sure to follow by his being felled to the deck and afterwards he felling the captain in his turn. Such brawls as I have sometimes seen on board that vessel would horrify the reader were I to depict them.

Captain Taylor was a man of illimitable passions, and had no control over himself in such moments. Besides that, I might add he was a low-bred man and possessed but little principle; hence follows the reason of the constant warring that made the *Adelaide* a floating hell. I have often seen him strike the heaviest man on the ship, in a moment of passion, which only a trifle was sufficient to excite, without heeding the consequences and often I have seen him grappled with another, fighting as it were for life or death, weltering in their own blood on the deck. I have also seen the knife, and the axe, at work whilst my hair has stood on end to think that murder might be the result. Yea, have I seen a man, and what is more an officer in the ship, knocked upon the head with the cook's hatchet by Captain Taylor's own hand.

Now, if such actions as these can emanate from a man of principle I know not what principle is, and can a man, be he a foremast man or no, I say, can any man be blamed, if when he is treated in such a brutal manner repays the author of it in his own coin? No, I say not, by the laws of our mercantile marine a man dares not lift his hand upon his master or officers; but by the same law, a master or officer dares not lift his hand upon his men. Nay, but the same law protects them both. I am master of a vessel myself at this moment, and yet I say and hold it to be right that a man is justified in pommelling well the captain that dares to strike him. If a master so far forgets or degrades himself as to fight with his men, he must expect to reap the reward of his actions.

Hilary vows to be avenged

I still recollect what my feelings were at that time when being driven and knocked about like a detested dog. I would have given worlds to have had sufficient strength to resent it, but I was growing up every day, and my strength was becoming equal to my spirit, and many times when receiving a blow did I mark it down upon the tablet of my memory as an additional one, one day to be repaid; yes, and I vowed that we should not quit each other that voyage till old scores had been settled, whether this prophecy was ultimately realised or no remains to be seen.

Back and forth across the Atlantic

In the meantime I shall go on by remarking that we sailed from Rio after the usual stay for Trieste in Austria, from there we sailed for Cette[1] in the Gulph of Lyon, South of France, and from there to Rio again. And again did we sail from Rio for Trieste, and from Trieste for Cagliari (Island of Sardinia) and from there once more to Rio. From Rio we sailed again for Cowes (Isle of Wight) from thence for Hamburg, then to Newcastle and Guernsey. I should remark briefly that we wintered at Hamburg having been caught by the ice in the Elbe and frozen there. It was a miserable time! This voyage took us five and twenty months to perform, during which time we had 51 strangers in the vessel, in every port did we take a new crew, either they ran away, or joined Her Majesty's Service or else were discharged by the British Consul. I and the carpenter were the only two foremast men that bore the voyage out.

[1] Now Sète, on the coast about 15 miles from Montpellier.

Hilary fights back

It was the last trip we were at Rio that an incident occurred which I am bound to relate in conformity with the above. We had stripped the ship and refitted all her rigging, had scraped and in part tarred and painted, all this with only the two mates, besides myself, when having one morning finished a job of work, the mate ordered me to go on scraping the jib boom; my hands and arms were besmeared with tar, and ere I went to scrape I sought to clean my hands.

Now gentle reader, our best soap at sea is grease, or more commonly called slush. I looked into the grease buckets one after the other but no grease was there, our allowance had been made use of, for all the grease made by the cook was taken into the cabin, and afterwards served out as it was required with as much stinginess as if it had been gold: a mean dirty practice I had never seen or ever have since. Not being able to clean my hands without, I took one of the buckets to the cabin companion and calling the steward begged of him to give me a small portion of grease, when the captain, who was sitting behind me on the skylight, asked what it was I was asking for to which I replied 'A little grease, Sir'. The next question was 'What do you want it for?'

'To clean my hands (showing them), Sir, before I can go on the jib boom a scraping.'

In a fury I did not the least expect he replied, 'The devil run a hunting with you, go clean your hands with soap.' Now this epithet coming so unexpectedly and the refusal of a bit of slush when so much needed, and in reality mine more than his, for he had our meat weighed out to us to the nearest part of an ounce, so that the fat that came off the meat did not in reality belong to him. All this I say aroused at once my hot blood and I replied (but coolly) that soap would not clean my hands in half an hour whereas an ounce of grease would do it in five minutes.

'Well, be off with you forward, you shall have none' at the same time pushing me. Now my blood boiled within me.

'The grease is mine, Sir, more than yours', said I but before I had time to say another word he had flown towards me, and picking up the first thing that came within his reach as was generally the case, he levelled it at me to strike me a blow. Now had I received the blow intended from the hand that was made furious by passion I dare say I would never have lived to recount this, for let it be understood that the weapon was the anchor stopper — a rope of at least five inches thick with a great knot at the end. It was this knot larger than my fist that waved over my head threatening destruction at its fall. I gazed at it a second, the next I had slipped on one side and the blow fell on the deck close to my feet. He attempted to rise the weapon again but before he had done so I had seized it with both my hands and was trying to wring it out of his. A struggle ensued, I was desperate, he was demented, it was the first time I had dared to lift my hands in self-defence but it was now the time appointed to come one day. I felt it was so, and now that I had commenced I would rather have died in the attempt than not revenged myself.

Let not my reader accuse me here of bearing malice in my heart, or revenge in my breast and tell me it is not right so to do. I will reply if I am so accused that if he had been in my place for the seventeen long months shut up from home, friends and all that is dear on the wide ocean and maltreated every day in the most brutal manner making life to feel a burden, he would like me, if indeed he were flesh and blood, have changed his character from gentility to ferocity.

This I did and ferocity gave me strength. I pulled and tugged, my eyes becoming bloodshot with rage, until I succeeded in pulling the dreaded weapon out of his hands. I flung it on one side of me, he that moment snatched up a billet of wood that lay close by, the carpenter being at work in the immediate vicinity putting a new plank in the deck, the old one being out leaving an opening of six inches wide and some twenty feet long. Seeing him take up this piece of wood I stepped on one side and looking at him full in the face addressed him in these words. 'If you attempt to strike me with that billet of wood I swear you will repent it, I am determined not to bear this infamous treatment at your hands any longer. I have done so now for seventeen months, but by the God that made me I will do so no longer, recollect that I am not a beast that I should be treated as such, I am not your slave that you should practice your inhumanity upon me with impunity. I am not a dog that I should be kicked about by you at your will, neither am I a child that I should be treated like a child — no, Captain Taylor, I am a man, and if younger than you, with at least as stout a heart, and far more honourable principles. You have behaved towards me in a most brutal manner during my stay on this vessel, I have borne it all with suppressed rage but now the moment has come when I can no longer stop the current of the stream, and therefore I warn you that if ever after this you lift your brutal hands towards me again I shall fell you to the earth if I possibly can, though I should be punished for it by law afterwards.'

During my speech the captain had been gaining breath whilst I had been expending it, and at my saying I would fell him to the earth he made a rush at me, exclaiming: 'You fell me to the earth, you young brat. I shall quarter you.'

'Will you?' said I, and I had clutched the billet of wood with my left hand whilst with my right I held him fast by the throat. We struggled together for some minutes when he let go his hold on the billet, feeling I suppose, my finger tickling his windpipe rather awkwardly. This manoeuvre of his I took the best possible advantage of, for having all to myself I hurled it up in the air at arms length and let it come down on his head with a force that made his teeth meet together closer than ever.

The captain is felled

On we struggled: he losing courage and I losing strength, until I know not how it would have ended for me, but fortune, which always favours the brave, favoured me at this instant, for in a moment when I least expected it he had inadvertently placed his foot in the aperture made in the deck by the removal of the plank spoken of, and falling into it until the crutch of his body prevented his going lower, was entirely at my mercy.

I did not lose one point of vantage ground on this occasion but commenced belabouring him about the head right and left whilst he could but try to hide his face with his arms. The old proverb 'that one might as well be hung for a sheep as for a lamb' was then uppermost in my mind, so comparing that with the present occasion I thought since the opportunity presented itself I might as well give him a complete thrashing and thereby repay old scores, as to leave my vengeance half satisfied. He, finding his situation an unpleasant one commenced bawling out for help from the mate, each time his mouth opened at so doing, my fist at once filled the aperture but the mate, who was no less ill-treated than any other, and at the time in the main rigging tarring down (an ill-becoming place for the mate of a ship), and whither he had been made to go against his will that morning by the same individual who would now fain expect his succour, was deaf to his cries, but in the contrary enjoyed the sport and by well understood signs gave me encouragement to complete the task I had undertaken.

I did not fail to do so, I pommelled him to my entire satisfaction and I am sure much more than to his. When I had ceased he at once made every exertion and soon extricated himself from his perilous situation. I stood a few yards from him in an attitude of defence, as immovable as a statue and with reckless determination depicted on my countenance, expecting of course the moment he had regained his footing, another attack from him. Such was not the case. He merely cast a momentary glance at me and uttering a few imprecations on my devoted head walked away abaft with his bruised leg in his hands. Now seeing no more use in maintaining my position I repaired on the forecastle deck where under the awning I betook myself to comfort and my pipe, ruminating in solitude over the past incidents and making resolutions for the future.

The captain had protested he was going to have me put in gaol, and severely punished for having dared to lift my hand against him, the master of the ship! I felt credulous that he would attempt it at any rate, knowing well his fondness for imprisoning his crew. But I feared not. I had a thousand of his brutal acts against me to bring forward as a justification of my present behaviour and I felt in reality more anxious to appear before the consul with him than he might have supposed. It was now noon and dinner was ordered to be served up, the crew leaving off work, my only shipmate the carpenter repaired on the forecastle with me.

'Well, Tom',[1] said I as soon as he had sat down, 'What do you think of my morning's work?'

'Well', replied he quite seriously, 'you have given it to him sure enough.'

'But do you think I have done so too much?' quoth I.

'Not at all in my opinion, he was deserving of all that, and more than that, but I fear that you may have committed yourself by daring to strike him.'

'Do you fear that?' said I. 'Well, Tom, I don't. I was first struck by him and you are witness to the weapon he attempted to fell me with, "the anchor stopper". Had I been foolish enough not to defend myself as I have usually done, he would probably have maimed me for life. No, no, Tom, I fear not in the least, and you will see that if he does not put his threats in execution of bringing me before the council, I will bring him there myself. As soon as he has done dinner you will see me walk abaft to him to know his intentions.'

'By George', quoth Tom, 'you had better not. I would not be in your shoes if you attempt such a measure.'

'Look here, Tom', replied I and Tom cast his eyes to the deck actually quailing beneath my look of determination, 'I am now and altered character, before you you now see the gentle lamb goaded by continual ill-treatment turned to the ferocity of the tiger. You are aware, Tom, that I have now for seventeen months borne continual ill-treatment, how little I have deserved such treatment I leave you to decide; you are also aware how I have borne the treatment without once opening my lips in complaint. How I have been always dutiful in every respect. Yea, how I have denied myself always, even to allow myself to be called a fool by my shipmates. But Tom, I had one motive always. Education has taught me that it was part of my duty to act as I have done. I expect one day to be master myself and when so, I shall look for respect, therefore have I always shown it whilst a servant. Yes

[1] Thomas Le Page, who later transferred with Hilary to the *Duke of Gloucester* to go to Ichaboe in 1844 (p. 172); the two remained together for several other voyages.

Tom, I've pride, and that self-same pride has always bound me to keep away the slightest opportunity from my superiors of ever saying that I had acted disrespectfully. But Tom, I am now changed, awfully changed! My good principles have been trampled upon. The feeling of pride has now altered within me, and I shall bear no more ill-treatment from any man. The tame animal may be goaded on to that pitch, that ferocity will become the predominant part of its nature. T'is so with me! No more will Captain Taylor's hands be lifted upon me, or I swear to strike him to the earth. Yea, these hands of mine shall return blow for blow from any man. But I perceive the captain has come up from dinner, I will go and speak to him.' And suiting the action to the word I repaired aft, Tom trembling the while for fear that another scuffle should take place.

I on my part, was not unprepared for such, thinking it most likely that I should be refused a hearing and perhaps an attempt made to kick me forward for daring to disturb the sanctity of the quarter deck by my unholy appearance. I was however received. I was permitted to speak and the first thing I said was to ask permission to go on shore. My reply was, 'No, certainly not. What do you want to go on shore for?'

'I want to go to the English Consul's to claim that redress which I cannot otherwise have. You said this morning you would take me there yourself. I beg of you to do so.'

'If it pleases you, I will not do it', said the captain.

'Then, Sir, I shall take French leave and will go at once.'

'You dare not, you rascal.'

'I beg you pardon, Sir, I am not a rascal, dare not call me so again.'

'How, do you threaten me?'

'I merely beg of you to judge between me and rascality before you apply that epithet to me again. The fact of it is, Captain Taylor, I am an altered man. You have made me so and as I now stand before you I have sworn never again to bear the least ill-treatment at your hands without retaliating. I have borne it for seventeen long months, you have treated me like a dog, yea worse than a dog, and you are witness to yourself that I have borne such treatment indeed like a dog almost to the licking of the hand that ill-treated me. But I can assure you that you have much mistaken your man if you have taken my behaviour as a proof of want of spirit. No but I had expected by my placid behaviour to have won your tenderness and esteem, but I have been mistaken, the first I find you are totally deficient of, the latter is not worth gaining, and now that spirit which you have thought me void of whilst it has only been curbed within me, is now aroused and has sworn never to seek for that favour which hitherto it has sought in vain. I stand before you an injured man, for recollect that such I style myself, not a mere boy any longer. I was indeed but a boy when I first placed myself under your care, and might have expected to have been led by you as by the hand of a father but alas I have been taught otherwise. Seventeen months have wrought a great change in me, and the boy that felt himself obliged to surrender to a brutal treatment in silence has now become the man of undaunted spirit to repay him who dares to offer the slightest abuse. These are my feelings, Captain Taylor, and I feel thankful to you amidst all wrongs for having heard them. Now I've only to add that as much as I had desired to complete the voyage in the ship, I am now determined otherwise. You have driven me to a resolution the shadow of which had often visited me, but which I had as often banished, therefore I beg you will give me no further provocation, but allow me to quietly quit the vessel and you. I feel t'would be the much better plan, for if we remain together I am confident some evil will follow. I will not, I swear again, allow you to lift your hand to me with impunity, therefore let us separate ere each of us may repent it.'

I remained silent for a minute awaiting some reply from him I had addressed, but to my astonishment no reply met my ears. I knew not what to think. Never had I seen Captain Taylor so docile in appearance, there he was sitting on the skylight, his eyes bent downward fixed on vacancy and beating his two feet together. I was about to break this silence when he all at once, without offering the slightest remark on what I had been saying and apparently not knowing what to say, asked me the reason why I did not do as I was ordered. Now this question I really did not know the meaning of, I could not see what reference it had to the present in any form, that I had always been obedient to the letter

I felt confident of, therefore what did he mean? These thoughts crossed my mind in less time than it has taken me to write them down, but during that time however great or small I stood mute, all at once a thought flashed to my brain that perhaps he referred to his order of washing my hands with soap and water.

I was about to expatiate on that point when he stopped me by making some other remark which tended to convince me that the soap and water was not the point he alluded to. I continued by remarking that he could not say I had ever refused to do what I had been ordered, it was wrong of him to hint at such, for he must feel well convinced within himself that he was doing me an injustice. And oh I remember it to this day how I could read it in his countenance that he felt so convinced.

'Well then', continued he, 'go and do your work now as you have been ordered' and would have added 'and all shall be forgotten' had not his false pride hindered him.

No this I replied firmly 'No, Sir, for once and the first time I refuse. My mind is made up and I cannot change it.'

'Then', quoth he, 'you refuse your duty?'

'No, Sir, I do not, for you yourself turned me off that duty this morning and there is your chief officer to witness it, and it is not because you wish to reinstate me now that I am obliged to put up with your caprices. No, Sir, I have suffered too much already, and having sworn to suffer no more, I do not wish to remain subject to that provocation that will lead me into constant broils with you. I know your character well; now you know mine, therefore better it is to separate rather than that each of us should blush at our conduct hereafter. Discharge me then if you please, and I promise to refrain from executing my intentions of bringing you before justice.'

At these words he started up as if struck by a cannon ball. 'You bring me before justice indeed. I think that if I were to do my duty it would be I that would take you there and have you severely punished. Do you know what you have been guilty of in lifting your hands against me?'

I replied coolly that I was not of the opinion that guilt would be attributed to my behaviour, but I knew what I had done. I had only defended myself, a repetition of which would follow at every future attempt of his to maltreat me.

Our conversation here ended but not until he had once more ordered me to go to work which I felt not inclined to do. I left him and repaired on the forecastle once more, and taking my pipe sat smoking in silence ruminating in my mind what course I should follow. I had not been there long before the carpenter came forward. He had, as well as the chief mate and steward, overheard the altercation which had taken place between the captain and me.

Taking advantage of the former's exit from the deck he sat down at my side, and commenced the conversation by asking me what I intended to do, or how I intended to act. I answered firmly 'I'm going on shore, Tom'. Tom cast his eyes downward for a minute and seemed to be buried in thought. Now Tom and I were much attached to each other, and the only two that remained of our original crew before the mast. We had always been accustomed to be alone in every port, the rest being always sure of leaving the ship the moment of her arrival, each crew never making more than one passage, so that each one's presence seemed to have become necessary to the other's existence. Tom at last raising his eyes on a parallel with mine exclaimed 'Well, Harry' (I was generally called Harry), 'You had better alter your mind and make it up to stay, after all, the old man (meaning the captain) has quite melted down and you should also melt a little, besides if you go, what kind of a life am I going to lead here alone amongst a parcel of all sorts, such as we generally have in the ship?'

'Well Tom, all that's very good, but you know how much cause for disgust I have against the ship, you know how much I have been injured and you also know that were I to remain, it will only be a continuation of unhappiness for me, for I swear to you again that I would avenge myself for the least act of tyranny, and that not being my natural character would only tend to make me feel unhappy.'

'Well, but you may depend', said Tom, 'the old man will alter his behaviour towards you now that you have shown such a spirit, he will not dare to trifle with you.'

'Tom, you are only colouring the monster some shades too bright, and wish to dazzle my eyes with their lustre. T'wont do, Tom, I am only too well acquainted with his character to expect that. Once he has me on blue water as he terms it, he will tyrannize in every form.' Tom still continued to argue his point in favour of future good treatment, I to discredit the hopes as fast as they were formed, and I know not how many points I would have been the winner by, if it had not been that Mr Leask, our chief mate to whom also I was much attached, came forward and joined his persuasions with Tom's, he (Mr Leask) promising always to befriend me in case of need.

However, I find that I am prolonging a detail which it had been my intention to have curtailed long since. I will not recapitulate all the arguments made use of to induce me to remain, suffice it to add that I eventually gave way, and when overcome by their persuasions I replied, standing up and assuming that attitude which I fancy Wellington must have assumed when the day of Waterloo had decided its fate in his favour, 'Well Mr Leask, and you my old friend Tom, breaking at once all my former resolutions of never more sailing in the ship, I am overcome by your undisguised affection for me. I will for *your sakes* remain. But by the ethereal blue of heaven above me, I vow to perform my former resolutions if ever after this the hand of tyranny dares to wave its unrighteous sceptre over my head.' This concluded the matter and half an hour after I might have been seen astride on the jib boom scraping away as if nothing had happened.

Eight peaceful months

I may as well here observe to finish my detail of a voyage that will always be present to my memory. We were eight months after the incident just related ere the voyage was completed and if it had not been for a few quarrelsome words that passed between Captain Taylor and me on the very eve of our arrival in Guernsey I might say that they were eight months of one continued sea of peace unruffled by the faintest breath of commotion. Never have I witnessed a greater change in life and perhaps I might say that I have never valued peace so much as I did those last eight months of a voyage of terror. Two greater friends never existed than

Captain Taylor and myself, at least so far as appearances went. He would sit on the skylight whilst I was at the helm and chat with me as familiarly as though we had never had a cross word together. He often in the evenings would bring me up in a small mug my glass of grog or wine, and in point of duty he always treated me like one of his best seamen. But notwithstanding this good treatment on his part and my apparent familiarity with him, there still dwelt a bitterness in my heart against the man who had been cruel enough to have made seventeen months of my life wretched in the extreme.

Yea, though I endeavoured all in my power to conquer this feeling it still remained predominant. I wished and I strived to follow the dictates of the first inculcations received in my youth 'to forgive as we hope to be forgiven' and to a certain degree I did forgive him, but I could not forget. Whenever I received any of those small gifts above mentioned, my conscience invariably told me I was acting in opposition to its feelings, and I would have spurned any donation that proceeded from a hand that was stained with injustice towards me, but on the other hand, better to conceal my real feelings and although against my natural character, act a little of the hypocrite in order that peace and tranquillity might reign, than by acting otherwise have courted that continued misery of which I had already been too familiar with.

Home at last

We arrived home on the Easter Sunday of 1844[1] — Oh what a joyful day that was for me. The slave who receives his freedom after a life of servitude under some austere master has never tasted of greater joy than I did that day when I once more felt the soil of my home supporting my feet. O glorious day, I never can forget thee! The *Adelaide* was not actually bound home, she was bound to Carthegena in the Mediterranean but merely called *en passant*

[1] 7 April.

to take a new stock of supplies.

The day after our arrival I repaired on board to take away my clothes and finally bid adieu to the prison that had held me bound in its narrow space for so long a time. The captain was on board at the time and the moment he cast his eyes on me he called me aft to him. I repaired in obedience to his commands on the quarter deck. He had called me for the purpose of enquiring of me if I meant to continue the voyage in the vessel, for said he if you will, I shall give you the second officer's berth, and to prove to you that I have your good at heart I will give you five shillings per month more than I have ever paid to my second officers. Of course I thanked him very much for his apparent good will towards me, but declined accepting his favours under the plea that his were favours like the devil's, sweet in appearance but bitter in reality.

We parted here after a conversation that lasted for upwards of one hour in which I did not forget to admonish him sharply. It may be strange that I should have become the admonitor but so strange, so true, I feared not to point out to him all his faults. I have never feared to speak out boldly to any mortal like myself, so long as I felt convinced that truth guided my lips. I have seen him but once since this epoch, and poor fellow, it was but a short time he was allowed to tyrannize after I left him. As far as I can recollect it was but eighteen months afterwards that he came home and died; his was a cruel death being gnawed by tortures for days and weeks by a cancer in the chest. May he during that time have made his peace with a justly offended God, and may he now be enjoying that felicity above which he never allowed himself or his fellow creatures to enjoy here below. I have now done entirely with Captain Taylor, *Deus Garde*, and before I proceed any further on my voyage of life I must digress somewhat for the purpose of bringing forward a few words of remark which ought to have figured in the preceding pages but which have escaped my memory as far as dates were concerned.

He Falls in Love

The remarks I have to make are in the introduction of a certain personage who though much over-shadowed in the present part of my narrative may yet ere its conclusion shine out in brightness equal to the noon day sun. I introduce this person to the reader, not that I wish him to expect to be introduced to some renowned hero or heroine, but because I trust that like me he will be led to believe that the first impression is always the best. What has impression to do with the present subject I hear the reader ask? Reader, be patient! What I mean by impression is not a kiss, no, no, fair readers, I would not say that that first impression is always the best. How can I even think so when I recollect that Judas betrayed our Saviour with a kiss? But kissing has nothing to do with the matter at all, I wished it had at the time.

It was, as far as I can recollect, in the year 1840 or 1841 that I one day whilst in company with a friend was introduced into a certain country house belonging to an old salt water fish like myself although then but a young one. Now this said old son of Neptune had four daughters, and it is one of these I am about to introduce. The companion that was the means of introducing me to this being of angels was a relation of theirs, but not another angel and had been sent by his parents on a message thereto; now it happened that I was at play with him at the time, consequently followed him for company's sake. It was about an hour after dusk if my memory serves me rightly, that we entered the kitchen of this said lodge. One fair being alone was within it, at the table like a thrifty housewife engaged at her needle. I had never seen this angelic creature before, I entered not with the purpose of seeing her. My heart was yet a stranger to such desires. No, not for any gratification of my own did I enter this house, but merely to accompany my companion at play. Still a certain something, I knew not what, struck me when I first caught a sight of this heavenly creature and unconsciously was my gaze fixed upon her. What feeling was that which then seemed to dispossess me of the boyish propensities that had been predominant with me all day, and which I had brought to the threshold of the room, and caused me to sit as sedate as a judge engaged in a criminal cause, and whilst my playmate was fondling and teasing his fair cousin, I sat in silence and gazing on his happiness, wishing in my heart that I too had been a cousin. I knew not how it was then (I can understand it now) but that meeting seemed to have wrought in me a magic change. I left that house altogether another creature, but how I was changed, of what my real feelings were I could not have expressed. Let me however endeavour to recall the impression my youthful mind had received that evening of the fair being I have promised to introduce. How sweet always are the reminiscences of youth. How sweet to me are these!

Her countenance was of the most illuminating beauty. The arched brows, the small ripe mouth, the rounded chin and the oval outline of the face were of classic faultlessness. Her eyes large and dark, were full of fire and yet had nothing of boldness in their expression, but bright as her glances were there was still a sweetness in them that bespoke a purity and an innocence of soul. Her shining dark hair clustered about her well shaped head shone with a natural glory of its own. Her complexion was dazzlingly pure and transparent, and the mantling colour upon her cheeks derived not its carmine hue from the effects of art, but was the rich vermeil bloom shed there by nature's own hand.

She was not tall, not slender, not thin, but while replete with bayadère[1] elasticity her figure seemed filled out to all its just proportions. There was a purity of soul shining as it were through her — a halo of innocence and chastity surrounding her, a perfume of virginal freshness filling the atmosphere in which she moved. Let me again behold her now as her cousin was teasing her in all the wicked ways he could think of, now pulling her hair gently on the opposite side of her head to which he sat, then twitching at her work which she held in her hands and again stealing her reel of

[1] A bayadère is a Hindu dancing girl.

cotton, determined not to give it back until she had consented to allow him to steal a kiss. Here again the power of language altogether fails me either to depict the winning graces of her style, the beauty of her attitude, or the sylph-like delicacy of her movements. I fancy I can not better express myself than by saying it was the poetry of motion expressed and personified in a being of beauty to embellish it, and of soul to comprehend it.

Now as her shining dark hair clustered over her polished brow, she shook it away with the sweetest and most innocently coquettish toss of the head imaginable, then as she appeared to warm to the excitement of her cousin's artful tricks a beaming smile appeared upon her budding lips suggesting to me the idea of a young love cradled in a just opening rose. To gaze upon her thus invested as she was with the most ravishing charms, to behold her starry eyes sparkling more bright than the diamonds on any high born maiden's brow, was to me a ravishing sight, and one which has never gone from the eyes of my memory unto this day. Having lost her mother when she was very young, and having a kind and indulgent father, Louise had received none of those delicate tutorings and refined teachings, those timely checks upon temper and those repressions of self-will which only a mother or a very near and affectionate female relative can give; but hers was a character that needed them not. She was well educated and at the very time I am speaking of had just returned from France whither she had been finishing her education. She was also lady-like in manners, and possessing good conversational powers, the development of which had been hindered by no bashful coyness. Thus altogether Louise Blondel was a woman in form, mind, and intellect, at the age of sweet seventeen when she was still a mere girl in years.

After a stay of about one hour or a little above and having delivered his message my friend proposed that we should now return homewards. On our way he asked me several question as to what I thought of his fair cousin, was she not a nice girl? was she not an angel? etc, etc, but there was a certain something which I knew not how to account for, that kept me from answering those questions with as much genuine frankness as he seemed to expect. Was I jealous of his privilege in claiming a relationship to that fair being? I must have been. Yes, I envied him. I was pensive and silent, and I felt thankful that the shades of evening prevented him from observing my altered countenance. Still, my altered mood from that in which I was ere we had entered the house we were now leaving fast behind us did not escape him, and he asked me several times what was the matter, but I as many times gave some evasive reply.

So arriving at the cross roads on which our way lay in opposite directions, I bid him a very good night and onward I sped, meditating all the way upon the charms of her whose image was now indelibly impressed on my young heart. I found myself at the door of the house before I knew that I had achieved half the distance.

Some time afterwards I was at sea again, but this fair form haunted me where ere I roamed. In the dreary night amidst the howling of the gale methought I sometimes heard the music of her voice in sweetest accents contrasting with the scene. In the stillness of the calm, in the midnight watch methought her fair form was flitting before me with aerial grace upon the mighty ocean. In fact, to be brief, neither time nor circumstances ever had the power to obliterate that first impression received on the eventful eve mentioned.

Years rolled on in succession and I had never had the favoured opportunity of meeting her again, but ultimately through the proposed alliance of my sister with a relation of hers[1] an intimacy was contracted which threw at once an opportunity in my favour of sometimes meeting with her, each time I saw her helped materially to strengthen the feeling of admiration which had long existed in my breast for her, and gradually that feeling I felt change from admiration to affection but twas not until when at sea many years after our first interview I began to fear that some more favoured being than myself might in my absence sue for her hand and be accepted, that I found my heart was susceptible of love. I wished in my heart that I was a few years older but young as I

[1] If this led ultimately to marriage it cannot apparently be identified from the Marquand family's own pedigree.

was how could I dare to entertain the faintest hopes of meeting with the approbation of my parents in a suit of love; and to act against their will it was my intention never to do if I possibly could avoid it.

It was in May 1847 that I left my ship in London to come home for the purpose of spending a few days amongst my friends ere I returned on another voyage. Now I had determined within myself that I should try to make a conquest this time, but before I allowed myself to run too deep in the passion that was growing every day within me, I resolved to sound the feelings of my parents with regard to the object of my choice. She and I often met during this visit of mine in Guernsey and, oh, how I felt each time we met that I loved her. Yea and I flattered myself sometime after we had met that I had found out some small proof that she was not totally indifferent to me. In this position and with equal feelings how many would have rushed at once into the delicious stream of open avowal which opened itself before me heedless of any consequences. But such were not my feelings, the power of self-denial has always been great with me, and the filial duty I felt I owed to my parents constrained me to do nothing without first consulting them, for fear by any wayward action of giving them a moments pain. But on sounding them imperceptibly I was mortified in finding that it would be useless to seek their consent. This was a great trial for me indeed! I found that the object of my love was despicable in their eyes. I grieved sadly and no one knew my secret grief but I denied myself, rather than act contrary to what I felt was my duty. I resolved to rejoin my vessel at once, and to wait patiently for a more favourable opportunity, which a something whispered in my mind would soon arrive; but ere I quitted the place that held the only object under the sun for whom I wished to live I sometimes reflected what if when I returned I should find her ravished by some other suitor? Would it not be better for me to avow that love my heart burned with ere I went away? I would not. I had rather never marry, than marry her who would be refused admittance at my father's house; I had rather lose the fair object of my heart's desire than to link her with a family who would refuse to own her as their daughter during my absence at sea.

Ah, had I been a landsman t'would have been different, she would have needed no other protection than that I would have been always near to afford. I thought of all this and weighed matters well in my mind, and whenever I reasoned with myself thus I invariably felt the whisperings of conscience telling me that all would yet be well. A few days afterwards I was on my way to rejoin my vessel, and a few days more I was on my way to the West Indies. T'was then when I felt myself on the mighty ocean that I regretted the part I had acted. Oh that I had even written to her a few lines on my arrival in London, merely to inform her of my safe arrival, it would have always proved to her that I had not forgotten her. But how was the innocent and artless girl to know that I loved her? Had I ever declared my passion? No, I had not dared to do so, nor had she ever ventured to encourage me in such daring. But yet I consoled myself; to those who love the signs and evidences of love in others are as intelligible as a language which though unknown to some, is yet a facile means of interchanging thoughts with those who can speak it. For love has its own peculiar language, which though often ineffable, is nevertheless potent in its silent eloquence — a language whose syllables, and words, and sentences are expressed by a thousand little circumstances that pass unnoticed by the common observer, but which are full of meaning to those whose heart affords the key to the reading of those mysteries. Thus a gesture — a suppressed sigh — a look hurriedly given and as hurriedly withdrawn — the flitting blush upon the cheeks — the thrill which is mutually experienced when the hands accidentally come in contact — the visible quivering of the entire form at such contact — the subdued hushed tones in which words are spoken at one moment, and the suddenly excited warmth with which they are uttered at another, although the words themselves may be but commonplace, all these are the signs and emblems, and soul waftings of love. But more! When two beings of kindred dispositions, and congenial spirits, and in whose union their appears to be a fitness marked by nature, and designated by heaven — when two such beings meet, although they may give no single one of those signs of mutual passion, yet is there not such a thing as the soft and mystic transfusion of souls, taking place by some unknown and ineffable agency, a blending of the spirits such as no gross passion can know, and no common nature experience, an interchange of silent whisperings from heart to heart, the whole passing all human understanding.

If the reader can comprehend all this he will not be surprised that I said in a preceding page I understood the cause of such strange (then to me) feelings at my first interview with the subject of my present narrative. He will neither be surprised that I found consolation intermingled with my very fears. Yes, I have often dwelt upon this epoch of my life and as often proved that there is indeed such a thing as the soft and mystic transfusion of souls, a blending of spirits, an interchange of silent whisperings from heart to heart the whole passing all human understanding indeed.

'I have now done with this interesting part of my narrative. The reader is now with me acquainted with the fair being I had promised to introduce, he must now allow a few years to elapse during which time he may follow me through the several windings and irregularities that have marked the path of my existence and then may be, a further introduction will take place between him and the party that he so reluctantly has left behind.

– 1844 –

The Nautical Story is Resumed

It was about Easter of 1844 that I led myself away from my regular track to fill up these last few pages. It must be about that same time that I find myself on the right track again. I had just arrived at home after a long voyage of upwards of two years. How I was kindly greeted by my parents and all the etceteras of a reunion I will not detail. Suffice it to say that I was very happy for the time being.

I was much altered in appearance, two years of feeding on salt junk and hard biscuit at that critical period of life often makes a wonderful change. I was looked upon now as a man, and indeed I thought myself such. There was not a point in a seaman's duty that I was not competent to perform, and as for the points in the top sails, they were but like shoe strings to me. My father was proud of me and often declared I was an honour to my profession for said he 'You seem to take so much pride in it'.

'I do indeed, Father, take a great deal of pride in it, and to myself for belonging to it, but you would not wonder at it', continued I, 'if you knew how great my ambition is to become a master to all intents and purposes; not merely master of a ship, but master of the profession.'

'Well', said my father, 'I am glad to see you push yourself on, I will always be a help to you when I can', and for my encouragement he added, 'as soon as you attain your first promotion of officer I will make you a present of my watch' (handing it out at the same time). 'Here is a watch that I have had for many long years, and which has never kept irregular time, one that I value a great deal, but it shall be yours at the time I have mentioned.'

I thanked him exceedingly. Little did he think how soon he would have to part with his treasure. My stay at home was not of very long duration for it was on the 14th May that I was sought after by the owner of a vessel that was then fitting out in our harbour for Ichaboe on the west coast of Africa, to know if I would make one of her crew. After enquiring who was going to command her (for I remembered my last voyage), I replied I had no objection. A few days afterwards I was sent for again when I was told by the owner that it was his wish I should go as second officer and that he would be glad if I went on board to see the stores and provisions taken in. Now this was unexpected, and I replied that I certainly hesitated in accepting his kind offer fearing that I was yet unqualified.[1]

'Oh', said he, 'You have qualifications enough if you wish. I am satisfied by what I have heard of you that you will do.' Very well, thought I, it won't do to refuse a good chance, so I agreed and the thing was settled.

I went home that evening quite elated, I found the family sitting round a small table diversified with all the paraphernalia of ladies' work boxes, my father engaged with his spectacles on his nose making a calculation of arithmetic about the value of some of the many productions of his estate, a piece of chalk for his pencil, and a pair of bellows for his slate. 'Now, Father', said I, disturbing him for a moment, 'I shall wear a watch tomorrow if you've no objection.'

He looked at me through his eye glasses for a moment, and then enquired what I meant. 'Why nothing more simple', continued I. 'You promised to make me a present of your watch as soon as I had become an officer in the merchant service. Now I stand before you as such, and consequently claim the promise.' Further questions were asked by him and a further explanation given by me. The old gentleman was satisfied, and true to his word he pulled the watch out of his fob, and in form, and with due honours placed it round my neck saying 'There, my boy, may you wear it as long as I have and a little longer.' I thanked my father sincerely

[1] See below, p. 168, for the possibility that Hilary may be misrepresenting his position at the outset of this voyage, which in turn suggests that the family celebrations at his promotion may have been somewhat overdone.

as well for the watch as for the good counsels that followed it, promising faithfully to do all that laid in my power to give him that satisfaction in his old age which he so much expected of me through a steady and persevering character.

– 1844 –

Fourth Voyage

May

Ichaboe, South West Africa

In a few days I was at my duty on board my vessel devoting myself to my new appointment with all the energy of a true British seaman. This vessel was called the *Duke of Gloucester*, her commander John Touzeau. She was bound to Ichaboe on the south west coast of Africa for a cargo of guano.[1] It was on the 21st of May 1844 that I again bid a farewell to my parents after but a short stay with them on this occasion and once more was launched on my favourite element, the mighty deep.[2]

It seemed to me quite a new thing, as it were a new life I was commencing, being now an officer in command instead of happy Jack before the mast. It might be thought that at my age, being then only nineteen, an appointment such as mine would have been inductive of pride in me, but no, such was not the case, the responsibility with which I felt myself invested rather humbled me than otherwise, certainly I had that pride which becomes every

[1] Guano is a natural manure found in great abundance on some sea coasts, consisting of the excrement of sea-fowl. Ichaboe is an island in Lüderitz Bay, off the coast of what later became (German) South West Africa.

[2] There is a crew list and agreement to serve for this voyage in BT 98/291 (Part 1). The crew signed on on 29 May 1844 for a voyage to Ichaboe; then either returning to Falmouth for orders (calling at St Helena for water if necessary) and discharging at a port in the United Kingdom or France, or alternatively, loading in Africa for Brazil, seeking freight there and returning to Europe. According to the agreement, however, Hilary did *not* sign on as second officer but as an ordinary seaman, although at £2 a month he was paid more than the other seamen and the same as the ship's carpenter. Any appointment as second mate must therefore have been in the nature of an informal arrangement with the master, which may explain why at least one of the seamen was reluctant to accept his authority.

man in whatever situation he may be, I knew my duty and would not let it go unperformed. Moreover I looked for a ready compliance from those beneath me to whom my orders were given. This on the first part of the voyage created some degree of unpleasantness between myself and a young man my senior in years who was before the mast, and certainly as smart a man as ever hauled a bowline. Being as good a man as I was he harboured the mistaken idea that he had no right to be ordered about by me who was yet his junior, but I soon taught him better, calling him to account one day after repeated insolence on his part.[1]

I spoke to him in the following manner. 'What is the reason, Edward, that you are constantly so rebellious against me? That you are as good a man as I am in point of duty I make no doubt, but that you are in point of education you do not show it, for it is proof of ignorance in you to act as you do, know you not that I am above you in position, and that it is a part of my duty to order whilst it is yours to obey? What would you feel some of these days when you are in a position as I am now, if you were treated by another as you wish to treat me? Now, I'll tell you what, Edward, I have withstood your behaviour towards me with no small degree of patience hitherto, but as I stand before you now a living sinner, I swear to put up with it no longer. You are my senior in years but that has nothing to do with it. I would not care if you were as old as Methuselah, you shall obey me when I command or by heavens I shall make you. And if you should think yourself a better man than me in this last respect I'm your man to try it on now.' And suiting the action to the words I clenched my fists and stood in an attitude of battle before him. Whether he found that I was in the right, and he in the wrong, or whether he thought that my skill at boxing was above his I know not, but certain it is that he declined the challenge and ever after that seemed to have formed a different opinion of me by a ready compliance to my commands.

[1] Cf. note on previous page.

They lose their anchor and make for Rio de Janeiro

We had a pleasant though long passage to Ichaboe but a very short stay there, having lost our two bower and stream anchors[1] before we had been in the roadstead 24 hours, consequently were obliged to run out to sea again, and our captain scarcely knowing how to act for the best, having no nearer port to go to for anchors than St Helena, or the Cape of Good Hope, with the uncertainty of obtaining a cargo at his return for at least five or six months, the place being crowded with shipping which was the occasion of our misfortune, having been obliged to bring up in the surf for want of room elsewhere, after some hesitation made up his mind to proceed for Rio de Janeiro and although at his return he was much blamed by his owners, yet I think he acted for the best, and only as I would have done in his place. We arrived at Rio after a speedy run across the South Atlantic and were soon supplied with anchors from the British men-of-war in the harbour who distinguished our signal long before we had entered it.

After Rio – London – Arriving January 1845

Having remained there some weeks we at last took freight for London where we ultimately arrived in January of 1845 without anything transpiring throughout the voyage worthy of note. Here on our arrival we learnt the consignees had orders from the owners to sell the vessel after the discharge of her cargo, consequently we were paid off and on our way home a few days afterwards.[2]

[1] The bower anchors (best and small) are those carried at the bows of a vessel; the term can also apply to the cable attached to either. The stream anchor is intermediate in size between the bower and kedge and is used to moor a ship in a sheltered position.

[2] The crew list (BT 98/291 Part 1) was handed in on 14 Jan. 1845.

Paid off – and home

Here was I once more on my native soil amidst my friends enjoying the happiness only known to them who return from exile. I enjoyed my stay at home this time the more because I had frequent opportunities of meeting in company with a certain young lady whose image had so long been daguerreotyped[1] on my heart and in consequence whose presence in reality tended in no small way to make me happy, although I feel convinced even at this present moment that whilst I enjoyed this happiness sweeter to me than any happiness I had yet ever enjoyed, none were cognizant of it, that is none of my parents or friends, but that she who was the author of such happiness must have had a kindred feeling, I believe. Yes, as I have said before, that soft and mystic transfusion of souls was taking place, and though we said nothing to each other that savoured of more than common courtesy, and though in fact there seemed to be the greatest distance between us sometimes, yet I feel certain that a silent interchange of whisperings from heart to heart was passing, and that our feelings were mutual.

She was a companion of my sister's and now and then would come to spend the afternoon at home. At other times my sister would go and spend the afternoon with her and family, where I sometimes did accompany them. By this means it was that an opportunity served which I valued greatly, that was of watching her, of scrutinising her very words, her actions, her movements, and all unperceived; I compared her with her sisters; sometimes I thought they shone on a degree of equality but soon after would follow some convincing proof that *she* was *the gem* of brightness, thus and thus, did I watch over the object of my esteem at that time, and thus did I try my young heart to prove if its feelings were but evanescent. Whether they were so or not, or whether I watched in vain, the sequel will prove.

Five or six weeks thus happily passed away and I began to

[1] An interestingly early figurative use of the verb derived from the photographic process named after its inventor, Louis-Jacques-Mandé Daguerre (1789–1851), which itself dates only from 1839.

grow anxious for future employment. I repaired daily to the harbour to note the arrivals and sailings of the different ships, and at the same time on the look out for a berth. I had not long watched before I learnt that a brig was arrived in London from the Brazils, a part of whose crew were just came over, having been discharged in that port. I fell in the same day I gathered this intelligence with two or three of my old shipmates, one of which the reader has already been acquainted with, my old friend Tom, with whom five and twenty months of misery had been passed on board the *Adelaide* and who I should have said was also one of the crew of the *Duke of Gloucester*.[1] I acquainted them of the news I had just gathered and asked them if they felt inclined to offer their services for this new ship, for new she was indeed, being only just returned from her second voyage.[2] They at once expressed their willingness at doing so, and without any more ado we set off three of us to the ship's husband to ascertain how many places were vacant, the nature of the voyage etc, etc, being told that several places were vacant and that the vessel was bound to the West Indies (island of St Kitts). We offered our services, I as second officer, Tom as seaman, and the third as carpenter.[3]

The next day our services were accepted and a few days after we were on our way to London again, the place we had so recently left. We arrived in due time with our bags and baggage, found our ship in the West India Docks, presented ourselves to the captain, were accepted, and the next day saw us at our respective duties. The ship I was now on board of was called the *Swift*, her commander John David.

[1] Cf. above, pp. 150, 154–4 for Thomas Le Page on board the *Adelaide*. The crew list for the *Duke of Gloucester*'s voyage to Ichaboe (BT 98/291 Part 1) confirms his presence on board the vessel: he was then 29, whereas Hilary was only 19.

[2] The *Swift*, a brig of 195 tons, was built by Henry Marquand and John de la Mare at South Beach, St Peter Port, in 1842. Her original dimensions were $82^{1}/_{10}$ ft long, $21^{1}/_{2}$ft broad, and $14^{1}/_{5}$ft deep in the hold; she had a figurehead and a square stern. (Ex inf. Dr Alan Jamieson from Guernsey shipping registers in BT 107.)

[3] The crew list (see below, p. 173) reveals that this was Henry Malny.

– 1845 –

Fifth Voyage

March

Bound for St Kitts

By the time we joined her she had nearly completed her cargo, so that in a few days we were in readiness for sailing and on the 9th day of March 1845 we did sail from the docks towards our destination.[1] We met with very severe weather going down the Channel which greatly retarded our voyage. I had not been many days on board before I found that Captain David was a thorough good man, and practised strictly that commandment which tells us to 'love one another.'

I was glad having fallen in with such a person, and I at once resolved to act in every sense to the utmost of my power to prove to him that the respect with which he treated me was not ill-placed.

Our chief mate[2] was a surly kind of a fellow and it was not in a few instances that I had to deny myself in order to keep peace. He certainly gave me provocation enough on several occasions to have shown my teeth, but for the sake of the captain who was a man of peace, I bore all with closed lips, and it was not with a little degree of satisfaction that on each occasion I perceived his marked satisfaction at my behaviour.

[1] Two crew lists and an agreement to serve survive for this voyage in BT 98/664. The list handed in before departure is dated 11 March 1845, as is the agreement to serve for a voyage from London to St Kitts and back. Hilary signed on as second mate at a wage of £2 10s a month; the crew also included a first officer, a carpenter, five seamen, a cook and an apprentice.

[2] The papers cited in the previous note identify the mate as Clement Day, aged 22, two years older than Hilary.

July — Dock in London, then to Guernsey

We performed our voyage to St Kitts and back again to London in four months exactly, and by this time I and the captain were thoroughly acquainted with each other's character and capacities, and I am not a little flattered when I say that mine were quite acceptable in his sight. After the discharge of our cargo and taking in of ballast we sailed for home where we duly arrived and spent again a few weeks of unmitigated happiness.[1]

I might here dwell for a while to describe the halo of sunshine that surrounded me during this my stay among my bosom friends, aye, *bosom friends indeed*, but as I have a long journey to go and very little paper to waste, besides less money to spend for more, I will pass over this happy part of my existence in order to preserve the nib of my pen to mark out a far happier one.

[1] The agreement to serve was handed in at the Custom House at St Kitts on 25 April 1845 and returned to the master on 31 May, presumably immediately prior to his departure. The crew were discharged at London on 12 July 1845.

– 1845 –

Sixth Voyage

September

Newport, South Wales – Málaga – London

Reader, allow a few weeks to pass unnoticed, or if you cannot do so, let your own imagination fill up the space my pen has refused to transcribe and then meet me again when the scene has changed to the 14th September of the year above mentioned, when with an overflowing heart replete with grief I am again about quitting the home of my 'Childhood' and the *bosom friends* just spoken of, meet me then I say and give me your sympathy — I need it! Have you, I ask, ever known the pang of tearing yourself away from a *bosom* friend? Then I have your sympathy. Yes, it has done me good, and now I can proceed.

On the day above mentioned the little *Swift* was again seen passing rapidly the extreme point of the beautiful island in whose port she had stayed for a short time, as it were resting her weary self from the labours she had previously achieved, bearing away with her many a noble heart now filled with grief which became greater and greater as each receding speck on the land banished from view, the memento of some joyous sport. Onward she went heedless of the sorrow that filled the heart of her gallant crew, and in a few hours no trace was left to view of that sweet home from where dwelt the bosom friend whose bereaved heart was perhaps now silently invoking a blessing upon us.

We were bound to Newport in Wales on this occasion but from thence we knew not whither. In course of time but after a severe passage in the Bristol Channel we arrived. It was some solace at least so soon after quitting home to be able to receive tidings from, and to be able to communicate with, those we had not yet done sorrowing for. Time, which like tide waits for no man, soon slipped by, and the 27th October saw us again hauling out of dock with a full cargo of 'black diamonds'[1] bound for Málaga.[2] Nothing particular occurred during our passage which was performed in sixteen days, of course we encountered some heavy gales and high seas etc, but such common occurrences I have become so familiar with, that I do not think them worth the writer's trouble of a recapitulation.[3] We were fortunate enough after the discharge of our cargo to obtain another for London, and certainly the most handsome cargo that it has ever fallen to my lot to handle. It consisted of raisins, almonds, grapes and nuts, the grapes so large that many of the bunches weighed two pounds: the raisins were nothing inferior in quality or size, in fact the whole of the cargo was one of choice fruit. After a long passage retarded by the homeward bound mariner's direst enemy, the east wind, we were once more on the Thames discharging our valuable freight only adding, as it were, a handful to the already innumerable quantities stored in the vast magazines of Lower Thames Street.[4]

[1] i.e. coals. [HM]

[2] There are two crew lists in BT 98/664 for the sailing from Newport to Málaga dated 25 Oct. 1845, and an agreement to serve (witnessed by W.H. Martin) dated two days earlier, in which Hilary, aged 21, is listed as second mate on a wage of £2 10s. a month; his mate's ticket number was 5,885. The diary kept by William Day, the chief mate (see Introduction, p. xxix), confirms Hilary's account: his entry for Monday 27 Oct. 1845 reads: 'At 4 a.m. hauled from the Docks and worked her down to Penarth Roads. At 9.30 a.m. brought up in 9 fathoms of water'.

[3] The agreement to serve was deposited with the British consul at Málaga on 14 Nov. 1845. Cf. William Day's diary for the previous day: '4 p.m. after working many short tacks brought up in Málaga Mole. Oh precious cargo of coals'. Earlier entries confirm Hilary's references to bad weather on the outward passage.

[4] The agreement to serve was returned to the master by the consul at Málaga on Friday 5 Oct. and the *Swift* departed the following Tuesday, when Day noted: 'At 1 p.m. unmoored. At 3 p.m. sailed from Málaga Mole. 8 o'clock close reef, dead too, continuation throughout Levanter'; there are also references on subsequent days to an easterly (i.e. Levanter) wind. The crew list and agreement were handed in at London on 3 Jan. 1846; Day notes that at 4 a.m. that day the *Swift* was 'hauled alongside cargo quay, delivered our beautiful cargo of fruit, too late for Aristocrats' Christmas dinner'.

Hilary falls down the hold
Three weeks in the London Hospital

It was on this occasion that an incident took place which calls my attention for a few moments to a retrospect of the particulars.

We had discharged our fruit and had hauled the ship out into the stream to discharge a quantity of lead (in pigs) which we had taken as ballast at Málaga, when one fine cold January morning a barge came alongside for the said lead. Preparations were immediately made for discharging, and I, being second mate and knowing my place, which was down the hold, repaired to the main hatchway for the purpose of descending, and when in the act my foot slipped, I scarcely can tell how, and in one moment I was precipitated headlong at the bottom of the hold, my head coming into contact with the sharp edge of one of the pigs of lead and my back across the keelson.

My head was cut open in a frightful manner, and the blood gushing out at once in streams whilst I lay motionless. For the time being, everyone thought I was killed on the spot. But not so, I was merely stunned by the terrible blow — and in a very short time was on my legs again and ascended a ladder myself and reached the deck where I was glad to find a seat as I began to feel faint through the loss of blood. The mate at once bound up the wound temporary and without any further hesitation I was conveyed to the London Hospital in a cab where the doctors, after dressing the wound properly, thought it advisable to detain me, but in fact my back had received so much harm that I could scarcely keep my body upright and therefore being such a cripple, I was fain to stop there where I was sure of receiving every attention my case demanded.

I was in that establishment three weeks, and during that time had ample opportunity to witness the care and attention with which every patient is attended, the regularity and discipline that is strictly maintained, and the efficiency of good servants whose number is not spared. Indeed I could never say too much in praise of the London Hospital, and I would strongly recommend any individual whoever he may be, whether high or low, rich or poor, whose misfortune it may be to meet with an accident in the vicinity of this establishment, to at once order himself to be conveyed there rather than lose time in fruitless (often so) searches after a doctor.

Here he will be sure of finding one ready at a moment's notice to attend to his minutest wants, and his wound will have been dressed, or his fracture set in half the time it would have taken to summon assistance elsewhere; after which he may then retire, if the nature of the accident will admit, to his own comfortable lodgings if he has one and would prefer it. Let not the individual whose pecuniary circumstances are good, refuse my advice because he scruples at receiving attention gratis; to him I say you owe your life to society, let not your scruples gain the ascendancy where life or death are so closely concerned. Do yourself justice; do justice to society; accept the proffered attention of him that seeks no reward, because no reward is allowed him for his services to you; then having acted wisely if your generous heart still prompts you to discharge its debt, remember that the establishment you owe your life to is 'Supported by Voluntary Contributions'.

– 1846 –

Seventh Voyage

March

Trinidad – Jamaica

It was not very many days after my dismissal from this establishment that I was again performing my duties on board the *Swift* and but a few more ere we were again ready for sea with a full cargo of what Jonathan would term 'Notions'[1] but what we more civilized Britishers call a 'general Cargo', and bound for the island of Trinidad. This voyage I was deprived the pleasure of paying my friends at home a visit, but a punctual correspondence kept me informed of their welfare and trusting to a speedy return I was fain to bid them adieu on the 3rd of March 1846.[2]

Our passage to Trinidad was rather tedious and long, only arriving on the 57th day after quitting the West India Docks.[3] Nothing particular transpired on the said passage, the usual routine of everyday life at sea, chequered as it is, becomes so natural to every sailor that he can find nothing to take notice of, although in reality every day affords changes and incidents enough for an active mind to feast upon, but as my present work was only taken in hand for the amusement of myself, I have but to note the more

[1] The *SOED* describes this plural use of the word ('Wares of various kinds forming a miscellaneous cargo') as American, dating from 1805. For Hilary's use of the name Jonathan when referring to American practice cf. p. 55 above.

[2] The crew list and agreement to serve (BT 98/938) are dated 25 Feb. 1846; Hilary, aged 21, signed on as second mate at £2 7s. month on a voyage to Trinidad and Jamaica. William Day's diary confirms the date of departure as 3 March.

[3] William Day's diary entry for 22 April reads: '4 p.m. hauled again by the winds, daylight close to Bocas, caught fine breeze. 2.30 been on the ground in Port of Spain. Thus ends passage'. The agreement to serve was handed in at Trinidad the following day.

conspicuous incidents of each voyage while the everyday particulars will fall quite fresh on memory's tablet at each page glanced upon hereafter.[1]

But as I have hinted before, should this meet the eye of any of my friends against my will let them not call me selfish, each of us has some desire to gratify. I am gratifying mine when I am writing this, without noting the everyday particulars of my varied life, and assuredly, if he requires more, he at once proves himself the selfish one, by not receiving the same satisfaction that was mine for whom it was only intended.

Our stay in Trinidad was about three weeks which time was employed discharging our cargo and ballasting the vessel.[2] I might here dwell for a few moments to give a description of the island but for the reason above stated I decline and carry my thoughts onward to our passage and arrival at Dry Harbour in Jamaica. The passage alluded to is certainly one often attended with diversified beauties of scenery. Sailing among the many islands which lie[3] in the route each of which is distinct from the other by its excellence in majesty and grandeur, the varied beauty adorning them enlivened to a surprising degree by a cloudless tropical sky, reflected in the ultramarine of the waters beneath, teeming with life, of which the smallest object is a gem of itself.

All, all these objects of admiration in nature's great field of surprising architecture strikes the mind of the observer with a sublime feeling of veneration for the creator and ruler of them all, while at the same time it enlivens and beautifies the scenery around. In due course of time and after leaving the above variegated beauties in the rear, we reached our destination.

Dry Harbour, on the north coast of Jamaica, is a small natural

[1] Although Hilary could recall nothing out of the ordinary on this voyage, Day noted on 4 April (in his only direct reference to him in his diary): '2nd mate bad eyes'.

[2] The agreement to serve was returned to the master on 7 May and the *Swift* left Trinidad on the 13th, when William Day noted in his diary: '5 a.m. left Chagaramus Bay when we have ballasted ship to sweat of our brows. Confound sandflies. Noon well out of Bocas'.

[3] Emended from 'lay' in the MS.

basin formed by a curve in the land and fronted by an immense coral reef having an opening of about 50 yards wide, which admits vessels of any burthen.[1] Here along the coast at certain seasons of the year a great swell prevails but inside of this natural protection, the coral reef, the sea is perfectly calm so that ships lay as comfortable as in a dock.

Hilary nearly drowns

It was on entering this harbour that I met with an accident which I will rank among the conspicuous incidents referred to in the preceding page.[2]

We were running before a gentle breeze at the rate of six knots or thereabouts and had just taken a negro pilot on board when the order was given to lower the stern boat down in readiness for carrying out a line the moment the ship should have entered the opening in the reef, so as to keep the vessel to windward. Now to all nautical persons it will at once appear evident that the order could not be executed without danger attending it: had the boat been suspended on the quarter of the ship it would have been a very different thing.

As it was, the order was repeated by both the pilot and the master after I had dared to make an observation on the difficulty existing due to the ship's way through the water. Of course, an order repeated was to me a command of immediate obedience, accordingly into the boat I jumped calling out at the same time to the men at the falls to lower away smartly, which certainly was

[1] Dry Harbour, on the north coast of Jamaica, is now known as Discovery Bay: see *Admiralty Sailing Directions. West Indies Pilot (North Western Part)*, I (1971 ed.), p. 244.

[2] William Day's diary notes that the *Swift* arrived at Dry Harbour on 21 May and includes what appears to be a brief note of the episode which Hilary now describes at some length: 'At 8 a.m. abreast Dry Harbour, couldn't make it at run passed it, consequently had to thrash up to windward. At 1 p.m. pilot came on board. 6 p.m. after heavy rain, thunder and lightning, anchor in Dry Harbour, swamped jolly boat and lost all gear'.

done as smartly as the falls could run through the blocks, but no sooner had the boat's keel touched the water than she turned half over emptying herself of all her appendages as well as of my humble self who, finding the water so very *wet* and cold, lost all at once the powers of speech else I dare say I should have cried for help in my present distress. As it was no one could afterwards brand me with fear for I bore my perilous situation so manfully that not a word ever escaped my lips, but if any one had been there that could read the language of the eyes I certainly should have been detected for, oh powers!, what glances did I throw upwards at every succeeding appearance I made above water. Consider my situation, hung by my arms to the tackle fall which I had caught hold of as the first thing that came in contact with my outstretched hands after my sudden immersion, and dangling in the air to a height of eight or ten feet, then under water to a depth equally great, scarcely time to regain my breath in one element before it was lost in the other. All the while the weight of my body was weakening my grasp to that degree that the sensation of 'I give up' came over me several times. Consider yourself in this situation, reader, and ask yourself if you would have borne it so heroically as never once to ask for assistance providing every time you opened your mouth it would not have been filled with salt water as mine was? I only know of one hero who bore his perilous situation with equal silence and that was Jonah when in the whale's belly.

You will ask me where all the crew were that they did not assist me, and I will tell you that the ship was in the mean time just in the most precarious situation, that of entering the reefs, therefore the master, mate, pilot and crew were all busied with attending to her safety, clewing up her sails, hauling round the yards, preparing the anchor for letting go etc, etc. A ship's safety in a moment like this requires the strict attendance of all her crew, a fellow creature's life is only looked upon in a secondary sense! I have said all the crew were attending to the ship, but I should have said with the exception of one, who was watching my diving feats over the stern with apparent wonder at my unparalleled dexterity, never once attempting to give me the least assistance, but every now and then enquiring why I did not come up instead of playing there the game of hide and seek. My strength was failing me fast and I had no alternative than to let go and take that repose in a watery grave which I had proved for the last half hour did not exist between earth and sea. I could not swim, and if I could my limbs were so deadened through my late gymnastics, that it was a certain case of going down the moment I relinquished my grasp of the tackle fall. Another minute and there is no doubt I would have let go, as I was fast becoming insensible, the gurgling sound in my ears at every immersion, and the swallowing of so much of the briny liquid, the former drowning the activity of the brain, the latter the pulsations of the heart. It was just then adieu to my youthful hopes! adieu brighter prospects! adieu to the world! and shall I say it? the image of one angel like being fluttered before the nearly blinded eyes of my reeling brain.

Methought I hesitated to whisper the cruel word adieu to her, when extending her hands she vanished from my sight, but left the word hope so legible in her trail that I felt the pulsations of my heart reanimated. At that moment I looked up and lo!, the chief mate and two or three of the crew were over me busy to my rescue. I felt a rope had been thrown over my head, instinct taught me to let it drop under my arms which I did, I cannot now tell how, but that moment I felt the rope secured to my body I let go the tackle fall and abandoned myself to the mercy of my rescuers; the next recollection that I have is finding myself lying on the deck covered over with a quantity of blankets etc and discharging enormous quantities of salt water out of my inward tanks, which never were intended for such a cargo of nauseous liquid.

A few hours of repose accompanied with sundry resuscitating measures brought me back to vigorous life, and a few hours more all would have been forgotten had not the image of that flitting angel kept constant place in my thoughts. Was it to her that I owed my life? Was it her guardian presence that gave me strength to hold fast the thread that suspended me between life and death? I decline giving my opinion. But certain it is that to the cheering word of hope she so deeply impressed on my dying heart, I responded with invigorating exertions. And who was the image of celestial appearance that so bid me hope when earthly hope was given up? Reader, I forbear to explain. Nevertheless true it is that destiny had formed the body whose representative that image was, to form no imaginary part in my existence in after years. Oh how wonderful is the electric power of sympathy? How mysterious and awfully grand is the power of union between two hearts, when as yet the tenements that contain them are estranged from each other; I have in a foregoing page dwelt on this true and wonderful subject and although I would fain continue it here, for the sake of my present task I must decline.

Long and happy stay in Dry Harbour

Our stay in Dry Harbour which exceeded sixty days by three, cannot be left unnoticed. I had never before that period, nor have I ever since, spent two months of equal felicity in any harbour, or in any ship; although true it is that this felicity was not an uninterrupted felicity, however of that hereafter.

I have already introduced Captain David, my present master, in a preceding page as a thorough good man practising the dictates of Christianity. It only now remains for me to add that through his Christian character flowed the cause of our happiness mentioned in Jamaica. Dry Harbour is but a small village of about a population of 300 souls, out of which number not more than 30 are white, the remainder being all emancipated negroes. The only business people were two merchants from Britain who having their families constituted nearly the whole white population.

The captain and his crew attend chapel

There was also a minister of the Wesleyan Society, a good and faithful disciple of Jesus, and all the population with few exceptions were Wesleyans. Our master, who was of the same denomination of Christians, and a strict attendant of the chapel, did not forget to give his crew the usual intimation on the eve of the Sabbath, which was that he expected to be followed the next day by all hands to worship.[1]

I say not that everyone felt inclined to follow him when the morrow came, but certainly every one felt inclined to obey him; consequently every one did follow him but the cook, who was left to attend to the dinner. Now to see the master of a vessel followed by his officers and all his crew on a good Sunday morning entering a place of worship is unfortunately such a strange sight that both the minister and all the congregation then assembled riveted their attention upon us, and each were struck with a feeling of such deep respect for such an orderly and Christian-like crew, that a bond of affection was at once established which soon became riveted securely. The minister, himself entering into the feeling of his people, preached that day a most delightful sermon expressly intended for the benefit of our seafaring souls. His text was 'They that go down to the sea in ships and do business in great waters, these see the works of the Lord and his wonders in the deep!'

Much may be said in favour of the negro zeal in religion, but especially in the West Indies or in particular in Dry Harbour, it was enough to do good to any heart touched with the least sensibility to see the crowded chapel of black heads and faces decorated of course, with white and gaudy colours and highly perfumed with the choicest perfumes of Paris manufacture, zealously catching every word that fell from their pastor's lips and securing them in their hearts as treasures for future mediation, singing at the tops of their voices in hymns of praise to God, their gratitude for the present opportunity of being met in His name and in His presence. Loudly re-echoed the words of John Wesley's 83

[1] The chapel which John David and his crew attended appears to have been the one at St Ann's Bay at the head of a Wesleyan Methodist circuit established in 1821 which included St Ann's Bay, Runaway, Dry Harbour, Ocho Rios Bay and Bellemont. The first chapel at St Ann's, a thatched hut built in 1827, was superseded in 1837–38 by a substantial stone building. See P. Samuel, *The Wesleyan-Methodist Missions, in Jamaica and Honduras, delineated* (1850), pp. 195–213, with illustrations of the first and second St Ann's chapels facing pp. 192 and 212. Despite what might be inferred from Hilary's text, there does not appear to have been a chapel at Dry Harbour itself at this date, although the congregation may have worshipped in a private house.

Hymn 'We bow before thy gracious throne, and think ourselves sincere; but show us, Lord, is every one thy real worshipper?'

Our constant attendance to chapel on Sunday and at the prayer meetings on the week days soon made us possessors of the hearts of our fellow creatures, and our every wish was read by then even almost before it was formed. Nothing was too good for us than was procurable, each tried to outvie the other in attention to us, invitation followed invitation for our company at their limited dwellings.

It really seemed to be a boon to any one of them to possess any of us for if but half an hour in their company.

Prayer meetings on board

On board prayer meetings were held and I'm sure it must have been a pleasure for any one to have seen the gallant vessel every Wednesday evening in nice, prim, tidy, orderly, and clean attire with the Bethel Flag waving above head and then to see Miss Nancy and Massa Thomas in flocks like sheep, making their appearance alongside in canoes, then, after ascending the side of the vessel, to see them take their places on the temporary benches arranged for the purpose, always kneeling first and offering their supplicatory prayer to that God they had crossed the water to come and worship, to see all this I say carried out in such an orderly manner was beautiful to the extreme, and to hear them groan the pathetic amen to the minister's prayer of 'Lord, Guide this ship by thy own unerring hand, Bless her master and crew in their inmost souls. Give charge to the wind and waves concerning them, etc, etc'. I repeat, to hear them express from their hearts the pathetic amen was touchingly beautiful.

Fond farewells

When the day of our departure came to hand it was hailed as a day of sorrow. I believe that day no work was done in the town, for every one came to wish us adieu, each bringing (out of his penury) some object wherewith to mark his affection and sorrow at parting. Some brought a young pig, another a bunch of bananas, another two eggs, another a fowl, another a pigeon, and so on, each equally showing his heart's good wish in the trifle he presented.

Never have I witnessed such a scene on board a ship, not even at leave taking from parents and relations. Ultimately the minister himself came off, and he too did not come empty-handed. No, he brought with him several tracts which he gave the captain for the reading of his crew at sea, but his more particular bequest was of a nice little work on religion to my unworthy self.

Why he selected me from among the rest for the exercise of his bounty I know not, but certain it is that he did so, and after presenting me with the book, following the gift with an admonitory speech, he bid me a good bye and God bless you, with eyes evincing real heartfelt sorrow. I can never forget that moment, although I'm ashamed to say I have forgotten the title of his book; but then memory is sometimes treacherous!

I have mentioned that my felicity during our stay in Dry Harbour was not uninterrupted, I will now briefly remark the interruption.

To Rio Bueno for water

On account of the total absence of fresh water in the above named harbour, from which peculiarity it has taken its name, we had to go in quest of that indispensable article of daily use to another port, called Rio Bueno or 'Good River', that lay about nine miles further along the coast. Accordingly, when the vessel was nearly ready for sea, the captain ordered me to take the long boat, fill her with water casks, and with my crew of three men, start away to fetch back a load of water; having been there on two different occasions I knew the route as well as the port perfectly and considered the task more of a pleasure cruise than any thing else. Our sails set and long boat manned and provisioned for two days, we started with a fair wind which soon brought us to our destination, when immediately we fell to filling our casks from the river stream which constantly runs there as pure as crystal.

Our boat being loaded and again ready for sea, we moored her safely along shore while we went to take a survey of the town and its environs; once work was done we had all the rest of the day for ourselves, as we could not start but with the land breeze, which usually came in about midnight, or one or two o'clock in the morning. Consequently on those watering excursions we generally spent a part of the time in the bush, and jungle, seeking for seeds, flowers, bird's nests and always expecting to fall in with a crocodile or alligator which we had made up our minds to capture, but which in reality we, I dare say, would have run away from pretty smartly. Be that as it may, our courage was never put to the test, although we often disturbed many a snake in its forest home, and drove him to seek shelter in some more retired spot.

The remainder of our time till dusk was generally spent in diving for coral and shells, but as not one of us was expert in swimming, it rarely happened that our diving feats were attended with any success. After dusk we laid down upon the water casks in the boat taking a few hours repose ere we set sail again. So were our watering excursions conducted and on the one in question the same routine had been gone through. When at midnight a nice land breeze commenced to blow, immediately I aroused my slumbering mates and the fastenings of the boat were let loose, our sails hoisted and away we went towards our ship in quite a gallant style. Being captain of the boat I took the helm and steered her on while my comrades slept anew, and I made sure that by three or four o'clock we should have gained the ship without any difficulty; but we are apt to make mistakes sometimes, especially when we make nature's laws the subject of our calculations. Our nice land breeze blew just enough to take us fairly out to sea, then it died away to a perfect calm and we lay motionless on the face of the starlight ocean, literally speaking as idle as a painted ship upon a painted ocean.

As soon as I perceived the dawn arising in the east I roused my crew from their uneasy beds to furl our sails which had now become useless for want of the breath of heaven and to take to the oars, in order if possible to gain our ship before the sea breeze set in, as I thought of course it would be dangerous to attempt to beat against it with our boat so deeply loaded that not more than six inches of her side remained visible above water. We pressed and exerted ourselves strongly but we were fated to disappointment on this occasion. By eight o'clock the sea breeze I so much feared had set in against us, consequently our oars were of no more service. We had but to make sail and weather it how best we could.

Our little boat acted much better than I had anticipated, she sailed remarkably well to the wind and took in far less water than I had calculated. After making a few tacks we got sight of our ship opening with a point of land we had to go round. At this sight my crew's courage was heightened and one ventured to pull out his pipe and flint and steel in order to treat himself with a jolly smoke. I was glad to see their animation and encouraged it, but my spirits could not share in it. My watchful eye had detected what had escaped theirs. Over the mountains on our weather I remarked heavy masses of greyish clouds rapidly rising and appearing darker and darker as they rose, exhibiting occasionally a vivid flash of light, sure signs of a thunder storm. As I was acquainted with the force of the thunder storms of the West Indies I looked upon this one with some degree of anxiety owing to our situation in an open boat not more than six inches above the surface of the ocean.

Thunderstorm nearly sinks the longboat

However, fear seldom prevailed in my young heart, though a certain degree of prudence was always present. I continued sailing and working my fragile ship to windwards with all dexterity, meanwhile the storm was rapidly approaching and becoming more and more dismal in appearance. At this time my crew began to take notice of it, whispering their fears to each other with very doleful countenance.

The lightning grew more vivid every moment, and had it been night instead of day, it must have been awful to the sight; distant peals of thunder were now heard rolling along in the distance, crack, cracking like the report of some tremendous cannon. Fortunately, neither the lightning or thunder has ever caused me any fears, or had it been otherwise I know not what had become of us, for my awe-stricken crew were now paralysed.

I endeavoured to cheer them by my own apparent cheerfulness, and answered to their pleadings of seeking shelter under the land, by making at once directly for it, but as I expected, the coast hereabouts was so rugged and iron bound that it was dangerous to approach it with our laden boat which must have been dashed to pieces owing to the high prevailing swell of the sea the moment the attempt would have been made. Consequently I hauled off the shore again and stood to seaward. One of my crew who (by the bye) is now master of a fine ship himself, suggested it was better to see the boat dashed to pieces and our lives saved, then courting the danger of getting swamped at sea when the storm fell upon us and all hands drowned. Perhaps he was right admitting that in the event of dashing the boat against the rocks we could have saved our lives, but as I was very doubtful of the chance I remarked to him that there was less danger in acting the part I was acting, as in the event of swamping the boat in the storm we could not lose our lives while we had such good buoys to moor ourselves upon as the water casks, while if near the rocks they also would be dashed to pieces and we should be left without any protection. Besides if we saved our lives by climbing the perpendicular rocks I bid him take note of the immense distance we should have to walk through a jungle infested with venomous insects and reptiles, leaving aside the wild beasts, without any food to eat, or any water to drink, while on the other hand we could float about comfortably on our water casks perfectly free from all the above dangers until some charitable person should come and pick us up, and if we wanted bread to eat at least we should have plenty of water to drink.

Poor Henry thought otherwise, so did the others and fancied if they were but safe on terra-firma neither hunger nor thirst would trouble them nor any of the above named creations.

Meanwhile the storm was coming on, the clouds had spread themselves as a deep dark mantle over the face of the sky, giving to earth the appearance of a gloomy cavern in some desert waste or other, so thick and so black were the clouds that daylight was eclipsed and the idea that was suggested to my mind was that darkness was really visible, beneath this sombre veil was earth entombed, above, the roaring of the increased thunder was appalling. It rolled along the sky with such hideous noise accompanied by the frightful forked and chain lightening, that the whole seemed as if the elements were at war promising imminent distruction to all around. Suddenly a dreadful noise was heard: a hissing as it were more terrible that the thunder itself. What was that? Every countenance wore an aspect as much in contrast to the scene as was possible, while marble white were the faces of my comrades. I knew not what colour mine was for I could not see it, but certain I am it was not black.

That dreadful hissing noise soon made its cause apparent, it was the rending of that dreadful pall that so effectually separated earth and sky, it was the confined air that had broken asunder its enclosing bands out of which it escaped in fearful gusts with maddened fury, at the first contact with our frail bark it was like the tremendous blow of some gigantic battering ram, which made her careen over so as to bring her lee side completely under water, thereby half filling her in an instant. One unanimous but dreadful cry was heard amongst my crew whose utterance pierced itself through the howling tempest, yet more dreadful than the latter.

Hope vanished

Hope had vanished with that cry and left the mortal tenements of clay as inanimate as the boat that bore them; there they sat with distended features and glaring eyes fixed as statues holding in a deathlike grasp the object they sat upon till the very nails from their finger ends pierced through the solid material. This all was but the instant of a moment although it has occupied several in describing it. The moment the first shock was over and our little boat had assumed its upright position, I called out to the top of my voice to them to turn to bailing out the water. I felt at the same instant confident of our safety for since she had not filled with the first and most tremendous shock which had caught her on her broadside, I knew the next would lose its power by striking us on the bow, for my presence of mind had provided for all this and I had kept part of the mainsail unfurled and hoisted up while the other sails were snugly fastened. The consequence was that when the storm came on catching into the after sail wheeled the boat head to wind, and there she lay like a sea fowl on the water, only rising and tossing on the crest of the wave, but not taking in any water.

The fury of the storm was now at its maximum scream, while my crew exerted themselves so dexterously that in less than ten minutes the boat was comparatively dry. The wind howled dreadfully, its deafening noise completely eclipsing that of the thunder, we could not keep our faces one instant to the wind as our breath was immediately stopped through its force, and the white spray flying like a mist over us washed so strongly against our flesh that the skin with which it came in contact was fairly cut as with a sharp instrument. Subsequently, the rain came down, How shall I describe the force with which it fell? It was a sheet of water. No words are sufficiently expressive to convey to the mind an idea of the reality. For some time we were as much in danger of swamping with the rain as we had been with the sea, our buckets were used very smartly, however, and we could manage after the heavy torrent ceased to look up to the elements and say 'We have conquered thee'.

This dreadful phenomenon which I have attempted to describe lasted about an hour, when after that space of time the clouds which had emptied themselves of their electricity and fluid, and had thereby become lighter vapours, moved away before the still existing gale; the sky began to make itself perceptible in patches of blue, the rain disappeared or only continued in a drizzling moisture, the wind, exhausted, blew fainter and fainter every moment, till at last followed a perfect calm on the face of the troubled ocean, and every thing around began to take its wonted appearance. Sol, however, whether from the infringement its lustre had received or otherwise, refused to make its appearance that day else it would have greatly added to enliven the dejected earth.

Once more in safety it was astonishing how my boat's crew smiled over their past fears, each trying to persuade the other that he had been the most frightened. I remarked to them that it was ill befitting of them to laugh over the dangers they had escaped but rather they should look up to the heaven with sincere gratitude for having made a way for their escape, for, said I 'Had you been treated according to your merits only, you should not now be here, but consigned where hope never cometh'.

This little remonstrance had the desired effect, and lighting our pipes, we once more plyed our oars to the tune of 'Row, Brothers, row' and an hour, or an hour and half brought us alongside of our 'bonnie barkie' once more.

Safe on board the Swift

On my arrival on the deck I found both the chief mate and the master had been very anxious for our safety, for they too had experienced the severity of the storm, it having taken the *Swift* in the same manner that it first took our boat on the broadside, careened her over so tremendously that they feared for a few moments for her safety. It blew away the quarter-deck awning, broke the stanchions, and otherwise did damage on board, so that both the master and the mate, who had seen us off the point at the opening of the harbour before the storm, and not seeing us after it had cleared away, concluded we had gone down. It was great satisfaction for them when they saw us once more make our appearance, and greater still for all concerned when we reached the ship.

A few days after these incidents and immediately after the leave taking of our friends mentioned in a preceding page, we set sail for London where we duly arrived after an ordinary passage of 46 days.[1] I felt very joyous at being once more in Old England and I trusted that the *Swift* would bear me this voyage to Guernsey where I longed to greet my friends again, but not so, a few days after the cargo was discharged the master announced to us that he had rechartered her for the West Indies, although not to the same port but to St Kitts where we had also been before, but as he said the vessel would be some time in loading, all the crew except the mate and one hand as cook, could go home.

Home

Of course this was good news for me and it was not many days before I was safely landed on my native soil once more. What a hearty welcome the sailor receives after a long voyage on his return among his relations and friends. What a hearty welcome was mine, but alas these joys are too sweet to be lasting and equally as great as these joys have been on arrival, are our sorrows at parting. I spent a very happy time which lasted five weeks; often did I meet in company the object on which my heart set such a great price, that aerial form that bid me hope at the eleventh hour, was itself in reality spreading its halo of sunshine around my path, and yet how strange no words of tenderness were ever interchanged, no outward or visible signs given to reveal the feelings of the heart within, yet the tenderness existed, the signs were circulated. It was my intention to have secured to myself this gem of beauty, innocence, and purity on this occasion, but circumstances were prevailing, and I was fain to postpone my felicity to a more distant period in order to secure hers uninterrupted.

[1] William Day's diary notes that the *Swift* left Dry Harbour on 24 July and entered Blackwall Basin on 6 Sept. The crew list (PRO, BT 98/938) was handed in at London on 11 Sept. 1846, the crew having been paid off two days earlier.

Letter from the Captain ordering him to London – Chief Officer

At length the day arrived, as every day arrives in succession one after the other, when I received a letter from my captain and master announcing at once both the cause for joy and sorrow. The former part of his kind letter appointed me as his chief officer, a promotion which I did not expect at the time, but which came very acceptable nevertheless, the later part ordered me to return to the ship by the very next conveyance.

Of course I did not hesitate in my duty, no sooner had I received this communication than I commenced making the necessary preparations for another voyage which were very soon accomplished as I had always kept myself as much in readiness as possible during my stay in case of a sudden call. The leave taking from my parents and friends was the most painful part of the business. I need scarcely remark upon the subject since everyone is more or less acquainted with this peculiar sorrow, by some termed sweet, for as one has it, 'If parting is such sweet sorrow, I could say good bye 'til it be morrow'.[1] There was one being however now added to the list of my intimate friends and with whom the yearnings of my youthful heart corresponded, from whom I would have fain taken the last farewell but my notice was so short it gave me no opportunity of meeting her in any company, and I could not dare the liberty of calling upon her for the only reason of wishing her goodbye.

I had gone my rounds and taken leave of all my friends and the eve of my departure had arrived. Uneasy, undecided, and scarcely knowing which way to turn, I sauntered out on this occasion by the light of the stars on the road towards her home. I chose the more solitary path out of the main road in order to be alone with my thoughts, arriving at the end of the path that opened out into the main road again, I awoke to consciousness as if from a dream.

[1] A slight misquotation of *Romeo and Juliet*, Act II, Scene 2: 'Goodnight, goodnight! Parting is such sweet sorrow / That I shall say goodnight till it be morrow'.

Why had I come this far? Where was I going? Which way should I turn now that I had arrived here? Strange to say the answer to which my actions responded was 'turn back' and back I did turn through the solitary path only enlivened by here and there a twinkling star peeping through the foliage above which met in its green embraces from one side of the path to the other forming a vault beneath, well adapted for the temporary seclusion of one so solitary as myself. Had anyone passed that way at this time they must have thought it strange to see me as I lay reclined against the trunk of an old tree with my face heavenwards, eyes gazing on vacancy, and apparently as motionless as the trunk which supported me.

> The hope of return takes the sting from adieu
> The bright star of eve from the blue sky was peeping
> The bee homeward had fled to add sweets to her store
> As sadly I strayed where no form was intruding
> To muse upon one I might never see more.
> O'ercome by my ramble, a slumber came o'er me,
> Methought a bright being appeared to my view
> And chiding my grief, in my ear sweetly whispered
> 'The hope of return takes the sting from adieu!'
> 'And who art thou fair one that thus would be cheering
> The spirit long bowed by affliction and care?'
> She answered me thus 'I'm the Guardian Angel
> Who bids thee look forward and cease to despair!'
> I rose to new life from that soul stirring slumber,
> And many a day kept this motto in view
> Twas a light in the darkness, a stream in the desert,
> The hope of return takes the sting from adieu![1]

Strange coincidence! I had gone to meet this angel of my thoughts, and baffled and obstructed by causes too numerous in this world of crosses, she had come to meet me, she had come

[1] The author of this verse has not been identified: was it perhaps Hilary himself?

again to whisper the cheering word hope in my troubled breast. I felt stirred to a sensation of perfect happiness and ease. I awoke from my slumber as it were, and I marched on towards my home with steps full of alacrity, and a soul with joy replenished anew, singing all the way to myself 'The hope of return takes the sting from adieu'. I now felt confident that all would be well, and that on my return, however long my absence might be, I should be enabled to act according to my heart's desire without meeting with any opposing measure in the rough and rugged course of love's warm stream. Next day I received the parting blessing from my venerable parents and I was on my way to London at an early hour where I duly arrived without any impediment on the passage. I resumed my duty in my new capacity as chief officer on the day following my arrival. My old friend and master Captain David and I being as happy to see each other again as though we had been separated as many years as we only had been weeks.

Eighth Voyage

St Kitts, West Indies

I found the vessel nearly loaded on my arrival, the ex-chief mate overlooking that part of the business. A few days more and we were again on our way to the West Indies, St Kitts[1] being our destination, where we arrived on the fifty-first day after quitting London.[2] Nothing transpired during the passage, or our stay there, on which I can make any remark. I will convey my thoughts and the reader, if such there is presiding besides myself, to our passage back to London; here I have food for many remarks, the passage being attended with exceedingly boisterous weather and more than once our lives being in extreme danger, but as a recapitulation of this bad weather and these dangerous moments savours much of an old story, I will spare myself the insipidity and weariness of going over them.

Back in London after dangerous passage

I have but myself to please in this instance, therefore I can be subject to the censure of none if I pass a few incidents in my life unnoticed. We, not withstanding the above hinted to bad weather

[1] Now officially St Christopher, one of the two adjacent islands forming the Federation of St Christopher and Nevis.

[2] The crew lists and agreement to serve in BT 98/1248 are dated 22 Oct. 1846 and give a departure date of the 26th for a voyage from London to St Kitts or Puerto Rico and thence to London and Guernsey if required. Hilary Marquand, aged 22, signed on as mate at £3 2s. a month; his mate's ticket number is given as 5,885, issued at London on 16 Jan. 1845. The agreement to serve was surrendered at the Custom House, St Kitts, on 18 Dec. 1846.

and dangerous moments, arrived at our old station the West India Docks in 57 days which was not so bad for the poor vessel that weathered out so much. I am not going to dwell on my stay in London since I have nothing worth remarking, but will, with dispatch, transport my mind on my passage out again after of course going through the usual formalities, discharging the cargo and loading again.[1]

[1] The agreement to serve was returned to the master on 1 Feb. 1847 on his departure from St Kitts and the crew list was handed in on their return to London on 30 March.

– 1847 –

Ninth Voyage

April

Nevis, West Indies

We are bound again to the West Indies, to Nevis if no objection. We leave London on the 25th April 1847,[1] we sail away down Channel, we meet a fair wind, we meet a foul one, we meet a gale of wind, and we meet a calm. We catch a porpoise, we catch a dolphin, we see a turtle without catching him, and I catch a confounded bad cold, which I did not easily get rid of for three weeks, and after catching and meeting all these very fine things, we catch a sight of the land, one of the West Indies islands, Antigua, and subsequently we meet with Nevis in whose port we enter and do the same there we had done in the sister isle:[2] that is discharge the cargo, go to chapel on a Sunday, and reload another cargo of sugar and cocoa nuts, and ultimately start away again for London where after catching less fish and meeting with less fair wind, we arrive on the 26th of August, thereby making our voyage in the exact space of four months.[3]

[1] One of the crew lists (BT 98/1248) actually gives 19 April as the departure date for a voyage from London to Nevis, calling at Guernsey outward; another says 17 April. The accompanying agreement to serve lists 'Henry Marquand', aged 23, as mate on £3 5s.; his old friend Thomas Le Page was second mate and carpenter. The *Swift* left Guernsey on 1 May.

[2] i.e. St Kitts: see previous voyage. The main port of Nevis is Charlestown, on the west coast. The agreement to serve was handed in at the Custom House, Nevis, on 15 June 1847 and returned to the master on 2 July.

[3] The agreement to serve was handed in at London on 30 Aug.

London – Guernsey

After a nine-days stay in London we proceeded in ballast to Guernsey and behold here we are once more in this blessed little earthly paradise.

> Where hearts with hearts unite, and joy and sport is seen
> Where angels smile at such a sight, as oft is met on village green.[1]

This time my stay on Guernsey was destined to be of peculiar delight to myself. Destiny, which had prepared its sweets and sunshine for two earthly beings, was now ripe for distributing them, the warm chords of sympathy which had hitherto been the silent conveyances of the soul's pure affection were now about to find a voice, the soft and mystic transfusion of souls was about to expand itself in words of blissful tenderness, in short young Captain Cupid was about to be set at liberty to enjoy at large its natural sport.

The confidence once hinted at in a preceding page with which I had possessed myself, that all would be well on my return, and obstructing measures vanished to the fulfilment of my desires was now to all intents and purposes established. The angel of my daily thoughts, and night dreams, was still the same enchanting seraph, only changed by the addition that three-quarters of a year could make in establishing the graces of womanhood, which graces took nothing, but added much to her already unsurpassed personal charms and soundness of character. The several trifling family impediments which had been previous cause of uneasiness to me were now vanished; nothing now remained to cross my path in wooing the heart I so tenderly loved.

[1] No author has been identified for this couplet, which is perhaps another of Hilary's own efforts (cf. p. 196).

He proposes to 'My dear Miss Blondel'

To the task I set myself most earnestly, and although her girlish coyness retarded somewhat the interesting moment yet it arrived in course of time. We had met at a sister's where she had been taking tea, of course I made it a very essential point of duty to meet her there, for I took care to acquaint myself with her everyday movements. When in the evening I begged in the most polite manner possible for the privilege of seeing her safely home, she kindly granted the privilege (sweet creature, how could she refuse me?) and after spending a very pleasant evening I offered her my right arm (my left was in reserve for her later) and on we walked towards her home, I chatting the while to keep her amused but on what subject heaven only knows.

I dare say she thought me very stupid and so I really was, since all people in love are. My mind was occupied in the task I had to perform, the momentous question was about to be popped. How could I settle my mind to talk on every day subjects like a rational being when such an important business had to be transacted? I shall never forget how occupied I was for a great part of our walk in preparing the words I wished to address her with, and after composing, fabricating, and jumbling together an address, I feel positive when I did bring it out, not one of my preparatory words was made use of. How foolish is a man in love! I feel certain if I had to propose to a dozen girls now I could do it with as much ease as proposing a toast previous to taking a glass of wine.

However, to continue, we had nearly reached at our walk's end when I thought we were only half way, finding this out I armed myself with courage and commenced the important task. 'My dear Miss Blondel, it cannot be strange to you ... .' At my suddenly breaking the existing silence which had lasted for some minutes, she visibly started at the words 'my dear' which must have fallen like angels music upon her ear, so sweetly did I speak them. I felt her arm tremble within mine, but at the words: 'I love you deeply, desperately, irrevocably', I distinctly felt her dear little heart thumping severely against my arm and at the words; 'Will you love me in return?' I heard it pit, patting like the noise of some terrible mechanical instrument beating against a wooden partition.

It is no use concealing that mine also was pit, patting pretty freely, but then the noise of hers drowned it completely. A–a–a–a–ah! what a plight we both were in at this critical moment! Who has not been in the like situation cannot understand it. After my speech was over, my protestations of desperate love, a pause ensued, the silence of which was equal to death itself, in the meantime we grew nearer and nearer to the house, and still did my timid, modest partner keep silence. My anxiety cannot be expressed at this moment. My future happiness or misery hung upon her tongue. Her 'Yes' would establish the former, while her 'No' would doom me to the latter for life, but it could not be in her, no, I felt convinced it could not be in her gentle nature to pronounce misery upon a fellow creature much less upon him who stood at her side, her faithful and devoted adorer. Still, on, on we went and deep silence reigned, or only broken by the noise of our footsteps on the ground. At last I ventured to break this silence by begging of her to grant me her answer. Sweet creature! I knew she loved me, did I not feel it in the twitching of her arm? But still I wished her to say so in plain English words. At length her answer came, it was such a mass of broken sentences. 'Really, ... I ... You have ... I am not ... .' I begged of her to be composed, and in a measure she did compose herself when she answered with such heaven like music in her voice, with such accents of tender emotions, that I freely forgave her for having kept me in suspense so long.

'Really, Sir, you have taken me so much unawares that I cannot possibly answer a question which is of such grand importance to us both, without first considering over it at leisure. I therefore beg you will allow me a few days to consult my feelings when I will be able to give you a direct answer.' Of course what could I do otherwise but in submission accord her request, naming however the day when I would expect her to answer me?

He is accepted

That day soon arrived and I was made the happy being I have ever been since and am still, by her giving me her hand accompanied with her heart, nevertheless making the necessary condition that I should obtain her father's consent who was then in London. I had no doubt as far as he was concerned therefore I was happy.

Thus were my early dreams realised, my early hopes accomplished. Thus was the fair being who I introduced in the year 1840 or 1841, six or seven years ago, one evening after dusk sitting at the table like a thrifty housewife engaged at her needle, and her cousin teasing her in all the wicked ways that youth could devise, whilst I remained a quiet observer of the scene, and wished in my heart, since cousins were so privileged, that I too had been a cousin. This fair being who I had never perhaps seen before who chance threw in my way, for I had not called for the purpose of seeing her, but merely accompanying my playmate who was sent there on an errand. This fair being who at first sight struck me so wonderfully, whose presence was ever afterwards my companion whose image remained indelibly impressed on my soul. This fair being who has been the theme of my daily musings was the being intended by destiny to become what the reader has already seen her, the betrothed of my heart, and at no great further period the cherished wife of my bosom. Thus and thus does fate mysteriously work its own ends, and who can contradict this truth? For I am with an ancient writer of opinion, that the management of our own fate is by no means required of us, but only self-culture.

I wrote of course to her father in London, and subsequently received his answer to the effect that he presented no objection to our happiness. All preliminaries adjusted, I was now enabled to continue my avocations with perfect delight, looking with enthusiasm upon the future as something worth toiling for, as a paradise which with unremitted exertions I was determined soon to obtain.

– 1847 –

Tenth Voyage

October

The Brazils via Newport, S. Wales

Shortly after the event mentioned I left the island to commence another voyage, not to the West Indies this time, but to the Brazils. In the same vessel and with the same master we left Guernsey in the month of October 1847 bound to Newport in Wales.[1] I shall not attempt to describe the parting scene between my beloved and me, suffice it to say it was one of heartfelt emotion, one in which vows of eternal faith were evoked, one in which the young heart poured forth its first pure stream of love, a stream which has never ceased to run with equal purity. Vows which have known of no other change but that impressed upon them through the sanctity of the altar.

During my stay in Wales the weariness of the long autumnal evenings was very much modified through the pleasing occupations of a loving correspondence. Oh, how insufficient is the vocabulary of the English language to furnish words expressive of the feelings in a case like this. How the young heart does melt itself away in words of tender passion, what an interchange of heavenborn feelings! What a foretaste of paradisaical bliss! Each successive post day was hailed with anxious delight, the sight of the postman going his rounds in the dock was always attended with a tremulous emotion and palpitating of the heart which could only be sup-

[1] There are three crew lists and an agreement to serve for this voyage in BT 98/1603. One of the lists and the agreement are dated 29 Sept., a second is dated 1 Oct., said to be the date of departure, and the third is dated 25 Oct. The voyage is described as destined for Newport, Cádiz, Bahia and Stralsund. Hilary (called 'Henry Marquand' but the ticket number identifies him), aged 22, signed on as mate at £3 5s. a month.

pressed by the tearing of the envelope which contained the missive which a world of bright gold could not have purchased. These pleasant reminiscences of halcyon days remind me of an incident relative to these billets-doux which I will briefly notice.

Departure: Letter from Louisa?

Our day of departure from Newport and mail day from Guernsey were one, consequently on the morning of said day I was greatly 'en embarras' for fear we should sail before the idolised postman made his appearance, and as chance would have it the hour appointed for our sailing from the dock was the same which he usually visited us, should the mail meet with delay, or our exit be hastened for half an hour, I should lose the so highly prized last and farewell communication from my beloved. I should have to go and brave the countless anxious hours of a tedious passage without having read her last endearing, soul enlivening words of farewell, to me these fears were dreadful; I would have given the whole worth of the vessel if she had been mine to delay sufficiently to answer my desire.

Meanwhile I was dexterously exerting myself in the performance of my duty in getting the ship in readiness for sea. The minutes were flitting by, but at so indolent a pace that five times I looked at my watch ere one quarter of an hour had expired; I felt certain that at any other time a quarter of an hour would have vanished ere I had looked at my watch a second time. How tedious the hours are to be sure when they give themselves the turn of indolence! It was now only 8 o'clock, I had yet one long hour, or hour and a half to wait before I could expect to see the postman, in that space of time the ship which was now unmoored and only fastened by lines in a temporary manner could be hauled out of dock and if towed by steam be halfway down the river. Yet there was no sign of opening the lock gates, surely my fear was premature, it would take a long time to open the gates, allow the water from the dock to take its level with that of the lock, and that of the latter with the river. Again I consulted my watch, only seven minutes had expired! I commenced making a calculation how long it would take to do all that I have mentioned above and ultimately get the ship fairly out in the river providing the minutes would be a little swifter in their course than they had been for the last hour. As I was in the midst of these calculations I was strenuously aroused by the boatswain-like voice of the harbour master who bid me haul the ship down to the dock head in readiness for going through the moment the gate was open. I looked round me and lo, the gate-men were already at their stations, the gates would soon recede to their unresisting force coupled with that of the massive machinery. There was no alternative, haul the ship down the dock we must. Consequently in a moment my orders reverberated through the ship to that effect — every man was instantly at his duty and the ship was answering to the work by gliding down on the surface of the mirror-like waters of the enclosed sea. By the time we reached the gate it had but partially opened, consequently we had to wait quarter of an hour. I was not sorry for this well timed detention, and less so, if possible, when I found my watch was maring twenty minutes to nine, surely in that time we could not be let out and the postman would be sure to make his appearance.

Two friends arrive to say farewell

In the meantime two friends of mine as well as the captain's came down to the dock to see us off. I may as well introduce them briefly as they will have to figure hereafter rather particularly. Wm H. Martin was a young man about three or four and twenty filling the situation of Custom House clerk in the establishment of our consignee and ship broker, Stonehouse & Co.[1] He was a handsome, good natured young man, of a middle stature with dark hair and eyes, and that pleasant expression of countenance which

[1] Neither this firm, nor that of Edwards, Rogers & Co. mentioned on the next page, can be found listed as ship-brokers or the like in Kelly's Newport Directory of 1848, although the sense implies that both were in business in the town.

betokens a frank and noble nature. The other friend, Thom. Williams was about the same height, rather younger by perhaps six or eight months; he was of a more reserved character, but of a genuine good disposition nevertheless, and filling the same situation in the house of Edwards Rogers & Co.

Now the former of these was my particular friend inasmuch as we were about the same age, perhaps very little difference in character, and both engaged in love's warm and fascinating bonds.[1] All these reasons combined, we had become inseparable during my stay at Newport and we had like two open-hearted friends made our bosoms the sacred repository of each other's private affairs. Consequently it is no wonder if the moment I saw him near the vessel on the morning in question, my heart leaped within me for the joy at being able to confide to him my extreme anxiety. The moment we had greeted each other with the formal ceremonies of the day, I called him apart and imparted to him all my fears, assuring him that if I did not receive the last farewell token of my beloved I should be miserable all the voyage. He listened to me the while with all the attention he was capable of, and understanding my feelings quite well, looked at the case as if it was his own, consequently heartily sympathised with me, then his generous disposition at once suggested the plan of his going at[2] the post office himself to wait till the mail was brought in, when by dint of entreating the post master with whom he was acquainted, try to get hold of the valuable missive and hasten down with it to me. It was very kind of him indeed, and I could have embraced him with tenderness, so much did I feel grateful to him.

[1] W.H. Martin later married Ellen, the daughter of John Davies of Cardiff, on 8 Jan. 1850.

[2] *Sic* MS.

Martin gets the letter

Away went he with all haste to said post office, and just as he arrived, the mail also arrived. Immediately did he seek for an interview with the post master and I still sometimes fancy how difficult it must have been for him to obtain this interview at such a moment when post masters are literally invisible, but if this part of his mission was difficult how much more so still that of being permitted of selecting a letter from the mass and taking it away when especially that letter was not for himself. I can well imagine all the words of entreaty it cost him to obtain for me this great boon and as well as I can imagine that, so well can I appreciate his generous nature and am filled with gratitude.

True to his good intentions he did obtain the sacred missive and hurrying down to the extent of his speed he reached the dock just after the *Swift* had left it and was towing down the river at full speed. I have not dwelt over the anxious moments spent from the time of his departure to the post office until now when all hopes were vanished, but such may easily be imagined in fact clearer than I can depict it.

Martin and friend commandeer small boat

Finding the ship just gone he beckoned Thom. Williams to follow him when away they ran along the embankment of the river outrunning the *Swift* about half a mile, then taking a small boat that lay on the mud they launched her into the water and jumping in made for the vessel as fast as they could ply their oars. Now to board a ship as she is towing down in a tide way is very dangerous, and knowing this, the moment I saw them pulling for the ship with such daring spirit that nothing seemed to mitigate, I begged of the captain to order the steamer to stop, which he certainly did. But a steamer is easily stopped enough, not so a sailing vessel which, when she has been impelled through the water by some forcible agent or other such as wind or steamer, retains her progress through the water for a long time ere she stops altogether.

Boat overturns

Meanwhile these two generous hearted young men were approaching the side in their crazy boat. Both being unacquainted with the management of it, I feared dreadful consequences and went myself to the gangway with a rope, ready to hand them the moment they were near enough, at the same time informing them with the mode of acting for the better. But just as I had feared, T. Williams, who caught the rope the moment it was thrown in the boat, instead of jumping in the bows with it, stood in the centre of the boat and thereby in a moment brought her broadside on, when she turned over and filled.

Here was a catastrophe! Williams had not let go his hold of the rope therefore he had saved himself, but poor Martin, who could not swim better than a stone, went away astern rolling and tossing in the foam of the sea like a man battling against the last enemy. It was less than a moment's thought, it was like the electric flash, which made me resolve to save him or perish in the attempt; had he not thus exposed himself for my sake? Should I not expose myself to save his life? Yes! and like a arrow darted from the bow, I sped along the deck and jumped over the stern heedless of any thing or consequence but that of saving the drowning man.

Now it is very likely as was reflected afterwards that had we both met in the water, both would have perished, for although I could swim it would have been difficult to put that acquirement into practice with a drowning man clutching with a death like grasp around me.

Saved by the pilot boat

As it was, however, instead of jumping into the water as I expected, I fell into the pilot's boat which had been fastened to our stern since we left the dock, unknown to anyone on board but the pilot himself. The young lad who had charge of the boat had, the moment he witnessed the accident, hauled her up close to the vessel in order to pick up the drowning man if possible.

Consequently as I have said before, I fell into his boat instead of falling into the river as I had expected which naturally made my fall heavier and longer remembered by my sore limbs.

However, my object was attained, for immediately upon attaining my perpendicular (which was but the work of an instant) I perceived my friend Martin floating by and at once caught hold of his clothes and with the help of the pilot's boy, got him safely into the boat. It is easily conceived that the poor fellow had but a very faint flow of animated spirit about him for some time, and certain it is that his appearance reminded me of the old phrase I have often heard which says something about 'a drowned rat'. Nevertheless a few minutes sufficed to restore him to consciousness and his first signal to that effect was a smile on his countenance no doubt at the happiness he felt in having cheated old Davey Jones of his expected prey.

We soon got him on deck and subsequently in the cabin when he and poor Williams enjoyed a hearty sympathetic laugh together. Between Captain David and me we fitted them out with a dry suit of clothes and in a very short time they were enjoying a cup of warm coffee before a nice clear fire, altogether in appearance as comfortable as if just returned from a voluntary sea bath. I feel persuaded that in all their joy and apparent merriment the feeling of gratitude to heaven for their safety was predominant. Meanwhile the ship was once more going on at the utmost that a powerful tow boat could give her, and consequently appearances promised us the company of our friends for a much longer time than either their business or their inclination would have otherwise allowed. However there was no help for it, and with martyr-like resignation they made a virtue of necessity by following the old adage of 'What can't be cured must be endured'.

Now it will be remembered that this affray which I have so briefly noticed and the present position of my friends was caused wholly and solely for the sake of a trifling piece of manufactured rags called paper, on which were traced a few lines of (by old bachelors termed) nonsensical words which to anyone but the party to whom they were directed would have been unintelligable, but to that party himself they were intelligible words of tenderness and of love, breathings of the souls's pure flame, of that inexpressible passion which when purely enjoyed is the paradise of man this side of eternity.

Oh! of how much value is the otherwise insignificant sheet when it bears upon its polished surface the testimony of love and truth! It bore that testimony then, it bears it now, and though years have rolled away and passed into oblivion the style of the writer is still the same, and I value a letter traced by that noble hand this day with equal worth as I did on that day I risked my life to save a friend whose pockets contained the treasure.[1]

The earth has treasures fair and bright
Deep buried in her caves
And ocean hideth many a gem
With his blue curling waves.
Yet not within her bosom dark
Or 'neath the dashing foam
Lives there a treasure equalling
A world of love at home!

True sterling happiness and Joy
Are not with gold allied
Nor can it yield a pleasure like
A merry fire side.
I envy not the man who dwells
In stately hall or dome
If mid his splendour he hath not
A world of love at home!

The friends whom time has proved sincere,
Tis they alone can bring
A sure relief to hearts that droop
'Neath sorrow's heavy wing.

[1] The following verse is attributed to the *London Journal*, which is too common a title to identify with certainty, but may be *The London Journal of Arts and Sciences*, published between 1820 and 1854.

Though care and trouble may be mine
As down life's path I roam
I'll heed them not while still I have
A world of love at home!

London Journal

It will now be asked, as no doubt it has been wondered for some time past, if the cause of such a narrow escape from a watery grave, the 'billet-doux', was safe, that is if having shared the same fate as the carrier of it, it had come off as fortunate, and now ready once more, after a resuscitation, to make its appearance in the world with all the enthusiasm of life. Let those who ask the question compare themselves to me, the principal party concerned, and they will at once perceive we differ widely, for mine is not a character of selfishness. Forgetting self entirely, I thought of nothing but saving a drowning man; when saved, my next thoughts were to administer the necessary attentions the case demanded, to divest with my own hands the rescued man of his wet garments, to provide him with others dry and warm, to chafe his lower extremities with a coarse towel in order to renew animation. To stir the fire and to add fuel in order that a glow of heat should fill my friend the sooner, and last but not least to procure for him a cup of well made strong coffee. These and a multitude of other more trifling attentions were the principal occupants of my mind.

Up to the moment I have left my friend with the reader on the former page enjoying his cup of coffee, I was still ignorant of the fate of the love letter. Indeed after the sad event for which I in a great measure blamed myself, I could not have conceived one single thought of enquiry after a missive which doubtless must have been carried away by the strong reflux of the tide which so nearly proved the destruction of my dearest friend. I was fain to lose the otherwise valued packet which at any other time an untold amount of gold could not have bought, so that my friend whose generous and sympathetic heart had led him to risk his life for me was safe.

The letter is safe – but wet

However, to satisfy my reader's curiosity, I was not doomed to bear the loss in compensation for his safety. No, the guardian angel whose ever watchful assistance had proved my friend's safe guard had also proved kind to me, for after the welfare of the rescued men was fairly established and Martin bethought himself of the letter and other valued documents which his pocket had contained ere he had taken his bathing excursion, he ordered his coat to be brought to him which had been spread in the rigging to dry and after examining the contents of its pockets found everything safe, my letter included, to the astonishment of all the beholders. Of course every paper was literally soaked with wet but as the waters of the Usk[1] are fresh it only required to place the drenched fragments before the fire for a short time in order to restore them comparatively to their former state. It may be imagined how pleased I was and with what agitated feelings I accepted the now doubly valued letter from Martin's hand. My pen would fail to describe the ecstasy of the moment, but let me add that I am sure however great my feelings of joy and pleasure were at that moment, his of satisfaction at witnessing it were not an atom less.

It is only a generous heart like his that can truly appreciate the genuine feeling of happiness caused by the conferring of it upon others. I am sure he felt it in all its pristine influence since he so largely had bestowed it upon me. In order to continue my narrative however, I must bring this topic to a close although the subject affords no mean attraction to continue it for some time longer.

The steam tug having left us once fairly out of the river, we sailed down the Bristol Channel with all the progress that a scant wind and a heavy laden ship could enable us to attain.

[1] The river on which Newport stands.

Windbound in Penarth Roads

In course of time we arrived in Penarth Roads where we anchored windbound at dusk, our friends remained with us throughout the evening when being relieved of duty we could enjoy in our snug little cabin a social pipe, and a social chat, and certainly a social glass also; providing it was filled with the only liquid we had on board, that is, water.

The evening passed pleasantly away and after we had pretty well exhausted our stores of rhetoric and dwelt *ad infinitum* upon the marvellous escape of that day etc, etc, and last but not least the stimulating fumes of the narcotic weed had pretty well inebriated us we all returned to rest, when next morning our friends, in company with the pilot, left us to return to their bereaved homes and neglected duties.

No parting can be more tender between male friends than this was, my eyes filled with the pearly drops brought up from the heart's gushing fountain of pure and undisguised affection as I tremblingly pressed the hand of my kindest friend. It needed not a very close observer to detect the feeling was mutual; the trembling lips quivering from their utter inability to speak; the long drawn scarcely audible 'farewell' followed by the more pathetic 'God bless thee ever' eloquently spoke the subdued feelings within. Once into the pilot's smart little vessel and the sails hoisted to the breeze they were not long in sight, but as long as they were our eyes were riveted upon each other, and the responding signal of the waving hat was the last proof of mutual affection paid.

Fair wind for Cádiz

The wind having continued from the south-west quarter for some time, we were forced to remain at anchor off the busy town of Cardiff, but at length a fair breeze took the place of the south-west wind and making sail we glided away like the dishanded[1] animal proud of his liberty, on our way towards the sunny south.

Cádiz was now our port of destination, and thither we arrived after a long and very rough passage of twenty days: the hardships of the passage were however soon forgotten in the pleasures that attended the perusal of an additional proof of my lady-love's sincerity on my arrival. We duly discharged our cargo of Newport produce, i.e. coals, and subsequently reloaded another cargo, not of coals but of salt, destined for a market in the Brazils, Bahia[2] being the first port we intended to touch at.

After a stay of twenty-one days we again spread our canvas to a splendid fair breeze then blowing and passed out of the beautiful bay of Cádiz to our familiar element, the open sea.[3]

On the third day after our sailing we met the serious accident of carrying away (alias breaking) our fore mast. Of course we repaired the fracture as well as we were able, but the accident tended greatly to lengthen our passage. Nothing worthy of remark transpired besides, therefore I will at once carry my thoughts in the bay of Bahia, anciently called All Saints' Bay,[4] where we dropped anchor on the 43rd day from Cádiz.[5]

Our master finding a pretty good market for the cargo, decided on remaining there and after going through the usual routine of discharging and loading a cargo of sugar and having replaced the broken fore mast by a new one, we were ready to make sail again for another part of the world, Stettin in Prussia[6] being that part.

[1] i.e. freed.

[2] i.e. the modern Salvador.

[3] The agreement to serve in BT 98/1603 was handed in to the Brazilian vice-consul at Cádiz on 23 Nov. and returned to the master endorsed with a certificate from the vice-consul dated 13 Dec. 1847 stating that the *Swift* cleared that date for Bahia.

[4] i.e. Bahia de Todos os Santos, in which Salvador lies.

[5] The agreement to serve (BT 98/1603) was handed in to the British consul at Bahia on 28 Jan. 1848 and returned to the master on 3 March.

[6] Now Szczecin, Poland, a major port on the River Oder; under Prussian (later German) rule between 1720 and 1945, during which time it was known by the German name used by Hilary.

Description of Bahia

Ere I proceed on my voyage it may be expected of me to furnish my MS with a description of the town of Bahia. Certainly I can do that, but as I am not writing to amuse others, but myself, I feel a certain insipidity in penning a description of a place which of all others in the Brazils is the least in my estimation, notwithstanding that according to tradition it is after Rio de Janeiro the largest city and the most important in all Brazil. I will, however, favour the reader with as good, though concise, a description of Bahia as lays in my power and although I admit I am prejudiced against the place yet I promise to divest myself of that prejudice for the time being and allow none whatever to direct my pen.

Bahia is divided into two towns, the Upper and Lower Towns. Most of the buildings are old and ill-constructed, but as in other Catholic cities the churches are distinguished above all other edifices. The cathedral is large but falling into ruin. The college and archiepiscopal palace are in pretty fair condition considering all things. They were all, at the period of their erection, spacious buildings and have a proud situation on the summit of a hill commanding the bay and surrounding country. The grand church of the ex-Jesuits is, by far, the most elegant structure of the city (if indeed elegance pertains to any of them). It is composed entirely of European marble imported for the purpose, at an immense cost.

In the Royal Square is the palace of the governor which is an old insignificant building, and opposite are the mint and public offices. The prison is an extensive structure exceedingly strong and secure. The Custom House and wharfs are on the beach, as is the dockyard as well as the house of the Commandant do Porto, or Captain of the Port. A few of the superior class of inhabitants have large, elegant mansions, appropriately fitted up. The habitation of other opulent individuals are generally roomy and convenient but most shabbily furnished. From the street, they have a dull and dirty appearance which is completely realized within.

The houses of tradesmen and shopkeepers are commonly disgustingly dirty. No matter what article you may have to purchase for home use, but it fills you with a nauseous feeling at the very sight of it. The very paper that encloses the package is besmeared with the excrement of the myriads of flies, tarantulas, centipedes, and scorpions that infest those dwellings and which have become so familiar to the inmates that half a dozen of the latter may be seen crawling across the partitions without meeting with the least impediment from the heedless occupants. Besides the insects and reptiles I have already adverted to, cockroaches, bugs, lizards, rats and mosquitoes, mice and numerous other creatures have free access in all parts of the house. The inhabitants are not free from vermin themselves — I mean the lower class. Scarcely can anyone walk the length of a street without witnessing the disgusting sight of one female cleaning the head of the other sitting at the open lattice, or more public still on the door step outside, without any other instrument but that provided by nature — her finger-nails which are left to grow long for the purpose.

Instead of glazed windows to the houses, they have wooden drop-lattices which want even the addition of paint to enliven or preserve them. The lowest order of soldiers, mulattoes and negroes have tiled cabins without a ceiling and with a single latticed window. These and other buildings with exception of a street or two are all intermingled throughout the Lower Town.

The British merchants have their counting-houses only in the Lower Town, it is so close and disgusting, but more from filth and the manners of the Portugese, than from the mode of building, for the very narrow streets insure shade, and declivity of ground commands the sea breeze every where by its nature, and would command cleanliness with very little art.

The Upper or New town is almost an English settlement and delightfully situated, with lanes at least clean if not trim, and gardens or rather shrubberies down to the sea. The mango and other tropical trees are beautiful and rich in their leafiness. The white cedar or bread tree of India grows here to perfection. In all the city there is scarcely any accommodations for strangers. A hotel is unknown. Those who choose to live on shore must take the whole or part of a house and furnish it. This however, is easily done, as a few chairs, trunks, and a table will be amply sufficient and in character. Eating houses there are a few and distinguished by a tricoloured flag over the door, but they are inconceivably dirty and disagreeable. The coffee shops which are numerous are very little better.

The city and country are alike infested with beggars; a subject of real or affected distress (generally the latter) presenting itself at every dozen steps.

Bahia has its comic theatre, which is little better than a barn, in a dirty situation. The actors, drama and scenery are all equally despicable, the music being the only tolerable part of the performance. The chief amusements of the country are the feasts of the different saints, professions of nuns, sumptuous funerals, the Passion Week etc which are all celebrated in rotation with pompous ceremonies, concerts and processions. In some season scarcely a day passes on which some one or other of these festivals does not occur, and thus is presented a continued round of opportunities for uniting devotion and pleasure which is eagerly embraced particularly by the ladies.

Bands of music frequently pass in large launches, playing on their way to the neighbouring villages on the bay to commemorate the anniversary of some saint or other festivity. It has also been a custom with the Portugese for European ships to have music on arrival, at departures, and the first day of taking on cargo, which sound charmingly upon the water. The musicians are all black, or Creole, and are trained by the barber surgeons of the city who are of the same colour, and have been itinerant musicians from time immemorial.[1]

The inhabitants of the city and suburbs were estimated a few years back at about one hundred thousand of whom thirty thousand may be whites, thirty thousand mulattoes and the remaining forty thousand negroes.

[1] Part of this description is transcribed from *Le Pilote de Brazil.* [HM] The work is in fact Baron Albin-Reine Roussin, *Le pilote du Brésil, ou description des côtes de l'Amérique méridionale, situées entre L'Île Santa-Catarina et celle de Maranhaõ* (Paris, 1826); the description of Bahia is taken from pp. 21–2. I am greatly indebted to Mr Max Justo Guedes, Director of the Serviço de Documentação da Marinha, Rio de Janeiro, for this identification and for kindly supplying a microfilm copy of the book, for which I have failed to trace a UK location.

Sail for Stettin in Prussia

Having now given a description of Bahia I may be permitted to proceed on my way to Stettin.[1] We weighed anchor and made sail for that port on the 11th March 1848 after a protracted stay of six weeks and duly arrived at Elsinore[2] after battling with the elements for seventy long days.

We were rather taken by surprise on our arrival when we learnt that during our passage war had been declared between Denmark and Prussia and all the latter ports blockaded by the former.[3] This was a pretty 'how d'ye do? Certainly, to Stettin we could not go, that was evident, unless we broke the blockade, and as our master was a man of peace and his crew were certainly not men of war, he decided upon accepting a proposal which was made him of discharging his cargo at Stralsund,[4] the nearest open port to Stettin, and paying part of the expenses for transshipping it to the latter port. This was a rather expensive business for the ship taking it in first light but by considering the pros and cons of the matter it was the cheapest mode of acting, for had the master refused to act as he did, there was no alternative left but remaining at Elsinore until the blockade was raised, which as time is money would have proved much more expensive.

Wheat for Guernsey

As it was it turned out very well, for immediately our cargo was discharged we took in one of wheat direct for Guernsey for which

[1] Cf. p. 217n.

[2] i.e. Helsingør, the port on the Danish coast of the Øresund.

[3] The dispute concerned the two Elbe duchies of Schleswig and Holstein, which in March 1848 broke from Denmark and sought support from the German *Bund*. By May Prussian troops had expelled the Danes from the duchies; when they entered Jutland, part of the Kingdom of Denmark itself, Great Britain intervened to secure an armistice, which was signed at Malmö in August (D. Thomson, *Europe since Napoleon* (1966 ed.), p. 242).

[4] On the Baltic coast of Germany, about a hundred miles from Stettin.

place it was both our intention and desire to go and as the freight for the wheat was a fair one, on the whole the owners were the gainers. We met with a succession of contrary winds and very rough weather on our passage. For a summer's passage I have never known one so rough. We lost some of our spars, cut-water figure-head etc. In fact we presented the appearance of a wreck on our arrival, so much so that the owners of the vessel did not know her at first appearance.[1] Once more on our dear native land however, the toils and hardships of the passage were soon forgotten in the warm and cordial reception given us by our friends.

Bliss

To me it was an Elysium of bliss! The proverb that says that 'absence makes the heart grow fonder' seemed to be perfectly realised. Eight months of absence seemed to have added to our love eight times the former force. I would fain entertain myself with a reminiscence of the meeting between my love and me on this occasion, the first in which both law and etiquette allowed us publicity. But as I should be wanting in words to express myself I shall decline that pleasure for the present and confining myself to the confirmed truth that courtship is the hallowed and proper preliminary to a happy marriage.

My stay was happily prolonged in the island to a period of near two months, and how swiftly did that happy time pass away. I have often found two weeks hang heavier on my hands than did those two months; I mean when I have been absent from home, for when there, it has always been to me (at least since the period alluded to) and is still, an uninterrupted time of pure happiness. Would that the lovers of single blessedness could understand this,

[1] Hilary does not mention that during this leg of the voyage, presumably because of the storms, the cabin-boy on board the *Swift*, John Brouard, aged 14, was lost at sea 'off the Sound' on 21 May 1848 (see the crew list handed in on return in PRO, BT 98/1603). The agreement to serve was handed in at Guernsey in July 1848 (the day is unclear but appears to be the 29th).

how soon they would change their condition in life! Would that it were my lot to enjoy this felicity without interruption, but alas! it is not the case. At the end of two months so swiftly sped away I was forced to undergo the cruel pangs of separation; to inflict upon a loving, tender heart equal pain. Oh why should stern duty impose upon us such a tremendous sacrifice? It is so nevertheless, as too numerous occasions have proved.

– 1848 –

Eleventh Voyage

August

Pernambuco

August the 7th we again made sail to pursue our course once more across the Atlantic, this time bound to Pernambuco.[1] As we left the receding shore where hearts were melting in anguish at our loss, I could not help looking back upon the distant steeples towering above the trees, the silent momentos of happy hours gone by, and with the words of the poet give vent to my feelings — Isle of Beauty, fare thee well!

I shall not occupy either time or space in dwelling on the incidents of our passage since it could only be a repetition of others already described. Let me therefore pass on from this gloomy moment at once to our arrival at Pernambuco on the fifty-first day after the aforementioned 7th of August.

Our stay in that port was not long, the master having been fortunate on arrival in obtaining a charter for London direct.[2] Consequently the ballast was soon taken out and a cargo of sugar quickly taken in.

[1] i.e. Recife, capital of Pernambuco state and the principal port in NE Brazil. Two crew lists and an agreement to serve, both dated 5 August 1848, survive in BT 98/1603: Hilary Marquand, aged 23, signed on as mate at £3 5s. a month (Guernsey currency).

[2] The agreement to serve (see previous note) refers to a passage to Pernambuco and thence on a trading voyage, ending at a port in the United Kingdom to unload. The immediate return to London was therefore a change of policy by John David.

Description of Pernambuco

Pernambuco is a nice little town enough, next to Bahia[1] in importance. I have often been there as well as to all the principal ports on the coast of Brazil, and as I have a pretty fair inclination of being eloquent today, I will indulge in a description of the place, but it must not be expected to differ a great deal from that of Bahia.

The islands on which the town is built are connected by two bridges, one of which is a beautiful structure constructed, I am informed, by the Dutch when they took the place from the Portugese in 1670.[2] It consists of fifteen arches, under which runs a strong and rapid river that comes many hundred miles down the country. On each side of this bridge are shops full of European merchandise, 'Facendas Inglesas'.[3] It is in the middle only that a person finds he is on a bridge; he there beholds an opening which during the day is often full of people enjoying the cool refreshing breeze that comes down the river and gratifying themselves with the prospect which from this spot is the prettiest in the town. The river is seen winding up as far as Olinda which is seated on a hill; on either bank cottages 'à la mode Portugese par example', whitewashed and looking beautifully white intermixed with mangrove and cocoa nut trees; the Indians paddling down the river with their unwieldy canoes, the fishermen on the beach drying their nets, and nature displaying her gayest verdure, form altogether a *coup d'œil* which is impossible to describe.

The other bridge is a long wooden one in which there is nothing remarkable more than its being quite open to the breeze which comes down the river. It is on that account much resorted to in the evening, especially by the English, who, seated on each

[1] i.e. Salvador; cf. above, p. 216.

[2] This passage is confused: it was at Recife that the Portuguese settlers in Brazil finally expelled the Dutch from the NE of the country in 1654.

[3] 'Fazendas Inglesas' (Hilary has mistaken the spelling of the first word) were fabrics, usually cottons but sometimes woollens, made in England and sold in the shops of the principal cities of Brazil in this period (I am once more indebted to Mr Max Justo Guedes of Rio de Janeiro for elucidating this phrase).

side, often amuse themselves by criticising, with the characteristic liberty of their country, the numerous passengers. Many of the houses in the town are well built, chiefly of stone, but the streets are comparatively wide and spacious. The churches are like those of other Catholic cities, magnificent enough, and contain many valuable images. I am told that the religious form one-eighth of the population. Half the inhabitants, say 30,000, are slaves, or rather were, for of late fever has made such dreadful havoc among them and the slave trade being now abolished, that their number is considerably reduced. Like in Bahia there are no glazed windows to the house, but lattices painted green and kept in pretty fair condition. When fresh painted of a nice pea-green they have a beautiful effect, since the houses are white and frequently surrounded with evergreens. During the morning the inhabitants are seen leaning out of them, muffled up in their cloaks and exhibiting a genuine picture of indolence.

The ladies are seen towards the evening only, peeping through the lattices; very few appearing about the street, and then generally veiled. There are some good coffee-houses which are known by a small round board with 'Casa de Café' written upon it. Pretty good wine, Sangaree,[1] and a tolerably good breakfast can be procured at all hours of the day.

Here are also billiards and backgammon tables, much frequented, especially on a Sunday, the day on which these and other amusements are mostly practised. At about eleven in the forenoon the merchants make a tolerable show and much business is transacted. They are generally English, rich and respectable.

The harbour of Pernambuco is wonderfully convenient; it is formed by a natural pier extending five miles in a direct line. This is a coral reef so exactly straight and even that one would imagine it the work of art, and not nature. The vessels lie alongside each other in tiers, moored head and stern, at about half pistol shot from the shore, and close to the reef which at high water spring tides is nearly on a level with the sea and forms an excellent barrier.

[1] A West Indian drink composed of wine, brandy and lime juice, sweetened and spiced.

The heat is sometimes excessive: the thermometer frequently being at 90 degrees in the shade. During the night it is pretty nearly always calm with much lightning. At about nine in the mornings the sea breeze gradually sets in, is strongest about noon, and dies away towards sunset.

The port is very well fortified in appearance but it would make but a sorry resistance in case of attack. I believe there are about five thousand military comprising the militia, of these the greater part are blacks and when I have sometimes seen them exercising I have thought how precious quick a few hundreds of our British red jackets would make them run for their lives.

Great numbers of the religious orders are always seen in the streets dressed up in their peculiar costume and soliciting alms, for which purpose they carry a small square box with the figure of Christ, or some saint, painted upon it, and I have often observed that although they consider the English as heretic, they do not scruple to receive their money for which they kindly bestow, in return, a benediction.

In every street there are images of the Virgin and saints, which on particular days are exposed to view, superbly illuminated with a large number of candles. At about eight in the evening on these particular days, the children in the neighbourhood assemble around these images and sing hymns. This has a pleasing effect, especially as they keep time with great exactness and have a person to direct them by the ringing of a little bell.

To a stranger, another custom which is common in Catholic countries appears very singular: twice every day at about eight in the evening, and ten in the morning, at the tolling of a bell, everything is in an instant at a stand. Men, women and children, whether in the streets or in the houses, instantly pull off their hats, cross themselves, and say a short prayer; this continues only about a minute. At the second tolling every thing goes on as usual. During this time a particular part of the mass is performing in the great church, the effect seems like that of magic, and the intelligent foreigner will, as a matter of course, treat it with respect.

The season of Lent is most rigidly observed, and that of Easter affords a perfect contrast. The religious procession which takes place in the latter, with the illuminations, fire works etc greatly surpass all that a native of Britain may conceive. Such shows are very frequently repeated and make a wonderful impression on the lower classes, more especially the slaves.

Fevers are common enough at Pernambuco, the cause of which I attribute to its situation on a low ground and quite surrounded by water. Since I have been there, however, it has been much affected with the African yellow fever which has caused a dreadful mortality, particularly among the negroes. There was but one hospital which consisted of a very large room with about 30 beds on each side filled with wretches suffering under the most loathsome diseases. A man stands at the door to solicit the charity of the passers by which contributes to defray the expenses. When a patient dies, he is laid on a table at the entrance with a plate on his breast to receive money for his burial, four or five are frequently thus exposed at once.

The country at a few miles from the town is covered with thick, impenetrable woods fearfully infested with wild beasts and reptiles, especially snakes, whose bite is fatal. The 'ignis fatuus', commonly called 'Jack a lantern', is very common, it is visible mostly at twilight and more than thirty exhalations of light may sometimes be seen at once. These luminations rise from the ground and continue to float in the atmosphere at the distance of eight or ten feet from the surface for some minutes, when they totally disappear.[1]

The most beautiful birds abound in the neighbourhood, some of which sing delightfully. Macaws and parrots are very common, nearly every house having one or two at the door, and as they often set each other chattering throughout the whole length of the street, they make such a din that an Englishman might almost imagine himself in a Welsh market, or at Billingsgate.

Fish on the coast are numerous. The river above mentioned abounds with alligators, which are often very destructive, and that

[1] The *SOED* defines an ignis fatuus ('foolish fire') as 'a phosphorescent light seen hovering or flitting over marshy ground, supposed to be due to the spontaneous combustion of an inflammable gas (phosphuretted hydrogen) derived from decaying organic matter'; Jack-a-lantern is one of several popular names for the phenomenon.

extraordinary fish the torpedo is frequently caught here. The electric power is so strong in this fish that even the line which catches it conveys a slight shock. The blacks have a curious way of catching fish which is thus performed. On a dark night they go on their catamarans (a sort of canoe composed of three or four logs of wood lashed together) on which they make a large blazing fire which instantly attract the fish when they strike them with harpoons or grains. Most of the fish with which the market is supplied is caught in this manner.[1]

I have pretty well exhausted my store of information relative to Pernambuco and the reader cannot be a perfect stranger with that town, after perusing my detail, which I have lengthened as much as possible, but which is all consistent with truth and without prejudice.

Arrival in London – Guernsey

I will now be allowed to perform my voyage once more across the Atlantic and be permitted to arrive in London on the 3rd December after a passage of 51 days.[2] Nothing presents itself to my memory on which I can make any remark during our stay in London which was but fourteen days, when we took ballast, and proceded for Guernsey, where an event was about to follow on which I will arrest my attention for a brief period.

Let it not be imagined that I am going to describe a matrimonial scene, or some event connected with the hymeneal altar; not at all, everything in its place, I am not arrived to that blissful period of my life yet. When I am, perhaps I may touch on the subject.

To initiate the reader in the outlines of the event which forms

[1] Partly from *Le Pilote de Brazil*. [HM] Cf. above, p. 219n. for *Le pilote du Brésil*; this passage is from pp. 24–5.

[2] The crew list was handed in at London on 4 Dec. and the agreement to serve (signed by Hilary as mate, together with the master) the following day (BT 98/1603).

so far a memorable period of my career through the vales and valleys of this world as to occupy my time to dwell upon it, I must refer him to the preceding pages No 49, 50 and 51[1] where he will find me a young lad of fourteen, with all the enthusiasm of a British sailor, watching the arrival of the brig *Nancy*, remarking upon her stateliness and majestic bearing on the waters of the British Channel, informing the amazed beholders with all the spirit of his boyish age that he was about to commence a seafaring life, and manifesting his particular ambition to, sooner or later, command as stately a ship as that now the subject of his earnest gaze.

Having referred to the above it will easily be perceived I did not commence life with thoughtlessness, but on the contrary with that soul-stirring ambition which was the leading point throughout my career; it will not, then, be wondered at if fortune, ever kept bright by the application of the oil of perseverance, shone upon me favourably at the early age of twenty-three, the period at which I have now arrested my attention.

On my arrival at Guernsey from London our ears were immediately greeted by the distressing intelligence of the cruel death of our captain's namesake and friend in the Baltic who,[2] after losing his vessel, lost his life by cold in an open boat. Now it happened that on the stocks in the course of construction was a splendid vessel of very large tonnage intended for this same person whom death had so prematurely visited on his way to Russia for the purchase of rigging for said new vessel.

Hilary appointed Captain of the Swift

In consequence the command had to be transferred, and the owners desiring to obtain the services of Captain David above all others

[1] The page numbers given in the MS by Hilary have been amended to refer to pages of this edition.

[2] This word does not appear in the MS but appears to be essential to the sense of this sentence.

entreated of him to take the charge, which he did without reluctance, especially as he was thereby obliging some of his greatest friends. But as a very natural consequence, by so doing he caused a vacancy in the mastership of his own vessel, the owners of which and he consulted together on the subject, when the conclusion they arrived at was that it was not necessary to move out of the ship to find a suitable person to take the command. Consequently the charge as future master of the gallant *Swift* was enjoined upon me.

All this was done among the owners at a meeting held by them to discuss the matter on the resignment of Captain David and entirely unknown to me. Captain David expatiated largely on the worthiness of him he recommended, assuring the owners that when they transferred the charge of their property from his into my hands, they had no cause to regret the exchange since he felt no reluctance in saying that though but young, a more experienced or abler person was not to be found, not excepting himself.

This was very kind of Captain David indeed, and the kindness was, and has always been, the more appreciated since it was conferred in my absence, and for which he has never sought any gratitude by the revelation of his eulogies in my favour. The gratitude has nevertheless been his, and while I have life I shall never cease to revere him as having been a kind and really good master, whilst he was a noble and generous friend.

I was rather surprised when I was greeted with congratulations on my new appointment by the public, not having yet heard any thing about it from a direct source. So much surprised that I denied the truth of the report for some time. At length, however, I was formally informed of my preferment and subsequently received instructions for a future voyage.

Shall I appear bashful, and say that I refused my new appointment, or at any rate hesitated in accepting it under the modest plea of feeling my own inability? Not in the least. Let me appear to the world as I really was, a truly happy being at having attained to the summit of my ambition at so early an hour of my life. Proud of the preference shown to me over the many eager aspirants which were about. Proud with the feeling of competency, which until then I had thought buried in the recess of my own knowledge, but which was now publicly declared to the world by other tongues than mine, and stood as a halo of sunshine around me. Nine years ago I was but a child of fourteen years of age commencing my apprenticeship to a seafaring life. Since then, I have gone through all the grades of my profession with more or less credit, and here I am now but twenty-three, chosen by a committee of competent judges of qualification to take charge of their property to the value of thousands and thousands and not only as in charge of that property, but as their agent to execute with that property whatever transaction my own judgement might enable me to think fit for the promotion of their interest. It is no small charge, that of master of a ship trading round the world, with *'Carte Blanche'* to act for the promotion of the owners' interest.

Rascality of Brokers etc

That man must be able to combine at once the essential qualities of merchant, and broker, to that of ship master, and I feel no reluctance to add that no man in whatever situation he may be, is surrounded with a greater set of disguised enemies in the mercantile world. From the tradesmen and the ship broker who present their cards with extreme professed civility on arrival, to the merchant into whose hand you place the consignment of your ship, and who receives you generally with all the courtesy imaginable, there is that avaricious feeling of imposition which if not wisely guarded against proves in the sequel of material consequence.

The former with whom you may transact your several purchases as occasion may require is not satisfied under four or five hundred per cent on the goods he may provide you with, and indeed on many occasions, depending on the quality of the purchase you may make, he extortionately demands a hundred per cent more whilst the same article sold to a resident would well repay him at 25 per cent profit. And if you remonstrate with this gentle and affable dealer, who is always ready to treat you with a cigar at any hour of the day or with a small drop of brandy and water at eleven o'clock to give tone to the stomach, he will excuse himself in the same way as any other honest man would under similar circumstances namely, that it is the risk of the trade.

The broker who generally acts in concert with the merchant, and who has a freight to offer not really worth accepting, will not scruple in calling falsehood to his assistance, to assure the unprotected ship master that it is really the best freight in the market, that he had better accept of it at once, as he is aware by secret channels that there is going to be a crisis in the freight market, and nothing will be done for five or six weeks. He commences by computing what the ship will carry, and in spite of your knowing the carrying capacities of your vessel, he will insist upon her carrying much more, showing reasons in numbers why he is right, and you are wrong, and with professed impudence he will maintain his superiority of knowledge.

Then he goes on by calculating the freight, which, with a dexterity only a broker's, he swells up the amount to such a figure that the whole at once appears a beneficial transaction. The expenses of the port he wishes to despatch you at[1] are nothing, literally nothing, and of course your passage is always at least 20 days under the average; he assures you that at this season you will be sure to meet with favourable winds etc, etc, and concludes his harangue by protesting with a countenance so well disguised that you might suppose every word of his to be gospel, that it is as a particular favour he has made you this offer and on account of old acquaintanceship, or for some other reason as well defined. 'For I assure you, my dear captain, that at this moment there are two ship masters anxiously looking out for this freight and would be glad in order to secure it, to take a figure less.' Oh unhappy and pitiable man, who is not initiated into the mysterious falsities of these unprincipled men. Who has not strength of mind to overcome their tempting persuasions, who perhaps judging others by himself, takes it for granted that he is dealing with honest people, and finally swallows the bait made to appear so delicious, and sweet, afterwards to find it disgusting, and bitter in the extreme.

Too many alas! have been the instances in which the flexible

[1] *Sic* MS, rather than 'despatch you to'.

ship master has been the dupe of these extortioners, who when once they have entrapped their game and secured to themselves a handsome commission, care not a straw about him or how matters end, but who has afterwards to meet the censure of the scowling ship owner, and perhaps pays the penalty of his flexibility in the loss of his situation and the degradation of his character.

The merchant, on the other hand, is more systematic in his unjust claims on the property of the shipowner which is entrusted in the charge of the ship master. The unexperienced eye can scarcely detect in the so very nicely made out account current (decorated here and there with a curving dash of the pen, and a double line of red ink, strictly parallel) any fault. Indeed many masters there are who would think it a breach of civility to doubt for a moment the incorrectness of the document, much less pass an examination over it. But the more philosophical is not so easily deceived and knowing that the pen refuses nothing, marks out with care and precision its traces, and finds out in the swelling amount opposite 'Custom House Charges' an unpardonable extension of figures, further on embedded in the flourished writing, scarcely perceptible, stands an item termed 'incidental and petty expenses' to which is added a flaming amount of cecy,[1] which is neither incidental in its relation, or petty in its volume. The real significance of the 'Incidental and Petty expenses' I will give translated into pure English, in order that the uninitiated in the language of mercantile houses may understand. It is this: 'Wine and cigar money for ourselves for the next three months'.

In the Brazils the significance of 'Custom House Charges' is in pure English: 'Bribe money paid the Customs officers to allow us to smuggle the next importation we make from Europe'. On further examination we find 'Commission five per cent on sale of cargo so and so, sold at eighteen months credit'! Of course at eighteen months because the discount follows: One per cent per month. But if written in English it would have been 'Sold at six or

[1] This word is clear in the MS, although the meaning is less certain. The French demonstrative pronoun *ceci* may be intended, possibly in a colloquial sense meaning bribe, backhander or the like.

nine months' but it could not have done so worded, because it would have been preposterous to have charged two per cent or two and a quarter per cent for discount. Then follows guarantee five per cent, brokerage two and a half per cent and last but not least of the commissions, commission on disbursement two and a half per cent, which means on all the money that has been needed to defray the expenses of the ship whilst in port.

Typical transaction

Now when we calculate these handsome remunerations, say on a cargo of wine value, or rather sold for, £30 per pipe, number of pipes we'll admit to be 350, the amount at once presents itself at £10,500, on which we will first charge the five per cent as commission which give us £525, then five per cent guarantee, which adds to the former an additional £525. Afterwards comes the discount of one per cent per month which swells to the vast amount of £1,890. The brokerage of two and a half per cent of course is not the merchant's but independent of that, we at once show a balance in favour of the merchant of £2,940.

A pretty fair transaction, certainly, considering that this is besides their 'Wine & cigar money' and other advantageous perequisites. Is it any wonder if these princes of the mercantile world keep house as they do in foreign countries especially, and lavish such sums of money upon their numerous wives, and display in general such independence that it is almost amounting to imminent danger to approach them on any unpleasant business especially.

Such are a few of the quicksands which stands in the ship master's course, and which renders his navigation very intricate. It requires all the art he may possess, having to steer among these many shoals, to reeve his bark between in order to avoid being crushed by any one of them, and although they differ from the rocks and shoals of the ocean, yet they are altogether more dangerous: for while the one stands always in the same position, wearing the same aspect and presenting the same danger, with due attention to the course steered and the distance run it may be avoided. Not so the other for its position varies always, for this voyage whilst steering a different course in order to avoid at, remembering how you stumbled against it last voyage, you invariably find it right ahead of you again but instead of wearing the aspect of danger, it presents to you its smooth and shiny side, inviting you to a nearer approach only to sink you deeper afterwards.

After all I have just described, it will be admitted that the man who has charge of another's ship and property to a vast amount, and who has that interest to guard amidst such impending dangers, has no small amount of anxiety and care weighing upon his mind, and his task is the more severe when it is considered that if he wishes to do his duty to all intents and purposes, he cannot enjoy real pleasure for a moment, as the necessity of being ever upon his guard imposes at once a certain distance between himself and his interested friends often approaching to enmity, which unless he is like themselves a finished hypocrite wearing two faces under the same hat he cannot well conceal.

It may be thought that I am rather severe in my comments, if so, I sternly refute the accusation. I am neither of suspicious or incredulous disposition as regards society in general, God forbid I should. My motto has always been that confidence is the basis of love, as well as of friendship. But unhappy experience has too often taught me, confidence cannot be practised indiscriminately. When I knew less of the world I had more confidence. I judged every one by myself and have paid dearly for the mistake.

I admit there are exceptions to every rule, fortunately it is the case, or what state would society be in? I have placed my owner's as well as my property into very honest hands, but I have placed it into very dishonest ones also, and candidly speaking, during my voyages north, east, south, and west, I have found less honesty among my countrymen than I have among foreigners. I strictly advise every ship master to be upon his guard in matters of business with all whom he has to deal and to treat all interested kindnesses with that contempt which it so richly deserves.

I once heard an unprincipled man of business, one of the profession I have described above, boast that a ship master could be bought at any time with a glass of grog! Alas! it is but too true that such has been the case. But thank heaven that season of intemperance, of ignorance, of folly, is in the wane, and we are now getting a class of ship masters of more educated minds, whom it will be difficult to purchase over even with a more deceitful weapon than a 'glass of grog'.

I have deviated somewhat from my course in order to point out the necessary cares that devolve upon the ship master. But having done so, I may be allowed to resume my narrative with a concluding remark upon my promotion.

It was with a great feeling of pride my parents learnt of the advancement their son was making in the world. They hailed the presence of a captain in the family with no small degree of joy — and where is the father who is not proud of his son's advancement in life? But there was yet another person equally interested; one in whom my appointment had created great satisfaction; one who would now feel really proud in giving up a lieutenant's arm to rest upon a captain's. She who looked upon me as her future husband, her future support, perhaps the father of her future children, could not but feel pleased beyond expression at the turn fortune had taken in her favour; she who loved the officer with tenderness could not but venerate the general.

Her father, an old veteran in the sea service,[1] greeted my appointment with much satisfaction and felt proud that one of his rank claimed the hand of his favourite daughter. Such was the state of affairs when I received my sailing order to proceed for Pernambuco in quest of a homeward freight, or in the absence of such to proceed on a trading voyage as circumstances might determine.

It was not long after receiving these orders ere I was on my road. It was a scene of tenderness, was this parting, all seemed to have increased their affection towards me since my promotion. Each wished the young captain success, and none prayed less fervently to God to give charge to the winds and waves concerning me, than did she whose future happiness was centred in mine.

[1] Abraham Blondel was himself a former sea captain: see Introduction, p. xvi.

– 1849 –

Twelfth Voyage

January

Pernambuco – Southampton – Guernsey

Joining in all their fervent prayers I left them on the 31st January 1849 once more to trace the uneven paths of the vast Atlantic.[1] As usual I had to contend with adverse gales, and other contrarities but nevertheless reached my destination after a fair passage of forty days. On arrival I was fortunate in obtaining an offer which I immediately accepted of a charter for a cargo of sugar destined for a market in the United Kingdom or the continent, calling at Cowes for orders.

I had quick despatch at Pernambuco and although I was unfortunate in making a long passage home, I nevertheless arrived back to Cowes after being absent only a few days over three months.[2] I was ordered to discharge my cargo at Southampton which was very fortunate, and in a very few days I had disembarrassed myself of the cargo, taken in ballast, and was safely enjoying the sunny smiles of love's beaming eyes in Guernsey again.

[1] The crew lists and agreement to serve (BT 98/1901) show that Hilary appears to have left Guernsey for Pernambuco, calling at Southampton outward, rather earlier in the month than he states. The first crew list and the agreement are dated 8 Jan. and the Brazilian vice-consul at Guernsey endorsed the agreement for clearance to Pernambuco the following day.

[2] The agreement to serve was returned by the British consul at Pernambuco on 24 March 1849 and was handed in at Southampton on 11 June.

Orders to sail

It seemed but as a dream that I had made a voyage to the Brazils, for my part I can scarcely believe I had been absent when enjoying the pure stream of happiness flowing around me. I was not destined to enjoy this happiness very long unfortunately, for about a week after my arrival I received fresh instructions to proceed to Cádiz, there to purchase a cargo of salt for account of the owners, with which I was to proceed to the Brazils for a market, calling at Bahia[1] as the first port.

I cannot forget what disappointment these fresh orders caused to my beloved and me who had been building castles in the air for our future enjoyment. The 24th of June being Mid-Summer's Day and always a grand holiday with us in Guernsey, on this occasion was hailed with greater glee inasmuch as a general order was issued that a grand review of the militia and a sham fight would take place.[2]

Not having since our engagement enjoyed one holiday together, we looked forward to the ensuing one with delight and who is ignorant of the pride and pleasure of the young lady who is escorted through the throng of the gay multitude on a grand holiday, leaning upon the arm of her beau? A dashing young captain too! But is not the feeling mutual? Yes, it is. Little less pride or pleasure exists on the part of the gentleman who feels reclining on his arm the sweetest and most charming of her sex, the idol of his fancies, the hope of his life. We were looking forward to enjoy inestimable delights on this gala day amidst the galaxy of splendour and fashion, when suddenly our disappointment fell upon us the more severe, because it was the more sudden. I had received my sailing orders and no other excuse but a contrary wind could keep me on shore.

[1] Salvador; cf. above, p. 216.

[2] According to a local newspaper (*The Star*, 26 June 1849), the 'sham fight' took place at Vazon Bay, on the west coast of the island, on Monday 25 June. After the 'battle' the militia marched past in review order and the senior officer, Capt. Ozanne, delivered a speech (I owe this reference to the kindness of Dr H. Tomlinson, Priaulx Library).

– 1849 –
– 1850 –

Thirteenth Voyage

June – March

Cádiz – Bahia – Rio de Janeiro Falmouth – Hamburg – Guernsey

It only wanted three or four days from the 24th and perhaps the westerly wind then blowing would continue its course, but to make our disappointment complete, on the morning of the 23rd it suddenly changed to the NE and *sans remède* I had to sail.

Oh how bitter, bitter are these disappointments to young impassioned hearts like ours were. It was a bright sunshiny day was the 24th, nature could never have displayed her brightness with greater perfection, the little birds cheeped in the green foliage of the bright and flowery orchards, the skylark sung her melodious tune high up in the air, appearing only as a dark speck on the otherwise spotless blue of the heavens, the little grey crested wren came warbling its puny notes on the very sill of the opened window as if to offer to the inmates a share of its joys, the surrounding fields were gay with the rich blossoms of the flowery world, and the new mown hay sent forth its fragrant perfumes over the earth adding to the excellence of the scene a perfection better imagined than described. How many thousands enjoyed the day, it was a grand sight amid the sunshine of such splendour to see accumulated on one particular spot the regiments of militia amounting to thousands, their splendid uniforms and arms of steel glistening in the sun, engaged in sham fighting, surrounded by thousands of admirers whose varied dresses contributed not a little to enliven the scene.

How many hearts were glad and gay, how many smiles lit up the countenance of myriads on that day? And yet amidst all, all this revelry and all this joy, one heart was sad, yea, two were gloomy and distressed. The one was buried in the solitude of her own boudoir, giving vent to her heart-rending grief in an uninterrupted flow of bitter tears, heedless of the gay world outside. The other was buffeting with the storms and waves of the troubled ocean not more restless than his feelings at the time. Such is life. Today we are joyful, tomorrow we are sad.

I had a splendid run through the Bay of Biscay with a favourable gale at NE and along the coast of Portugal down as far as within a few hours sail of my port of destination, when it suddenly fell calm which retarded my passage of one day. Notwithstanding, I arrived in Cádiz Bay on the 9th day after leaving Guernsey which was reckoned a good passage.[1]

Description of Cádiz – and the Spanish

The Bay of Cádiz is a very spacious bay and has a good roadstead. Ships lay quite comfortable except during the strong Levant winds which cause a short rough sea and prevents the loading or discharging. The town is well built and appears, from the roadstead, a magnificent object to arrest the attention.

It is entirely surrounded by a strong-built wall, inside of which it is immensely fortified with innumerable cannon, which would seem to ensure the safety of its inhabitants from the approach of the enemy. The houses are all white, and here and there interspersed are magnificent trees whose green foliage and variegated blossoms form a most delightful contrast. The streets are wide and very clean. The inhabitants are naturally lazy and indolent. Groups of fine athletic and well built men may be seen at all the hours of the day lounging in the streets, ever smoking their cigarette with an air of as much independence as though they were enjoying an income of ten thousand a year while in reality ten sixpences would

[1] The crew lists and agreement to serve (PRO, BT 98/2184) show that the *Swift*, with Hilary as master, left Guernsey on 22 June 1849 destined for Cádiz, Rio de Janeiro and Hamburg.

buy all they are worth.

The women are generally reputed handsome. I have heard much, and read more, of the beauty of the Spanish ladies; but in my humble opinion, their beauty is far from being comparable to the standard of beauty of our English ladies and whatever it may be, in my estimation it is much lessened by their inconstancy and faithless disposition. They have that horrid propensity of smoking also, which is so disgusting in a lady, and which no true English character can tolerate. There is a old saying which says 'Handsome is that handsome does'. Therefore by that rule handsome cannot be attributed to a Spanish lady since she is both inconstant and faithless, and smokes besides!

Sails for Bahia

As soon as I had completed my cargo of salt I made sail towards Bahia, where I duly arrived after a passage of thirty-nine days, but finding no market for my cargo, I proceeded towards Rio de Janeiro intending to continue my route to the River Plate if I could not sell in Rio. As it happened however, I did meet with a marketable price in Rio and consequently remained there to discharge my cargo after I had sold it, after which I loaded a cargo of coffee, bound to Falmouth to call for orders.[1]

Description of Rio de Janeiro

Before I proceed however, I will occupy a little time and space in giving a description of Rio de Janeiro. As I have described Bahia and Pernambuco[2] I think it would be inconsistent to pass the

[1] The agreement to serve (PRO, BT 98/2184) was handed in to the British consul at Cádiz on 11 July and returned on the 16th. It was surrendered and returned at Bahia on 27 Aug. and returned by the consul at Rio on 8 Nov. 1849.

[2] Above, pp. 219, 228. Although no attribution is given, the following paragraphs are once again based on *Le pilote du Brésil*, pp. 15–16.

former unnoticed, it being the seat of government and the capital of Brazil and to all intents and purposes a magnificent place.

It is very spacious, and one of the most magnificent bays in the world. Its extent in diameter is from four to five leagues in several directions, between mountains of majestic elevation, covered with the richest verdure, and terminating with an easy declivity, occupied by numerous villages down to the sea.

Plantations of all sorts, handsome country houses surrounded with trees, many isles, woody and inhabited, ornament and diversify the surface and the coast of this little inland sea; and there is not on the globe a more beautiful residence, or an aspect more imposing and agreeable.

The city is fine and large, the population about 180,000 persons. It possesses in abundance all the resources which mariners can require. Vessels may here be careened,[1] and remasted, and furnished with all things requisite; but all is expensive, and repairs are very dear, on account of the high price of workmanship. Provisions, although plentiful, are not cheap, cattle excepted: and the flesh of these is not only indifferent in quality and flavour, but frequently unwholesome, a disadvantage common in hot climates, and in particular on the Brazil coast.

Their mode of killing the meat conduces a great deal towards it. It is one of the most revolting and disgusting sights that man can witness. There are wharfs and stairs for the purpose of landing at, but their accommodation is only poor, and when there is a swell in the harbour which generally happens at every change of the moon and prevails for three or four days, then the landing is very bad.

The Palace is extensive and has nothing magnificent in its appearance to indicate its being the royal residence. The houses are in general well built, most of the the streets are good, but are improving very much by undergoing repairs and a new pavement for which purpose a great deal of the stone is imported from England at a great cost although there is no want of splendid granite in the immediate vicinity of the town, but such is the want

[1] i.e. turned over on one side for cleaning, caulking or repair.

of energy of the Brazilian that he would rather pay dear for the article ready for use than have the trouble to make it ready.

The shops are well supplied with British as well as other wares, and whether the vendor be English or Portuguese, he is equally unconscionable in his demands.

Most of the streets are designated by the trades which are exercised by those who occupy them. As in Rua de Zapatos (Shoe Street) you find shoemakers; Rua d'Ouvidor (Gold Street) gold smiths, jewellers, lapidaries etc, Rua de Saboò (Soap Street) soap dealers etc. Gold Street is the most attractive, and is generally the resort of strangers who are anxious to supply themselves with jewellery or precious stones natural to the country, but it is not always that they are fortunate enough to succeed in obtaining them genuine; for, since the city has become the royal residence, it has attracted a host of English, Irish, and Scotch adventurers, and the Portuguese are apt scholars in knavery, so that from any of them you are now very likely to acquire a bit of paste instead of a diamond.

There are a considerable number of churches, but they are by no means splendid. Excepting the Chapel Royal, which is in the vicinity of the Palace, there is little worthy of notice. The theatre and opera possess no particular elegance. The market is splendid and well supplied with every article of the vegetable kingdom and is in so eligible a situation that with a comparatively small portion of trouble, it might be kept in fine order; but the people are naturally idolaters to filthiness, so what can we expect?

The country for a considerable distance round is peculiarly beautiful; the mountains high and woody, the valleys perfect gardens. The most delicious fruits are abundant. The quantity of oranges exhibited for sale in the orange market is quite astonishing. The same tree often exhibits at once the blossom, the fruit in its primitive state, some half ripe, and the rest fully so, or fit for use. The pine apple is here in great perfection. The various kinds of richly flavoured bananas abound also, in fact all the productions of nature are abundant. In a certain quality of the orange there is a peculiarity which is not generally known, and which I will briefly mention; it consists in the part where the seeds are formed being removed near the crown, and in some instances outside the pulp, but beneath the rind, giving it, upon the peel being removed, the appearance of two oranges, one large and the other small. The part containing the seed is a kind of excrescence into which is drawn all the objectionable portion of the fruit, leaving the legitimate production free from every impurity, and rendering it the most delicious in its kind.

In the suburbs are several botanical gardens belonging chiefly to private individuals and containing many rare plants etc. If the heat were less oppressive Rio de Janiero might be esteemed as one of the most desirable places in the world; a nice sea breeze generally comes in about noon which cools the atmosphere and renders it endurable. It has like most of the other ports on the coast unfortunately been visited with the African yellow fever and cholera of late, which at its first onset caused a dreadful mortality, but within this last year or two that disease seems to be vanishing rapidly, and has lost a great deal of its terror in the knowledge gained by the physicians for its treatment.

Thirty or forty English mercantile houses are established here and the export trade is almost entirely in their hands. The imports consists in English manufacture and all the produce of Europe which can be required in Brazil. The exports are chiefly coffee, some sugar, and some hides, but of the two latter, comparatively small quantities are exported. Brazilians are the growers of the raw produce, which is conveyed by them to the port and sold to the English merchant.

I cannot extend my description of Rio de Janeiro. I believe I have said enough to acquaint the reader with that beautiful place. I can only conclude with the language of Mr Forbes, the lamented botanist. He says: 'On entering the harbour the mind is at once struck with its magnificence and beauty. The vast expanse of water bordered with bright green, the numerous inlets and islands, the rich verdure of the hills studded with villas, and the lofty chain of mountains form a dark and distant background, and make altogether a picture more like the poet's fancy than a reality on earth'.[1]

This language of Mr Forbes, I admit, is very impressive but in my opinion who has visited Rio de Janeiro many times, it yet fails to do justice to the beauties of the scenery. In fact I cannot think any description can convey an adequate idea of this splendid country. I have visited several parts of the world, and seen many specimens of romantic scenery, but none have at all come up to the neighbourhood of Rio de Janeiro.

Arrival in Falmouth

After a long stay in port and having completed the loading of my cargo, I sailed on the 10th November and meeting with a great deal of opposition only reached Falmouth on the 13th January 1850 where I duly received orders to proceed to Hamburg, but owing to the Elbe being closed with ice I could not proceed until the 20th of February which was yet very early certainly, as some winters that river remains closed up to April. I safely reached Hamburg on the 25th after a speedy run of six days, being more fortunate than many others who had sailed at the same time from Falmouth as I did, some arriving after my cargo was out, and others not yet arrived when I sailed.[2]

[1] The author referred to is apparently John Forbes (1799–1823), a botanist who left London in 1822 for the east coast of tropical Africa and sent home considerable collections of specimens to the Horticultural Society from Madeira, Rio, the Cape and Madagascar, but died at Senna in August 1823, during an unsuccessful attempt to march up the Zambesi (*DNB*), although I have failed to trace the book or paper from which this quotation is taken. Hilary appears not to be referring to Edward Forbes (1815–54), who was a geologist, rather than a botanist.

[2] The agreement to serve (BT 98/2184) was surrendered to the British Consul-General at Hamburg on 2 March and returned on the 13th.

Hamburg

Hamburg is a magnificent city and the suburbs are really indescribably beautiful. Part of the ancient city was burnt down in 1840 which has since been rebuilt on a much more grand and elegant scale, and the contrast which exists between the old portion of the town and the new is altogether remarkable, showing at once the more refined taste of the modern and more enlightened age over that of our ancestors.

The streets are wide and exceedingly clean, the houses are lofty and well built. The public buildings are splendid. Places of amusement are numerous. The Germans are naturally a gay people and passionately fond of music, hence all the places of entertainment with which the town of Hamburg teems, where music and dancing form the principal features. In the summer time Hamburg is a delightful place, but in winter it is so very cold that very little enjoyment can be looked for out of doors.

Guernsey via Shields

I sailed again from Hamburg on the 14th March bound to Shields[1] with a view of loading a cargo of coals on owner's account. I duly arrived after a boisterous passage across the North Sea of five days, and loaded according to intention, when I proceeded to Guernsey to discharge, where I arrived on the 30th of the same month.

I was again happy in being reunited with those near and dear to me. Passed troubles, cares or anxieties were forgotten in the full enjoyment of rapturous delights. The midsummer's day so much regretted nine months ago was now entirely banished from our thoughts, and nothing but beauty, sunshine, and pleasure encircled our path whilst others were complaining of the cold, dreariness, and gloomy aspect of the season.

[1] i.e. North and South Shields, the modern Tynemouth.

Everything has its season of enjoyment. So has the weary and worn out mariner when he arrives from a long voyage. Whether it is winter or summer, if the clouds be bright in the clear sunshine, or lowering and dark in the gloom of a tempest promising sky, it is all the same to the young sailor's heart filled with the sublime passion of love. He reads in his beloved's eyes the realisation of present and the hopes of future happiness, and from those glowing orbs, bright with the glow of innocence and purity, the sweetness of her voice, the kindness of her disposition, flows a radiancy which throws such a lustre on everything around, that in her presence it is an unchanging summer of happiness.

The little birds may refuse to chirp, the minstrels of the wood may refuse their melodious tunes, the blossoming flowers may refuse their fragrance and perfume. But in the parterre of true love these things are not missed. Every word is melody in each other's ears, the breathing of the lips has more fragrance than the richest violet.

It is a season of perfect happiness is the return of the sailor to his home, and oh! how much is he deserving of all that happiness to compensate for the privations and hardships he has had to contend with. There are few who can judge how miserable is a sailor's life, constantly exposed to the fury of the elements, with broken rest, oftentimes no rest at all, or even if the body is at rest from fatigue, the mind is denied that luxury. Thrown repeatedly from one contrast to the other. Now freezing with the cold of a northern climate, the very blood losing its animation, then into a tropical climate, under a vertical sun exhausted with heat, panting for breath; the perspiration streaming at every pore, and what is still worse than all, obliges to bear the tediousness of a long passage without a soul with whom to pass away the leisure or tedious moments, in fact totally deprived of society, the greatest boon man can enjoy.

It is true that the master of a ship has his officers with whom to associate, but oftentimes it will happen they are such that a respectable and intelligent ship's master cannot make companions of them. Or if perchance they possess those qualities which will enable a companionship to exist, it may be that the temper of one will not agree with that of the other, but supposing even this last drawback to have no existence, there is the urgent necessity of a master to prevent too much familiarity which entirely precludes the possibility of his officers to take the place of confidential friends. Thus without remedy is he left alone to brood over his misery, to brave the howling of the tempest, the roar of the mighty ocean dashing in milk white spray with furious power over his tiny bark throughout the awful gloom of night, made gloomier still by successive flashes of powerful lightning, preceded by dismal peals of thunder, and torrents of deluging rain, the whole imposing upon the mind a heavy burden.

But thanks to an all wise and gracious providence amidst this awful darkness, the mind finds refreshment in a cheering ray of light just sufficiently visible in the heaven of the soul to mark the words of the prophet, 'Behold thine arm is not shortened that it cannot save, Neither is thine ear heavy, O Lord, that it cannot hear'.[1] It is awful to feel alone! and after the fury of the tempest has subsided, and a perfect calm succeeds, there is also an emptiness in the sound of the yet agitated waters against the motionless ship, the flapping of the lazy sails against the creaking masts, that is truly awful, and I can scarcely tell which is preferable.

Ships' masters and the bottle

I do not wonder, nor can it be wondered by any, that many of my brother ship masters in their solitude fly to the recourse of stimulants to alleviate their gloom. But it is a great folly, as well as a great sin so to do, for while that remedy cheers the spirits for the time being, it ultimately causes a reaction which is distressingly depressing and sinks the mind into a brutal state of morbidness. There is no other poison more efficient in its effects than the abuse of ardent spirits to brutalise man, or to render him inferior to the brute. The very disease for which he takes it as a remedy is mightily aggravated by it. It robs him of that energy which God

[1] This is an almost direct quotation from Isaiah, ch. 59, v. 1.

has given him to overcome the trials which lie[1] in his path. Since man is born to earn his bread at the sweat of his brow, how then can he expect to keep free from difficulties? But God in his great mercy had made him equal to the task he has to perform, and He lays upon us never more than we can bear. There is no difficulty in which we may be placed, but what He can find a way for our escape. But man in his ignorance and sinfulness repines at the last weight of difficulty he feels imposed upon him, and refuses to bear it, flying at once to Satan for assistance, borrowing from him a weapon of destruction to prop him up in his difficulty. But alas! he will soon find (perhaps when too late) that the assistance he has procured, while it has availed him nothing, has to be repaid with interest, the price of which is his own soul! Oh unhappy man who so far forgets himself, and his God, as to be guilty of seeking any other help but His.

In praise of exercise

I have invariably found in the monotony of a seafaring life that there is nothing better adapted to disturb it than exercise; and I have had a considerable share of trial, for I have had some officers with me with whom it was not only impossible to associate, but on the contrary who tried by all the well devised means in their wicked compositions to make me as unhappy as they possibly could, but I can assure my readers they have invariably fallen short of their desires, and have ultimately found themselves wounded with their own weapons.

Exercise has been my remedy against all evil. Exercise has made me proof against their sourness of temper, against their railings and backbitings. Exercise has made me proof against the dangers of the tempest, and against the dreadful stillness of the calm. Exercise has made passages of 143 and 150 days upon the sea appear comparatively short. Exercise has filled me with hopes full of soul-stirring animation towards my happy return to my

[1] Emended from 'lay' in the MS.

peaceful home and friends. Exercise has given me health, and spirits, joy and happiness. What an inestimable remedy then is exercise!?

It may be improper of me to give a prescription of so much value without stating how it is to be used after it is made up. In order to show the validity of my recipe I will first remind my reader of what he and everybody knows, but perhaps do not always keep in view. The mind of man was naturally made for occupation, and occupation it will have. If you will not occupy it, it will occupy itself. Does everybody know that?

But as man was born in sin, it is a natural propensity of the mind, when left to its own resource, to revert to evil. Now as Satan is ever on the watch seeking whom he may devour, he soon perceives that neglected mind, and with very little trouble calls it into his own granary and gives it occupation, knowing well it is that which will please it most. Does everybody know that?

Now once the mind of man is under the charge of the devil, it is easily supposed that not much good will result from the relation! and he is such a liar and deceiver that the consequence of so much familiarity with him will be in the end bitterness and sorrow. Does everybody know that?

Now comes the value of my prescription. To avoid the mind reverting to evil, as well as to avoid the devil taking possession of it, give it exercise. Occupy it to good purposes, and it will not seek evil purposes. Do not allow the mind to be idle for one moment. (See its tendency for occupation; when in your sleep you have lost control over it, it is ever on the alert, it employs itself even then.) In the morning when you awake, let your first care be to offer up your thanksgiving at the throne of grace for the night which has passed and rolled into eternity, for the comforts you have enjoyed etc. After which let the duties of your situation be attended to with vigilance, neglecting nothing that can tend to the safety and protection of your charge, if you so devote your energies you will find constant employment throughout the day, on which the mind will feast in its natural element, while the body receives a corresponding benefit.

When evening approaches, and the hours of labour are over, retire not in idleness, but retire to your cabin to treat the mind with a change, by taking up a book and reading, keep always a good stock of useful information by you, so that you can vary your readings now and then. But rest assured that you will read in no better book, nor derive more or better information than in the volume of the sacred law, the more you read in it, the more attached will you become to its words of soberness and truth, and daily gaining a knowledge of your maker, you will not fail to gain a knowledge of yourself; whereby you will learn to estimate the glory of the one, and the unworthiness of the other, which will lead you to call in the right place for assistance, instead of flying to the wrong. But as it is necessary that we should store our mind with moral, as well as religious learning, in order to move in society as ornaments of the great creator, it is as well to have occasional recourse to works of literature and art. And when you find a weariness in your reading, mark carefully the page you have concluded, and move on deck to take a walk, during which continue to meditate over what you have read.

If you tire in that, take up your pen and write something. Force your brain to bring out a verse of poetry; or write a mercantile letter to a supposed business man; failing in that, change the pen for a pencil and draw out a sketch of your ship in the last gale, or attired in all her suit of majesty make her gliding proudly on the white crest of the blue wave — at any rate do not remain idle. How many times have I been remarked at for being 'un corps sans repos', which epithet I possibly deserved, but it has been from that ever bustling disposition, that ever keeping the mind in exercise that I have gained an ascendancy over many of my brethren.

And God be thanked also for his goodness in having watched over me, and strengthened me with His strength to resist temptation at its very appearance. I would not ascribe any perfection to myself. I would not say that I am above my neighbour in any quality. But what perfection may be mine, or how much I *may* outvie another, I have gained by the grace of God and that is to be acquired in the manner above stated. Watch and pray that ye may not fall into temptation. Watch what? Watch whom? Why, watch against Satan! And by taking care to keep the mind in wholesome exercise, you will succeed in keeping him aloof. While your hands are engaged in the employment of your worldly duties, you can be meditating, and employing the mind on heavenly things, you can be holding sweet communion with your God. You can be pressing forward towards the mark and prize of your high calling of God in Christ Jesus. What a grand and inestimable privilege, that the Lord is not limited to time, or place. He regards not the length or form of a prayer, but is always ready to hear and accept the faintest breathings of the heart. How then shall we be estranged from Him who is so near unto us, even at the door of our hearts, and desirous of entering in.

– 1850 –

Fourteenth Voyage

May

Brazil via Newport

On the 31st May my holidays were over, and I had once more in obedience to orders to proceed to sea. I had spent two months or nearly of continued happiness, but now they were past, and the cruel ordeal of separation was felt the more intensely bitter. On this occasion I was bound to Newport to load a cargo of coals intended for a market on the Brazil coast. I duly arrived at Newport in five days from Guernsey and I had the pleasure of meeting my friends of the cold water bath, Martin and Williams.[1]

The former I employed as my broker, we had many a causy[2] chat over old times, and did not scruple now and then to indulge in a hearty laugh over an accident which should have been remembered only in awe.

Through the exceeding kindness of Martin, and the hospitality of his amiable wife,[3] I spent a very agreeable time in Newport during my stay, which tended greatly to sooth my aching heart. I was forever taking tea, or spending the evening at their home, and I believe that both Mr and Mrs Martin's principal object was to try to exceed each other in rendering me happy, for both well knew that I had only just left the object of my affections and that the wound in the heart was still fresh and bleeding. Their gentle and

[1] Above, pp. 207–14 for Martin and Williams. There is a crew list for this voyage (Gernsey to Pernambuco) in BT 98/2522 dated 30 May 1850.

[2] The word is clear in the MS and appears to be a variant (not recorded in *SOED*) of 'cozy', which is itself from the French *causer*.

[3] Martin married Ellen, the daughter of John Davies of Cardiff, on 8 Jan. 1850.

sympathising natures were daily proved, in the essences of kindness with which they bathed me which succeeded in a measure to lighten my affliction.

Ship springs a leak. Two crew ill. Return to Guernsey

After my vessel was loaded I cleared at the Customs for Pernambuco[1] or a market and taking leave of my friends proceeded on my voyage. A few days after I was out, accidents took place which retarded my voyage greatly. The ship sprang a leak and made considerable water. Two of my crew who had been slightly indisposed during the last few days I remained in port now got from bad to worse, and showed evident symptoms of fever. One of them became so bad that he lost all consciousness, and was in that state of helplessness which demanded a constant watch over him. The other was little better.

In such a predicament, and with a leaky ship, and a long voyage before me, besides the fear of contagion among the crew, I resolved to put back and chose Guernsey for refuge, very naturally as it may be supposed. For more reasons than one but principally because I wished to land the unfortunate sufferers among their friends who would take better care of them than strangers might have done and as I certainly believed they were marked out by the hand of death, I felt a desire that their dying bedside should be surrounded by their friends with whom the last breath might be used in prayer.

My next reason was that the leak in the vessel would be easily found in Guernsey without incurring much expense, while in any other port it would have been the contrary. In fact I had obvious reasons for preferring *Guernsey* as my *port de relâche.* I arrived on the roads one fine morning early to the surprise of all the inhabitants, who could not make out the nature of the distress that

[1] i.e. Recife: see above, pp. 223–8.

had brought me back to their shores whilst they considered me half-way to Pernambuco. Soon however, the truth was ascertained and a medical man sent off to examine the sufferers who declared the one under a serious influence of typhus fever, and the other under the less dangerous influence of intermittent fever. Both were conveyed to the hospital and afterwards removed to their respective homes.

Meanwhile the necessary arrangements were taken to facilitate the discovery of the leak, and in a few hours of the reflux of the tide it was found and stopped. I employed myself replacing the two sick men and other necessary business, and was again ready to proceed ere the noon of the day following my arrival had arrived. The wind blowing fresh in a contrary direction, I did not however sail till the following day. I had a good opportunity of enjoying a tête-à-tête with the object of my affections and although it was only *en passant* felt the meeting was as pleasant as it was short and unexpected.

Voyage recommenced

On the 29th June I again started on my voyage.[1] With a fresh crew and a tight ship I could not but go on comfortably. The passage was gone through in the usual routine of passages, and on the 49th day I arrived at Pernambuco, from which port, finding no market for my coals, I sailed the next day for Rio de Janeiro. I met with very severe weather on the coast and a deal of SW (of course contrary) winds.

Some authors have pretended that a gale never blows on this coast, and that ships, once on the parallel of Bahia, never meet with obstruction in getting to the southward, and among them the

[1] This date is confirmed by the existence of a second crew list for the voyage in BT 98/2522 dated 28 June 1850 and a note on the earlier list of 30 May showing that two new crew-members joined the *Swift* on 28 June.

illustrious Hosburgh in his *East India Directory*.[1] But I can safely assert that such is not the case, for experience has taught me that severe gales may be expected on that coast, both from NE and SW as well as anywhere else. I do not say they are so common, but that in certain seasons they do frequently happen I can vouch, and as regards his (Hosburgh's) remark of ships *never* meeting with obstruction it is perfectly ridiculous. I have been eighteen days getting to Rio from Bahia, when I could with ordinary weather have made the passage comfortably in five or six days. His rule may have been very correct in his time, but the seasons are changing daily and what applied correctly to the system of the world twenty years ago, will not in any wise bear the resemblance of truth now a day.

Sells cargo in Rio

Arriving at Rio after a long passage, I sold my cargo to advantage, and then made a stay in that beautiful port, (so imperfectly described on a preceding page)[2] of 39 days, which allowed me another opportunity of familiarising myself with its beauties. More correctly, I have some very intimate as well as influential friends at Rio, and through their kindness I have been enabled to see more of it, and acquainting myself better than I otherwise might have done.

[1] James Horsburgh (1762–1836), a Scottish hydrographer, compiled many charts and papers but is best remembered for his *East India Directory*, originally published as *Directions for sailing to and from the East Indies, China, New Holland, Cape of Good Hope, and the interjacent ports, compiled chiefly from original journals and observations made chiefly during 21 years' experience in navigating those seas* (1809–11), which, under the better known title of *The India Directory*, had reached a fifth edition by 1852 and continued to be published down to the late nineteenth century (*DNB*).

[2] See pp. 241–5.

Arrives Falmouth – orders for Hamburg

After loading a cargo of coffee as usual, I proceeded on my way for Falmouth, again calling for orders, and arrived at that port on the 13th December after a passage of sixty days from Rio.[1] I was not many days arrived before I received my orders to proceed to Hamburg. Considering the late season of the year I was anything but pleased at this. I made up my mind fully to have to winter there; and to an impassioned and restless body like mine who was corresponding with my lady love to the effect that she would hold herself in preparation for walking to the hymeneal altar with me immediately on my arrival. The prospect of remaining buried in ice and snow for seven or eight weeks were anything but sunshine. Had I been chooser I would have preferred being buried in the pleasures of a honeymoon for the same amount of time, but as it was not the case I had but to resign myself to circumstances with heroic spirit.

I wrote to my intended bride, making her the confidante of my fears, but not without assuring her at the same time, that all the ice and snow of the Polar regions, supposing they were accumulated at Hamburg, could not tend to mitigate the ardent love with which my young heart was burning, or the impassioned hopes of leading her to the altar soon.

As soon as wind and weather permitted I sailed from Falmouth and was favoured with a speedy run to Hamburg where I arrived in seven days, on the 28th December. The wind being from the south-west quarter there was no indication of the ice yet setting in, but it would only depend upon a continuation of that wind if the river kept open for any time longer. Had the wind veered round to the north-west, or more northerly, I knew the river was sure to be blocked in the course of twelve hours, and my fate was certain.

There was nothing but a quick despatch could save me, consequently I set all my energy at work to procure this. I left no

[1] The agreement to serve for this voyage (BT 98/2522) was returned by the British Consul at Rio on 9 Oct. 1850, immediately prior to the *Swift*'s departure for England.

means untried. I employed labourers from the shore to bundle the cargo out, and where commands or entreaties failed in hastening on the work, I had recourse to the more potent measure of getting it done by the aid of shining coin.

At any rate I allowed no obstacle to stand in the way between despatch and me, so that eventually I succeeded in obtaining my ends. I completed the discharge of my cargo, ballasted the vessel and sailed out of the river just as an easterly wind set in which brought on frost and snow *ad libitum* and twenty four hours after my departure no ship could have got out of the Elbe if it had been to save the world.[1]

I hurried on to Shields where I was ordered to procure freight for any port of England or France in the English Channel, or in the event of failing in that, to load on owner's account and proceed to Guernsey.[2]

Guernsey

It was the latter order I complied with; freights were very low at the time, and I found by calculation that I could not enhance the owner's benefit by chartering the vessel. Consequently without loss of time I decided on purchasing for account of owners a cargo of West Hartley steam coal with which I proceeded to Guernsey and safely arrived on the 27th day of January 1851.

I was not a little surprised as well as mortified at finding on my arrival that the owners had decided on sending me on with the cargo to Havana. I that had made such tremendous exertions to arrive there expecting a long stay, discharging the cargo and afterwards hauling the vessel on the stocks to lengthen her, as had been promised by my employers the voyage preceding and had

[1] This quick turn-round is confirmed by an endorsement on the agreement to serve (BT 98/2522) showing that the document was deposited with the British vice-consul at Hamburg on 30 Dec. 1850 and returned the same day.

[2] The crew list (BT 98/2522) was handed in at the port of Newcastle-upon-Tyne (which included North and South Shields) on 16 Jan. 1851 and the agreement to serve two days later.

consequently chosen the opportunity of fulfilling my vows of constancy to the object of my tenderest affections by taking before the altar of God the solemn pledge of marriage.

The owners understood the case and sympathised with me in my disappointment, wished they could for my sake have found a purchaser for the coals in the island, but the coal stores were overstocked and it was out of their power to act otherwise than they had done etc, etc, etc.

'Humbug!' said I.[1] 'This won't do. I have a promise to fulfil, a solemn and sacred promise, and not less solemn and sacred a duty to perform. It has been my intention to perform both, and I will not be deterred from the good cause in which my Samaritan heart has been engaged!'

I made known my determination to the owners, beseeching them to look for another master for their ship but as it was their intention to use this expedient only as a last recourse, they used all the winning persuasions that the power of language could produce to tempt me to change my mind.

All of no avail; I was inflexible. At last they were fain to let me do as I wished in all respects, excepting in that of giving up my situation. I might go and marry, and enjoy myself, in the meantime the ship would wait but they insisted I should not leave them.

Of course when I saw so much real value set upon me and not less affection, my heart yearned towards them and I determined to marry at once and with as little delay as possible take charge of their property again. Consequently I repaired in haste to my beloved to acquaint her with the facts of the case. Need I say how she received the tidings? The crimson blush that overspread her lovely face, the modest downward look of her bright eyes, the trembling and agitated movements of her tiny fingers at their work, guilty of guiding the needle in false direction, told but too plainly the feelings of the heart within. Pride and joy were mixed with grief and sorrow! The former related to the attainment of her brightest hopes. The latter of the thought of such a speedy separation to follow. Preparations were at once entered into, or

[1] To himself, one suspects, rather than to the owners.

rather completion, for everything was in a forward state on my arrival.

Marriage

On the second day following my arrival which happened to be the 29th of January 1851 I led my affianced to the altar where our happy courtship was terminated by holy marriage. And thus gentle reader have I brought myself in the end, on the pinnacle of my desires. It is therefore impossible to rise any higher. Allow me then to rest quietly on the couch of perfect happiness which my good fortune has laid out for me. And behold in the maiden which I have introduced to you as 'the Gem of Brightness', whose genuine qualities I have made a very imperfect attempt at describing, behold in her the wife of my bosom. The bright star of my future destiny! The cloudless sun of my present joys. May the Almighty, that great architect of the universe, who in His wise providence has so ordained all things that the most inconsiderable falls under His immediate inspection, whose watchful and fatherly care over the works of His own hands is so great that 'not a sparrow falleth to the ground without Him',[1] grant that we may live a long life of uninterrupted happiness together, and like Isaac and Rebekah of old, being full of days we may be gathered unto our fathers. Amen and Amen.

[1] Cf. St Matthew, ch. 10, v. 29: 'Are not two sparrows sold for a farthing? And one of them shall not fall on the ground without your Father'.

Appendix

A Letter from Hilary Marquand to his Wife, 1866

Ship 'Channel Queen'
Mangalore Road (Malabar Coast)

February 20th 1866

My dear Louisa,

The mail closes on the 22nd inst. and I engage in preparation for your entertainment, and when doing so I feel more than ever thankful to Almighty God who has spared me to enjoy the pleasure. I also call upon you my 'best beloved' to join with me in deep, heartfelt gratitude, and also to teach our young children to join their thanksgivings to ours, for they had very nearly been *Fatherless and you a Widow.*

On the 12th inst. I and my boat's crew (four) were miraculously saved from a watery grave!; and this is how it happened. On the day mentioned I left the ship at half past one o'clock p.m. in my jolly boat[1] under sail to go on shore, it being the fifth day since I had communicated with the shore owing to strong winds, and high seas on the Bar in consequence. I had had no cargo sent me, and had heard nothing concerning progress or otherwise so that I was quite fidgety with anxiety. Well on this day (the 12th) the wind was much moderated and there seemed to be less sea on the

[1] A clinker-built ship's boat, smaller than a cutter.

Bar, therefore I resolved to try and reach the shore. I was in the habit of crossing this Bar and always under sail so I thought I knew it well and apprehended no danger whatever. Alfred Guilbert, Beamont de Putron, and two young men I shipped in London were my boat's crew. The Bar is about one mile, or one and a quarter, from the ship, and the shore about three-quarters of a mile further.

We left the ship with a fine breeze and a flowing sheet all as gay as larks, my little boat speeded onwards like a young frolicsome buck. We reached the approach to the Bar in about a quarter of an hour, then I saw the sea was yet very high but still feared no danger. Away we went, one sea came curling after us, and reaching us my little boat lifted itself upon its crest and rode on the surging wave majestically. Another tremendous sea came curling along seemingly in pursuit of the former, but higher and fiercer in appearance. I prepared to put the helm hard a-weather and to run right before it. It came booming along with a mighty curl of white foam which looked like the mane of some angry monster of the woods, it came, it came, it dashed upon our little boat; alas it filled it! sank it! and we five were hurled away by its force, rolled over and over again like mere straws, and lastly came up to the surface once more only to look upon another huge wave preparing itself to finish what the other had not completed, namely our annihilation! Left to the mercy of these waves we managed to cling to the boat which by this time had rolled itself upright, having emptied itself of ballast etc, and now floated between wind and wave. Another wave came and, dashing over us and the boat again, turned her over on her side, in which position she remained from the weight of the mast and sail. In this position we could not hold on well and seeing this I asked if any of us had a knife. Being answered in the affirmative I encouraged the young lad who had it to at once cut the ropes which attached the mast to the boat and so free her of this weight that she might right again and so serve us to hold by. This was done, and the mast and sail went away, the boat righted and we thought ourselves in a better position. I at this time perceived the oars floating by and called out to my lads to swim after them and to cling to them for their life. Meantime I got hold of one and Guilbert of another, but the others preferred holding on to the boat.

Our position was a dangerous one for every half minute a huge curling wave came dashing over us, which made it very difficult to hold on to any thing, and by being tumbled about so, exhausted us much. Seeing that no one would attempt to pick up the oars and knowing that our safety depended much upon them, I struck out with my one under my arm, and succeeded in picking up another, and then another, and finally seeing the mast and sprit at a distance I swam after that also and got hold of all, but by this time I was separated from the others many yards. I called out to them and cheering them encouraged them to come to me who had three oars and the mast and sprit upon one of which each of them could hold on. This they did not do, and finding they preferred to hold on to the boat which I expected every moment would be dashed to pieces, I dashed away the mast and sprit from me, being too much to hold on and placing one oar under each arm allowed myself to float for a while, while I was reflecting what was best to be done. I was most anxious about little de Putron, poor little fellow, it made me sad to think he should drown. I did not then know he could swim, but it appears he can swim like a fish. We all could swim but one, but being so far from shore we could not have saved our lives in such breakers.

While I was reflecting on my oars (literally laying on my oars) and thinking of you, my dearest, and of my dear little children so soon to be deprived of their Father, I felt as cool and collected, and as resigned as if nothing had really happened and I looked up to Heaven and every pulsation of my heart said 'Thy will be done, O Lord!'. At this moment I heard a cheering cry from my lads, from whom I was separating fast, and looking round I saw a native boat under sail coming towards us, each of us bellowed out, in fact screeched for help, and I heard little Beaumont's voice in the distance and amid the roar of the waves call out, 'Oh, they've seen us, they've seen us, they wave their hands, here is help, Captain, here is help.' I called out, 'All right my lads, hold on like brave fellows, don't be frightened or excited, our safety depends upon our coolness, they come to pick us up.' Alas how little did we know the feelings of the men upon whom we depended. These natives came on seemingly dashing through the foam thinking it was so many of their fellow men who were drowning, but finding we were not men of their caste, and white men, they luffed their boat too and passed within five yards of de Putron and another one, not deigning to offer us any rescue whatsoever. Poor little de Putron was calling out, 'Oh, Captain! Look at that boat! She is passing us and does not offer to pick us up!' I merely coolly replied, 'Well I see it, my boy, but I cannot help it.' Another one called out, 'Offer him some rupees, Captain, perhaps he'll pick us up?' 'Offer him a thousand if you like' said I, 'I'll pay it, if he will turn round his boat and save you.' We then all called out to them, offering them any quantity of rupees to save us, but it was like wasting our voices in the echo of the waves. No, these ruffians went on, no doubt rejoicing in their hearts that so many Englishmen the less would be in the world on the morrow, or at the setting of that day's sun.

This incident having transpired, 'I lay on my oars' once more considering what I should do, but I began to feel very exhausted, not having been in the water for years, and with all my clothes on, and a heavy pair of shoes on my feet, besides being rolled and tumbled about by the sea as I had been, I found I was becoming very weak. Not so my lads who are in the habit of bathing very often and of course taking exercise in the water, they felt comparatively strong. After reflection I came to the conclusion I had better strike out and try to reach the beach before me (we were all fast drifting towards it). I struck out accordingly, but before I had gone many yards I found I could not move my legs and feet from a weakness which had taken hold of me in the small of the back. (My lads say I had a blow on the back when the boat turned over but of this I have no knowledge.) Therefore, finding this to be the case, I gave up the thoughts of swimming and rested on my oars, giving myself up to the mercy of God. Perfectly cool and resigned I knew that He had been very merciful to me all the days of my life, and out of greater danger and as near death He had rescued me on former occasions, and I did not dare to think that He ought to rescue me now. I felt my heart responding to the silent prayer on my lip, 'Thy will be done!' By this time we had been from half to three-quarters of an hour, I dare say, in the water, a very long time this when life and death are waging fierce battle for victory!

I could no longer communicate my feelings to, or cheer, my lads. I was too far away from them; each seemed to be now drifting separately. Beaumont de Putron and the two strangers always clinging to the boat. Alfred Guilbert and I resting on our oars, and each of us drifting towards the beach upon which was rolling a tremendous sea even greater than that rolling on the Bar, so that if we did reach the beach it would have been a miracle had we not all been dashed to pieces in the tremendous breakers.

At this period, and certainly when last expected, I heard the voice of Alfred Guilbert calling out in cheering language, 'Never say die, my boys, here's help', and in a few moments more I had the inexpressible pleasure to see my own gig[1] and five of my men in her picking up the first two they came to (de Putron and a stranger). They then pulled after Guilbert and the other stranger, both of whom refused to be picked up until I was safe (noble trait in their character this). None could tell if I was still afloat or not for we had not seen each other for at least a quarter of an hour, but while I could not see a mere speck like a man's head on the water among the waves, I could distinctly see the gig and the men in her. I therefore bellowed out to the top of my voice and held up my hand, which they at once saw and heard and in less than five minutes I was laying in the bottom of the gig prostrate and exhausted, but alive and thankful. They then pulled and picked up the two remaining sufferers and in another half an hour we were all safe once more on board the 'Channel Queen.' And thus, dear Louisa, was your husband saved from a watery grave! Can you read this and not feel thankful to Him who has through His mercy restored to you a loving husband and to your children a loving father? No, I know you cannot, and I know when you realise the case in all its terrors you will join your prayers to mine in fervent gratitude.

One thought crossed my mind several times when 'resting on my oars' and buffeting with the waves, it was this. Oh what awful news is coming to you, dearest girl, by next mail! But away sad thoughts. I am still among the living and spared to provide for you

[1] In nautical usage, a light, narrow, clinker-built ship's boat.

and to cheer you on through life's rough path for many a long year.

I lost my hat, umbrella, and 21 pieces of clothing which I was taking on shore to the Dobé[1] (washerman), white shirts, coloured ditto, white waistcoats and trousers, shirt collars, etc etc. Of the ship's I lost one small cask of water, one funnel, one bucket, and some of the boat's gear. The boat I sent after as soon as we had reached the ship in safety and my mate picked her up on the beach some miles away but she is all broken to pieces and useless. I may get her mended on my return home.

I have not told you how the gig came to our rescue. George Payne, my second mate, happened to be watching me with a glass, feeling a curiosity to see me cross the Bar, and saw me capsize; then of course calling the mates attention to the catastrophe they immediately got out the gig (which by the bye was stowed in its place on deck) and pulling with all their might, rescued us. This I trace the hand of God in for had not Mr. Payne been watching us we must have perished, as my chief mate had not been concerned about us since I left the ship's side. In fact, having the ship's work to look after I could not expect him to do so. I have now given you a detailed account of the accident in all its minutes and have no doubt you will have perused it with deep heartfelt interest. Have I not a reason to say I am thankful to be permitted once more to entertain you. How different would it be if another had been commissioned to write instead of me, and in telling of the accident had added 'thus the Captain and four hands lost their lives!!!' Truly in the midst of life we are in death! And now I will leave this doleful account and may it only present itself to our memories to enable us to draw nearer to God in fervent gratitude for all his benefits and mercies.

I am still without any news of or from you. I expect, however, by the end of this month to have a letter in answer to mine of November 26th dated at Rangoon. I hope you wrote immediately after you received mine? If so, I may hear of you at the end of this month. The letter which I imagine you wrote to Ceylon in answer

[1] i.e. dhobi, a Hindi word correctly glossed by Hilary as a native washerman.

to my first from Adelaide and was sent on to Rangoon, reaching there after I left, I have not yet received, but I think I will get it ere long. It cannot have reached me yet so I don't despair.

I am getting on very slowly in loading. I have done very little since I wrote last about a fortnight ago, and I can see there is no chance of my getting away before my laying days expire, which will be on the 15th March. Coffee is abundant enough, but the transport from the country is a tedious work and hence the delay.

I am enjoying very good health (thank God) but a martyr to rheumatism in the right arm and shoulder. I have been obliged to discontinue my morning bath since a month which is giving up a great luxury in this warm climate. I suffer so much at times that I could cry with pain. This does not affect my appetite or my spirits and hence do I call my health good.

Young de Putron may not write to his mother, or perhaps young Guilbert either to his father, therefore if you should see any of them you might tell them the news, but making it appear as light as you possibly can, for it is no use making any *Helas* about it, if so the whole town will resound with exaggerated accounts and all will come from *the Captain's wife*. You might just say we had a narrow escape from drowning by being capsized on the Bar on the 12th February and were picked up by the gig after being left to perish by a native boat's crew who refused to pick us up though passing within five yards of two of us. Even this I would not tell unless you are sought after or asked. I will of course write to John Marquand and tell him of the accident but I will not give him a detailed account as I have given you. To him you may be as communicative as you like if he should ask you about it.

I will now 'my dearest' conclude. I have written a long letter and I dare say an interesting one. May God continue his protection and may we soon be again reunited, and after the perils and hardships of a long voyage join each other in fervent gratitude to Him for all His mercies.

I notice by the papers which I occasionally chance to glance at that much severe weather has prevailed on the coasts of England, Ireland and Wales and that many valuable ships and lives have been lost! How thankful I am to have been this side of the world during your severe winter enjoying very fine weather and a fine warm climate. I had forgotten to mention that among other things mentioned as lost my poor watch may be considered of the number for it had such a soaking in salt water I doubt if ever it will be right again. I have put it in sweet oil until my return to London. I am very thankful it was my silver watch and not that I inherited from my dear father.

Give my kind and affectionate regards to all my friends, and to all who may enquire after my welfare. Kiss all the children for me. How thankful I shall feel if I am spared the pleasure of kissing them myself by and bye.

Adieu for the present
I remain dear Louisa
Your devoted Husband
Hilary.

PS. Do not forget dear old Miss David when I speak of my friends, see her and give her my warmest regards.

I am not writing to Auguste, perhaps you will, and if so excuse me for having kept silence.

Index

Adelaide: *see* ships
Adelaide, Australia 266
Africa, places in: *see* Barbary Coast, Cape of Good Hope, Ichaboe
Albion: *see* ships
All Saints' Bay, Brazil 216
almonds 176
Antigua 72–3, 200
Antwerp, Belgium xiii–xiv, 51, 53
Australia, places in: *see* Adelaide
Austria: *see* Trieste, formerly in

Bahia: *see* Salvador
Bahia de Todos os Santos, Brazil 216
Barbary Coast, Africa xiv, 90
Bay of Gibraltar 99
beans 86
Belgium, places in: *see* Antwerp
Bellot, Dr 128–36
Bermuda 77
Berchervaise, John x
Blondel, Abraham 236
  Louisa, wife of HM xvi, xix, xx, xxii–xxvi, xxviii, xxx, xlii, xlv, 158–64, 171, 174, 175, 183–4, 195, 201–4, 205–6, 216, 222–3, 236, 237, 237–8, 240, 255, 257, 259–60, 261–8
Bourdic, Mr 27–32, 37
Brazil, bribery at Custom Houses 233
  places in: *see* Recife, Rio de Janeiro, Salvador
bribery, in Brazil 233
Bristol Channel 175
Bristol Channel Tug Owners' Association xxv
Burman, Mr 26, 26–7, 46
  Mrs 46

Cádiz, Spain xviii, xx, 216, 238, 240–1
Cagliari, Sardinia 145
Cape Bon 90
Cape of Good Hope 170
Cape Trafalgar, Spain 116
Cardiff, Glam. xviii, xx–xxvii, xxxiii, 215
  Bute Docks in xviii, xliv
  Butetown in xxi–xxiii
  Cathedral Road in xlv
  Cowbridge Road in xlv
  High School xxvi
  Marquand family homes in xlv–xlvi
  Mount Stuart Square in xxi
  Penylan in xxv, xlvi
  Tredegarville in xxi–xxii, xxiv
  University College xxvi
Care, Edward Richard xxvi
  Richard xxvi
Care & Marquand Shipping Co. Ltd xxvi
cargoes, general xvii–xviii
  named:
    almonds 176
    beans 86
    coal xviii, xx, 176, 216, 246, 253, 255–6, 258–9
    cocoa nuts 200
    cod-fish 139
    coffee xvii, 77, 123, 241, 257, 266
    fruit xvii, 176
    grapes 176
    guano xvii–xviii, 168
    lead 177
    'notions' 179
    nuts 176
    potatoes 122
    raisins 176
    salt 216, 238, 241
    sugar xvii, 77, 123, 200, 216, 223, 237
    wheat 220
Cartagena, Spain 156
Castel, Guernsey xix, xxxviii
Cayman Islands 74
Ceylon (now Sri Lanka) 266
Channel Queen: *see* ships

Cheminant, Nicholas Le xiv, xxx–xxxi, xxxii, 62–118
church attendance, in Marquand household 10–12
coal xviii, xix, 176, 216, 246, 253, 255–6, 258–9
cocoa nuts 200
cod-fish 139
coffee 77, 123, 241, 257, 266
Cohu, Henry xiv, 62–116
Cowes, Isle of Wight 145, 237
Cross, Catherine Douay: *see* Marquand, Mrs C.D.
Cuba 74–6
  places in: *see* Havana, Isla de la Juventad

dame school, attended by HM 2–8
Dauntless: *see* ships
David, John xv, 172–4, 184–5, 187, 195–7, 205, 211, 223, 229–30
  Miss 268
Davies, Ellen: *see* Martin, Mrs Ellen
Day, Clement xxix, 173
  William xxix–xxx, 176, 180, 181, 194
Denmark, places in: *see* Helsingør
Dispatch: *see* ships
dolphins 67–8, 200
Dry Harbour, Jamaica 180–1, 184–7
Duke of Gloucester: *see* ships

Earl of Bute, Earl of Dumfries, Earl of Dunraven, Earl of Jersey, Earl of Roseberry: *see* ships
Edwards, Rogers & Co. 208
Elbe, River 145, 245, 257–8
Elsinore: *see* Helsingør
Europa Point, Gibraltar 100

Falmouth, Cornwall 241, 245, 257
Forbes, John xxviii, 244–5
Fort George, Guernsey 31, 53
France, places in: *see* Le Havre, Sète
fruit 176

G—s, — 31–4
  Maria Ann 31
gangrene 129–31
Gardner — 35–44
  Colonel 35
Germany, places in: *see* Hamburg, Stralsund
Gibraltar xiv, xxx–xxxi, 87, 98, 100–116
  Bay of 99
Gilmour, Mrs 140
grapes 176
guano xvii–xviii, 168
Guernsey, militia 238
  places in: *see* La Brigade, Castel, Fort George, St Peter Port, V—t, Vale Castle
Guilbert, Alfred 262–5
Gulf of Venice 87

Hacquoil family, of Jersey and Cardiff xx
  F.P. xxv
Hamburg, Germany xviii, 108, 145, 245, 246, 257
Hartley, West, Northumberland 258
Havana, Cuba xli, 51, 74–6, 122–3, 126–36, 258
Havre, Le, France 83
Hayes, Mr 129
Helsingør (Elsinore), Denmark 220
Hill's Dry Dock & Engineering Co. xxiv–xxv
Hispaniola 74
Horsburgh, James xxviii, 256
Hugo, Victor xix, xxxix

Ichaboe, South West Africa (now Namibia) xvii–xviii, 168–70
illnesses:
  gangrene 129–31
  smallpox xxiii
  typhus fever 255
  yellow fever 126–36
India, places in: *see* Malabar Coast, Mangalore Road
Isla de la Juventad, Cuba 74
Isle of Pines, Cuba 74
Isle of Wight 145
  places in: *see* Cowes
Italy, places in: *see* Gulf of Venice, Trieste

Jamaica xv, 74
Dry Harbour in xxx, 180–1, 184–7
Rio Bueno in 187–8
Jamieson, Alan x, xv
Jessie: *see* ships
Jersey 139, 143

La Brigade, Guernsey xii, xxxvii
Lacheur, Nicholas Le 103
Le Havre, France 83
Leask, Mr 155
Lièvre, Thomas Le 131
London 86, 201, 228
London Hospital in xv, 177–8
Lower Thames Street in 176
St Katherine's Docks in 116–18
West India Docks in 179, 199
London Journal xxviii, 213
Lüderitz Bay, South West Africa (now Namibia) xvii–xviii

Malabar Coast, India 261, 261–8
Málaga, Spain xviii, 176, 177
Malny, Henry 172, ?190
Mangalore Road, India 261, 261–8
Marquand, family xi–xii, xxxvii
Alfred, son of HM xxii, xxv
Amelia, daughter of HM xxii
Augustus John (Auguste), son of HM xxii, xxv, 268
Catherine Douay (née Cross), wife of H.B. Marquand xxv, xlv, xlvi
David, brother of HM xii, 11, 12
David, father of HM xii, xiii, xxxvi, 1–2, 8–9, 10–14, 21, 46–9, 51–3, 56, 58, 61, 118–19, 165–7
Elise, daughter of HM xxii
Eric Blondel, great-grandson of HM xxxiv
Ernest David, nephew of HM xii
Hilary, author of autobiography: *see next entry*
Hilary, uncle of HM xiii, 50–3, 117
Hilary Adair MP, grandson of HM xxvi–xxvii
Hilary Blondel, son of HM xxii–xxvi, xlii, xliii, xlv, xlvi
John 267
John, brother of HM xii, xiii, 11, 47–8, 59
John, son of HM xix
Leonard Blondel, grandson of HM xxvi, xlvi
Louisa (née Blondel), wife of HM: *see* Blondel, Louisa
Louise, daughter of HM xxii
Margaret (née Thoume), mother of HM xii, xxxvi, 2, 7, 8, 10, 56, 58–9, 118–19, 137
Nicholas, brother of HM xii, 11
Pierre xii
Rachel, sister of HM 66
Marquand, Hilary, author of autobiography
ancestry xii; family home xxxvii
parents: *see* Marquand, David; Marquand, Margaret
early childhood xii–xiii, 1; schooldays xii–xiii, 2–46; home life as a child 8–14; determines to go to sea 46–9; placed in lawyer's office xiii, 49; persuades father to allow him to go to sea 50–3
prepares for first voyage 53–7; departs for first voyage 58–61; first voyage 58–118; second 122–37; third 139–57; fourth 168–72; fifth 173–4; sixth 175–8; seventh 179–97; eighth 198–9; ninth 200–4; tenth 205–22; eleventh 223–36; twelfth 237–8; thirteenth 239–52; fourteenth 253–60
appearance in 1842 139
reception by family at end of first voyage 118–20; father's pride in career 165–7; at appointment as master 236;
falls in love 158–64; courtship xvi, xxx, 171, 195–7, 221, 254–5; proposes to Louisa xxx, 201–3; is accepted 204; emotions while engaged 205–6; assures Louisa of his love 257; marriage xix, 259–60
appointed ordinary seaman 139; second mate xv, xxxi, 168–9; chief officer xv, 195–7; captain

of the *Swift* xv–xvi, xxxii, 229–31
conflict with Captain Taylor xv, xxxii, 140–3, 146–55
learns to speak Spanish 76, 122–3; Italian 123–4
contracts gangrene 129–31; yellow fever xiv, 128; injured while discharging cargo xv, 177–8; is home-sick and seasick xiv, 61–6; threatened with amputation of leg xiv, 131–6; treated at the London Hospital 177–8
nearly drowns in Jamaica xv, xxix, 181–4; in a tropical storm 187–94; off coast of India 261–6
advice to masters in dealings with brokers etc 235; on dangers of drinking by ships' masters 248–9; of importance of taking exercise at sea 249–50; concerning the burdens of command generally xvi
opinion of Hamburg 246; of Recife (Pernambuco) 224–8; of Rio de Janeiro 241–5; of Salvador (Bahia) 217–19; of the Spanish in Havana 75–6; of women of Spain 241; of foreigners generally xxxii
views on ship-brokers and others 231–5; on value of reading and writing at sea x, 251
reflections on life at sea 247–8; thanks God for His goodness 251–2, 260
married life in Guernsey xix, xxxix
later life in Cardiff xx–xxiii, xlv
death xxiii
portraits of xxxv, xlii
autobiography, assessment of x, xxvii–xxxiv
Martin, Ellen (née Davies) xxi, 208, 253–4
William Henry xvi, xx–xxv, 176, 207–14, 253–4
Martin & Marquand xxi–xxvi, xliv
merchants, HM's views of 231–5
Methodism, Wesleyan, in Jamaica xv, 184–6
militia, Guernsey 238
Montserrat 73
Morel family, of Jersey and Cardiff xx

Namibia, places in: *see* Ichaboe
Nancy: *see* ships
Navy, Royal: *see* Royal Navy
Nevis 200
Newcastle upon Tyne, Northumberland 145
Newport, Mon. xvi, xviii, xx–xxi, 175, 205–14, 216, 253–4
nuts 176

Ozanne, Capt. 238n.

P., D.L. 107, 109
Page, Thomas Le 150–1, 154–5, 172, 200
Payne, George 266
Penambuco: *see* Recife
Penarth Roads, Glam. 215
pirates 91–6
Plate, River 241
Poland, places in: *see* Szczecin
porpoises 67–8, 200
potatoes 122
private schools, attended by HM 14–46
Puerto Rico 74
Putron, Beamont de 262–5

raisins 176
Rangoon, Burma 266
Recife (Pernambuco), Brazil xvii, xli, 223–8, 254, 255–7
Redonda Island 73
Reeves, Moses xiv, 122–36
Relentless: *see* ships
Rio Bueno, in Jamaica 187–8
Rio de Janeiro, Brazil xvii, xviii, 139, 143–5, 146, 170, 217, 241, 241–5, 255–6
Roberts, Dame, schoolmistress 2–8
Rogers: *see* Edwards, Rogers & Co.
Rosehill: *see* ships
Royal Navy, at Gibraltar 101–16
at Rio de Janeiro 170

see also ships
Russia 229

St Christopher: *see* St Kitts
St Helena 170
St Katherine's Docks, London 116–18
St Peter Port, Guernsey, xix, xxxviii, xxxix
St Kitts 172, 173–4, 194, 198–9
salt 216, 238, 241
Salvador (Bahia), Brazil xvii, 216–19, 224, 238, 241, 255–6
Santo Domingo 74
Sardinia, Cagliari in 145
Schleswig-Holstein dispute (1848) xviii, 220
schools, attended by HM 2–46
Secret: *see* ships
Sète, France 145
sharks 68–71
Shields, North and South, Northumberland 246, 259
ship-brokers 207–8, 253
  HM's views of 231–5
ships:
  Adelaide xiv–xv, xli, 137, 139–57, 172
  Albion 108
  Channel Queen xix, 261
  Dauntless xxiv
  Dispatch xv
  Duke of Gloucester xv, xviii, xxix, 168–72, 172
  Earl of Bute xxiv
  Earl of Dumfries xxiv, xliv
  Earl of Dunraven xxiv
  Earl of Jersey xxiv
  Earl of Roseberry xxiv, xxv, xliv
  Jessie xix
  Nancy xiii–xiv, xx–xxi, xxx–xxxi, 50–6, 59–121 passim, 122–7, 228
  Relentless xxiv
  Rosehill xxiv
  Secret xix
  Silvia xxiv
  Swift xiv, xv–xvi, xviii, xxix, 172–260 passim
  HMS *Vanguard* xxx–xxxi, 101–15
Sicily 89, 90
Silvia: *see* ships
smallpox xxiii
South Africa, places in: *see* Cape of Good Hope
South West Africa (now Namibia), places in: *see* Ichaboe
Southampton, Hants. 237
Spain, places in: *see* Cádiz, Cape Trafalgar, Cartagena, Málaga
Sri Lanka (formerly Ceylon) 266
Stettin: *see* Szczecin
Stonehouse & Co. xx, 207
storms, tropical 77–85, 187–94
Stralsund, Germany xviii, 220
sugar 77, 123, 200, 216, 223, 237
Sunday observance, in Marquand household xiii, 10–12
Swift: *see* ships
Szczecin (Stettin), Poland xviii, 216, 220

Taylor, Robert xv, xvii, xxxii, 137–8, 139–57
Touzeau, John xv, 168–72
Trieste, Italy (formerly Austria) xxx–xxxi, 77, 86, 87, 88, 98, 123–4, 145
Trinidad 179–80
turtles 200
typhus fever 255

V—t, Guernsey 35
Vale Castle, Guernsey 54
Vanguard, HMS: *see* ships
Venice, Gulf of 87
Virgin Islands 74
Wadeson, Mr 22–39, 43–5, 137
  Mrs 44–5
Wakeham, Mr 19–21
Wales, coal trade of xviii
  market at Recife compared to those in 227
  places in: *see* Cardiff, Newport, Penarth Roads
Wesleyan Methodism, in Jamaica 184–6
West Hartley, Northumberland 258
West India Docks, London 179, 199

West Indies 49–50, 72–4
see also Antigua, Bermuda, Cayman Islands, Cuba, Hispaniola, Jamaica, Montserrat, Nevis, Puerto Rico, St Kitts, Santo Domingo, Trinidad, Virgin Islands
wheat 220
Wight, Isle of 145
see also Cowes
Williams, Thomas xvi, xx, 207–14, 253

yellow fever 126–36